SSSP

Springer Series in Social Psychology

Springer Series in Social Psychology

Attention and Self-Regulation:
A Control-Theory Approach to Human Behavior
Charles S. Carver/Michael F. Scheier

Gender and Nonverbal Behavior
Clara Mayo/Nancy M. Henley (Editors)

Personality, Roles, and Social Behavior
William Ickes/Eric S. Knowles (Editors)

Toward Transformation in Social Knowledge
Kenneth J. Gergen

The Ethics of Social Research:
Surveys and Experiments
Joan E. Sieber (Editor)

The Ethics of Social Research:
Fieldwork, Regulation, and Publication
Joan E. Sieber (Editor)

Anger and Aggression:
An Essay on Emotion
James R. Averill

The Social Psychology of Creativity
Teresa M. Amabile

Sports Violence
Jeffery H. Goldstein (Editor)

Nonverbal Behavior: A Functional Perspective
Miles L. Patterson

Basic Group Processes
Paul B. Paulus (Editor)

Attitudinal Judgment
J. Richard Eiser (Editor)

SSSP

Attitudinal Judgment

Edited by
J. Richard Eiser

Springer-Verlag
New York Berlin Heidelberg Tokyo

J. Richard Eiser
Department of Psychology
University of Exeter
Exeter EX4 4QG
England

With 13 Figures

Library of Congress Cataloging in Publication Data
Main entry under title:
Attitudinal judgment.
Bibliography: p.
Includes index.
1. Attitude (Psychology) 2. Judgment. I. Eiser, J. Richard.
BF323.C5A84 1984 303.3′8 83-20266

Typeset by Publishers Service, Bozeman, Montana.
Printed and bound by R.R. Donnelley and Sons, Harrisonburg, Virginia.
Printed in the United States of America.

9 8 7 6 5 4 3 2 1

ISBN 0-387-90911-7 Springer-Verlag New York Berlin Heidelberg Tokyo
ISBN 3-540-90911-7 Springer-Verlag Berlin Heidelberg New York Tokyo

In memoriam

Henri Tajfel
Born Włocławek, 1919
Died Oxford, 1982

Erich Eiser
Born Bratislava, 1908
Died London, 1983

Preface

Despite the central place that the study of attitudes has long held in social psychological research, the last decade or so has been relatively quiet as far as the development of attitude theory has been concerned. If one looks back to the Yale studies on communication and persuasion in the 1950s, followed by the massive literature derived from cognitive dissonance theory and its alternatives, there may be a temptation to think that the well of researchable questions has run almost dry. The purpose of this book is to convince the reader that this is not the case. On the contrary, a new look at the concept of attitude offers the prospect of as rich and varied a range of questions as ever before.

The term "new look" is an old one in social psychology. It was used 30 to 40 years ago as the designation for the school of thought which held that "basic" psychological processes such as perception, cognition, learning, and memory could be influenced by attitudes, motives, and values. There are still lessons to be learned from that period, and the new "new look" that is now emerging incorporates some of these same themes, albeit in the context of changing issues and emphases.

The title *Attitudinal Judgment* implies a commitment to the notion that attitudinal and judgmental processes are closely interrelated. It is with these interrelations specifically that this book is concerned. This results in a narrower focus than one would expect from a book on "attitudes." Nevertheless, the various approaches represented here certainly have implications for more general views of attitudes and attitude theory. A very great deal of attitude research invites a characterization that stems from an interest in individual attitudes "for their own sake," irrespective of what they tell one about more general cognitive processes on the one hand or social relations on the other. The work on which this book is based resists such a characterization.

The first aspect of this interrelationship to be described is the notion that attitudes are themselves *the products of judgment*. This is introduced in Chapter 1 by Parducci, who interprets our experiences of happiness and unhappiness in terms of classic principles of the relativity of psychological judgment. Although the traditional stimuli for psychophysical research have often been arid and devoid of intrinsic interest, Parducci shows how fundamental evaluative reactions may be predicted from the range and distribution of positive and negative events which a person has experienced.

The theme of relativity of judgment is pursued further in Chapter 2 by Upshaw and Ostrom who describe their theory of how different attitudinal judgments result from differences in psychological "perspective." This is a vitally important theme: The same objects or events can be judged completely differently depending on the context within which they are experienced. Differences in judgment, and hence in expressions of attitude, can arise from differences in the perspectives from which objects and events are viewed.

This chapter also introduces the idea which is developed further in Chapter 3 by Eiser and van der Pligt, of attitudes not simply as the products but also as the *objects of judgment*. How do we judge people's attitudes from the things they do and say? This question has been around from the earliest work on attitude-scaling. It is within this tradition that Eiser and van der Pligt consider how opinion statements (of the kind used in attitude scales) are interpreted as expressing different kinds of attitudes. An important factor considered here is the response language (and particularly the implicit value connotations of that language) in terms of which judgments of attitude statements are expressed. Such judgments *of* attitudes are also influenced *by* the attitudes of the judges themselves. Thus, attitudes are also an *influence on judgment*. Eiser and van der Pligt argue that people categorize statements on the basis of personal acceptability and this theme of *categorization* is reiterated in many of the following chapters.

Chapter 4, by Judd and Johnson, shows how the intensity with which attitudes are held can influence the extremity of "polarization" of judgments, including estimates of the extent to which others hold similar or dissimilar opinions to one's own. Thus attitudinal judgments take place in a *social context* where other people and their attitudes become part of one's own perspective.

The next three chapters on "intergroup attitudes" explore the social context of attitudinal judgment in terms of its broader relevance to intergroup relations. In Chapter 5, Granberg uses national survey data on the issues of racial desegregation and of abortion to illustrate how people may overestimate the support for, and underestimate the opposition to, their own views among the rest of the population. In Chapter 6, Rothbart, Dawes, and Park deal with the issue of how people may come to see greater homogeneity among members of other groups than they see within groups of which they themselves are members. Their theoretical analysis of the emergence of stereotypes rests heavily on notions of categorization and "sampling bias"—in other words, the *selective* search for, and processing of, information. Ethnic and group stereotypes are looked at again by Ryan, Hewstone, and Giles in Chapter 7, who show how attitudinal judgments can be importantly influenced by the language, speech style, and accent of a target person. The point is that such cues have no necessary connection with the more "psychological" characteristics attributed to group members; however, since linguistic cues serve to differentiate groups from one another, they acquire the potential to evoke value-laden attitudinal judgments and stereotypes.

The assumption that judgmental processes are *selective* is central to these discussions of stereotyping and intergroup attitudes. The final three chapters deal further with the notion of selectivity in the context of more general theories of attitude formation and change. In Chapter 8, van der Pligt and Eiser discuss the notion of "dimensional salience," arguing that different individuals may see different dimensions or aspects of an issue as "salient" or important. Such differences in salience may both be predictable from, and also help explain, differences in attitude. This view is compared with views of attitude based on expectancy-value models of decision-making.

In Chapter 9, Palmerino, Langer, and McGillis explore the implications for attitude theory of the "mindlessness-mindfulness" distinction. According to their thesis, people process much information relatively mindlessly at a reduced level of cognitive activity, and the way in which such information is initially processed constrains the way in which it can later be used as the basis for judgments and behavior. This chapter reemphasizes the importance of the judgmental context in determining how information will be processed and includes a plea for renewed attention to be paid to Lewin's field theory.

Finally, in Chapter 10, Crocker, Fiske, and Taylor discuss how our knowledge of our social world is organized into cognitive structures, or schemas, and how the processing of information in terms of schemas shapes the way in which attitudes are formed and can change. Much of our cognition and behavior is "hypothesis-driven," based on expectations that may be confirmed or challenged by events, whereas events themselves are experienced within the context of our expectations and hypotheses.

The ten chapters in this book thus cover a range of topics and approaches, but still there is an important consonance in the themes they propound. Not only can attitudes be both the products and objects of judgment, and an influence on how judgments are made; the relationship between attitudes and judgments goes further and deeper than this. Attitudes are also themselves a form of judgment, a system of structures that are at the same time cognitive and evaluative and that represent the structure of social relationships in terms of which they are enacted.

Attitudes are not simply a phenomenon of interest in their own right, they are the meeting point for theories of cognition and theories of social behavior. A unification of such theories may still be a remote ideal, but if a meeting can be arranged, the signs now are not unpropitious.

Exeter, England J. Richard Eiser

Contents

Part III. Salience, Schematic Processing, and Attitude Change

Contributors

Jennifer Crocker, Department of Psychology, Northwestern University, Evanston, Illinois 60201, USA.

Robyn Dawes, Department of Psychology, University of Oregon, Eugene, Oregon 97403, USA.

J. Richard Eiser, Department of Psychology, University of Exeter, Exeter EX4 4QG, England.

Susan T. Fiske, Department of Psychology, Carnegie-Mellon University, Pittsburgh, Pennsylvania 15213, USA.

Howard Giles, Department of Psychology, University of Bristol, Bristol BS8 1HH, England.

Donald Granberg, Department of Sociology, University of Missouri at Columbia, Columbia, Missouri 65201, USA.

Miles Hewstone, Psychologisches Institut, Universität Tübingen, 7400 Tübingen, West Germany.

Joel T. Johnson, Department of Psychology, University of California, Davis, California 95616, USA.

Charles M. Judd, Department of Psychology, University of Colorado, Boulder, Colorado 80309, USA.

Ellen Langer, Department of Psychology and Social Relations, Harvard University, Cambridge, Massachusetts 02138, USA.

Daniel McGillis, Center for Criminal Justice, Harvard University, Cambridge, Massachusetts 02138, USA.

Thomas M. Ostrom, Department of Psychology, Ohio State University, Columbus, Ohio 43210, USA.

Mark Palmerino, Department of Psychology and Social Relations, Harvard University, Cambridge, Massachusetts 02138, USA.

Allen Parducci, Department of Psychology, University of California at Los Angeles, Los Angeles, California 90024, USA.

Bernadette Park, Department of Psychology, Northwestern University, Evanston, Illinois 60201, USA.

Myron Rothbart, Psychology Department, University of Oregon, Eugene, Oregon 97403, USA.

Ellen Bouchard Ryan, Department of Psychiatry, McMaster University, Hamilton, Ontario L8S 4KJ, Canada.

Shelley E. Taylor, Department of Psychology, University of California at Los Angeles, Los Angeles, California 90024, USA.

Harry S. Upshaw, Department of Psychology, University of Illinois at Chicago, Chicago, Illinois 60680, USA.

Joop van der Pligt, Department of Psychology, University of Exeter, Exeter EX4 4QG, England.

Part I
Value, Relativity, and Polarization

Chapter 1

Value Judgments: Toward a Relational Theory of Happiness

Allen Parducci

This chapter presents a theory of happiness. Its basic premise is that the experienced value of any event depends upon comparisons with other events. Values are relative. This is a theory about what they are relative to.

The origins of the theory lie in everyday observations about the relativistic nature of value experiences. We observe that as we earn more, it takes more to satisfy us: we find ourselves adapting to whatever level we have been earning so that it comes to seem only "average," whatever its absolute level might be. This kind of everyday observation was formalized by the late Harry Helson (1947) in his theory of adaptation level. Adaptation-level theory assumes that experienced values are proportional to stimulus deviations from the average or mean stimulus, which implies that the algebraic sum of all experienced values must be zero (Brickman & Campbell, 1971; Parducci, 1968, 1983b). This may be too pessimistic an assessment of life's possibilities, for there is ample evidence that value judgments do not balance around adaptation level (Parducci, 1983a). What was shown by the work of Helson and others was how psychophysical methods, in particular the method of single stimuli (Wever & Zener, 1928), can be employed to study the relational character of value judgments (e.g., Beebe-Center, 1932; Campbell, Hunt, & Lewis, 1957; Hunt & Volkmann, 1937; Johnson, 1944, 1955; Sherif, 1936; Volkmann, 1951; for a general review, see Eiser & Stroebe, 1972; Zoeke & Sarris, 1983). Although in their practical implications quite different from adaptation-level theory, the principles of judgment on which the present theory of happiness is based were developed and tested in this kind of psychophysical research.

This research suggests specific relational considerations for understanding the value experiences of everyday life. The immediate context of stimuli determining the judgment of any particular stimulus in a psychophysical experiment is assumed to have a direct counterpart in the broader contexts of everyday life. For example, the context determining how satisfied we are with any particular income may consist of other incomes that we ourselves have earned in the past, incomes that we imagine ourselves making in the future, and so forth. Although psychophysics cannot tell us what gets included in these broader contexts, it can serve as a source of hypotheses about them. The very simplicity of psychophysical experiments encourages a sharpening of hypotheses beyond what we might otherwise require for the interpretation of everyday value experiences.

Overview of the Theory

Our value experiences are elicited by events around us and also by imaginary events that exist only in our own private experience. Although our own experiences of subjective value may seem like intrinsic characteristics of the events being experienced, we know that extraordinarily similar events may have very different subjective values when experienced in different circumstances. Wine from the same bottle can be delicious when it follows a mediocre wine, yet disappointing when it follows a superior wine. We sometimes try to arrange the context to bring out the best in the wine. So too with the grander contexts of life—might we not be able to arrange them so that they bring out the best in whatever we experience?

The context for a wine may be short-lived. Some of our grander contexts seem to plague us for years. For example, a spectacular opportunity that is just missed may provide a new upper endpoint to a context in which lesser opportunities are forever unsatisfying. It is not clear whether we can simply wipe out those parts of a context that rob other events of satisfaction. But the optimistic assumption is that with better understanding of the relational character of value experiences, we increase our power to control them.

What gets included in a context? Some of the important domains of experience seem relatively independent—in the sense that the subjective value of what is experienced in one domain does not seem to be affected by what is experienced in another domain. For example, eating a particularly wonderful dinner in the evening would be unlikely to affect one's satisfaction with work the next day. On the other hand, an especially satisfying dinner might diminish the satisfaction obtainable from a subsequent dinner, particularly if it had promised the same culinary gratifications.

The purpose of this theory is to provide a framework for speculating about which conditions are conducive to happiness. In its definition of happiness (given in the following section), the theory tries to adhere to common use of the term—but without bringing in *moral* considerations. Thus, there is no claim that one ought to be happy. Nor is this a theory of motivation: It does not assume that everyone seeks happiness. The theory follows Bentham (1789/1961) only in defining happiness as the balance of satisfaction over dissatisfaction, or (more generally) of positive values over negative ones. As with Bentham, it is degree and duration (but not qualitative considerations) that enter into the calculation of the balance.

The theory attempts a solution to the problem of how these subjective values can be measured. Its starting point is the expression of value judgments by means of category ratings. It assumes that expressions such as "very pleasant," "slightly dissatisfying," or "absolutely terrible" can accurately communicate degrees of subjective value. Psychophysical research in which subjects rate simple stimuli in terms of verbal categories demonstrates that these categories are used with such precision that they can be predicted from simple algebraic models (Parducci, 1983a). Skeptics can argue that there is no proof that a category rating is a direct expression of a value component of experience, but the fact that this is the way we ordinarily express our value judgments suggests that it is the closest we think we can come to direct expression of our subjective values.

The happy life, according to this approach, is one in which a preponderance of all value experiences would be described using positive category ratings. Not that the happy person necessarily goes around announcing positive assessments; rather, it is the potential for such assessments that is essential to happiness, that is, positive categories would predominate if a happy person were to express his value experiences as overt ratings. Of course, even the happiest life also has the potential for negative assessments, experiences that would be rated "unpleasant" and occasionally even "dreadfully painful." It is the overall balance of the positive over the negative that distinguishes the happy life.

There is also a distinction between momentary value experiences and the overall assessments that people make of their lives as a whole. An overall assessment is more a philosophical decision than a direct psychological report, and it may be a poor representation of the countless individual experiences that constitute each of the different domains of a life. The primary concern of the present theory is with the value experiences themselves rather than with how people make overall assessments of happiness.

Formal Statement of the Theory

Definitions

1. Value Judgment: the internal value experience elicited by an event.

This is the basic primitive at the heart of the theory. It represents the value attribute of phenomenal experience. As such, it is a mentalistic concept and thus outside the received doctrine of behaviorism. But behaviorism has not produced a theory of happiness. A radical behaviorist, such as Skinner, may speculate about the conditions for happiness (e.g., Skinner, 1948, 1971), but always with a promissory note: If happiness has any meaning, it can be reduced to objectively (i.e., "publicly") observable events. No such promise is made here. Indeed, it seems unlikely that any theory of happiness can ever be tested directly by the methods of science (Parducci, 1983b). The only test is subjective experience with all its shortcomings as a basis for inference.

The theory is concerned with *value* judgments because it assumes that these are the constituents of happiness. The term value judgment is not restricted to assessments of moral or aesthetic values. Perhaps "utility" would be a less restrictive term; however, utility has come to be associated with choice or preference, as in the theory of subjective expected utility. "Pleasure" and "pain" (i.e., hedonic judgment) would be other acceptable alternatives, except that they are sometimes construed to be restricted just to sensual experiences. Value, in the present sense, is meant to cover all experiences that can be ranked on a scale of preference but with no implication that people in fact choose alternatives with higher expected values.

The theory refers to the degree of subjective value as a value *judgment* because it assumes that subjective values follow the same relational principles as overt judgments, that is, as category ratings. Although experienced directly by the person making the judgment, other people can sometimes infer the judgment from the overt behavior of that person, especially from a category rating, or even from their knowledge of the context in which the judgment occurs. The overt rating may be simply a public expression of the private value judgment, in which case both could be predicted if the context were known. However, various pragmatic considerations, especially the concern to affect the value judgments made by others (analyzed by Stevenson, 1944), complicate any such prediction.

2. *Event: any stimulus, image, or state of affairs that can be compared with other stimuli, images, or states.*

The term event is used here by analogy to the physical stimulus that elicits a category rating in psychophysical research. This use is partly metaphorical because many of our most intense value experiences occur in the absence of any obvious external stimulation. For example, one may suddenly experience a strong feeling of shame at the thought of some failure that had taken place, perhaps years earlier; one experiences once again in the imagination that earlier failure and with it the negative value judgment, in this case the shame, that may now be greater even than in the original experience.

Ordinarily, the imaginary experience shares much of the character of a publicly observable event. Its value component is experienced as an objective attribute of the pseudopublic event just as the shamefulness of some misdeed or failing seems like an objective attribute of the act of failing. It is this attribute that we experience as having a certain *degree* of value, identified in the present theory as the judged value of the event.

3. *Context: the set of events affecting the value judgment of any particular event.*

In a simple psychophysical experiment, it is often possible to equate the context with the particular series of stimuli presented for judgment. Stimuli experienced outside the laboratory or even in earlier experimental sessions may not be incorporated into the context for judgment, which means that they do not affect the ratings of the present stimuli. The category ratings of stimuli in the present experimental series can be predicted from their physical relationships: A change in any of these stimuli produces highly predictable changes in ratings of the other stimuli (Parducci, 1974, 1983a).

It is rare that the context for judgments made outside the psychophysical laboratory can be specified so completely. Nevertheless, the theory ascribes to change in context any change in the experienced value of what in other respects seems like the very same event. Application of basic principles of judgment suggests how one can infer certain features of a context from value experiences or from overt category ratings. Thus, if one experiences some event as "ecstatically wonderful" or if someone else rates an event in such terms, the obvious inference is that the event in question must be at the top of whatever context is affecting how it is experienced. If on a later occasion this same event has much less positive value, one can infer that a greater event has taken its place as the top of the context.

4. Dimension of Judgment: those characteristics of events for which variation produces correlated variation in value judgment.

In psychophysical research, the dimension of judgment is usually specified by the experimental instructions; for example, the instructions might stipulate that each of a succession of squares be rated in accordance with how large or small it seems in comparison with the other squares. Unless restricted to a prescribed set of categories, different subjects use different numbers of categories (Parducci, 1982), but all of the resulting scales are ordinal to the physical sizes.

The introduction of a value dimension may result in systematic nonordinality. Although ratings of the sweetness of drinks laced with different concentrations of sucrose are ordinal among subjects, ratings of pleasantness are not; the optimum concentrations are much lower for some subjects and contexts than for others (Riskey, Parducci, & Beauchamp, 1979). With more complex psychophysical stimuli, such as perfumes, people vary in their orders of preference, and with the very much more complex events of everyday experience, "one man's meat is another man's poison." What this means is that certain dimensions of judgment may be peculiar to the individual. Perhaps in some of the most important applications to happiness, the dimension of judgment can be inferred only by the person making the value judgments. Inferring the dimension is part and parcel with inferring the context for judgment, with the same problems of inference.

It should be emphasized that in the present theory the dimension of judgment is entirely subjective. Even when it is perfectly ordinal to some fundamental physical measure, the relationship is rarely linear. As Bernoulli conjectured centuries ago, losing a certain sum of money is more painful than winning the same amount is pleasurable: utility functions are usually curvilinear, with decreasing marginal utility.

The dimension of judgment is thus not to be identified with any physical dimension (though it may be highly correlated with a physical dimension). Nor should particular points on this dimension be identified with value judgments. The value judgment is assumed to be a conscious experience and as such open directly to introspection. On the other hand, the dimension of judgment is only an inferred construct, useful for explaining value judgments and overt category ratings, but not itself experienced directly. In this respect, it should be identified with the hypothetical discriminability dimension posited by Thurstone (1927) and by the closely related theory of signal detection (Green & Swets, 1966): Ratings change but discriminability often remains invariant. Similarly, in functional measurement (Anderson, 1981), which is the most general theory of this type, rating scales or other response measures need not be linear to the inferred scale values of the stimuli. In the present theory, positions of events on the dimension of judgment represent what their value judgment would be if it were not for the tendency to distribute events equally across the scale of judgment (described in the next sections by Principles 1 and 2).

Although the location of any event on the dimension of judgment may be fairly constant, even psychophysical stimuli sometimes change their scale values (cf. Mellers

& Birnbaum, 1982). In everyday life, what seems like the same event may change its location on the dimension of judgment as the result of changes in background events. For example, a particular wine may be much higher on the dimension of taste when served with cheese and crackers. This is not simply a change in the context of other wines with which it is compared. It is rather a change in the event itself, wine with cheese being different from wine alone.

5. Contextual Range: the difference on the dimension of judgment between the two events in a context that elicit the highest and lowest judgments.

Like the dimension of judgment on which it is measured, this strictly hypothetical difference or distance is obtained only by inference. It should not be confused with the difference in value judgments elicited by the endpoints of the context. However, these highest and lowest judgments can identify the two endpoints of the contextual range.

6. Happiness: the general level of all value judgments taken across all contexts, covering some restricted period of time (e.g., this moment, the past few minutes, this day, this year) or a whole life or even covering many lives (e.g., the happiness of a people). This general level may be defined as either the

a. Average Level of Happiness, in which case it is the algebraic mean of all value judgments covered, or

b. Sum Total of Happiness, in which case it is the algebraic sum of all value judgments covered.

The notion of taking an algebraic mean of experienced values as the measure of happiness derives directly from Jeremy Bentham's hedonic calculus (Bentham, 1789/1961). One can think of a teeter-totter for which positions on the plank represent different degrees of experienced value, with the neutral value represented by the position at the fulcrum, and positive and negative values proportional to distances on either side from the fulcrum. Happiness for Bentham would be measured by the tipping moment, the resultant degree of force making the teeter-totter tip. The present theory attempts to go beyond Bentham in assuming that each value experience can be represented by a judgment that follows the same relativistic rules as overt category ratings.

It should be noted that, as with Bentham, qualitative distinctions between different experiences enter the calculation of happiness only with respect to *degree* or amount of value. The place of any given event on the teeter-totter depends solely on the value judgment it elicits, that is, on the place of that event in a context of related events. Eating ice cream may be perfectly delightful, and hearing that one has gotten an unexpected raise may also be perfectly delightful; therefore, both would be represented by the same position near the good end of the plank. No matter that a raise is infinitely preferable to ice cream. Ice cream is not ordinarily compared with a raise, for it would not be judged so highly if a raise were part of context for eating ice cream. The direct contribution of each event to the average level of happiness is simply its judgment at the time it is experienced. However, duration should also be taken into account (again following Bentham), as though longer events could be divided into separate events of shorter duration each then located at the position on the plank representing its separate judgment. In this sense, the raise is represented by much more weight on the plank than is ice cream.

The happiness of a life, or of some period of a life, might alternately be defined as the *algebraic sum* of separate value experiences represented as judgments. This alternative measure is sensitive to the total number of events. A life spent mostly in sleep or in experiences not on any value dimension, that is, a life with relatively few value judgments, would consequently have less potential for happiness than one that was full of value experiences. Even if the algebraic mean of all judgments were the same for the empty as for the full life, the latter would have a higher sum total of happiness (or unhappiness, if the mean were negative).

7. Category Rating: the verbal expression of a value judgment in terms of a value adjective (e.g., "good" or "bad") or an adverb-adjective combination (e.g., "very good" or "slightly unpleasant"), or a numeral representing the verbal expression (e.g., "1—terrible," "5—average," or "9—wonderful"

a. most value judgments are not expressed as category ratings, but any value judgment could be so expressed

b. some category ratings do not express value judgments accurately (e.g., they may be used to influence or deceive rather than to express the actual judgment)

c. value judgments that are not expressed as category ratings may nevertheless be inferred, sometimes from those value judgments that are so expressed.

This is where the world of subjective events, the concern of the present theory, is translated into objective, intersubjectively observable behavior. The translation is far from perfect. We each know that relatively few of our value experiences are ever described for other people. Most such experiences are not even rated covertly, that is, to ourselves. And yet we know that there is often the potential for making such a rating. We can tell others how we feel about something, and sometimes we think we are expressing the degree of value with considerable accuracy. Our confidence in these self-reports is greater when the value experience is an intense one, when we are euphoric or when we are in agony. It is when the experience is so neutral that we are not even sure that it has any value component that we have least confidence in our category rating.

Since most of the category ratings that express value judgments have a strong hortatory component (Stevenson, 1944), there is every reason to believe that this reduces their validity as a direct index to value experience. For example, we may take inordinate delight in deriding a particular work of art if it violates some canon of beauty to which we subscribe philosophically; this does not necessarily mean that we experience ugliness while viewing it or while rating it. We may want others to admire our taste or at least to accept our aesthetic standards. So many category ratings have a strong component of "social desirability," that is, putting ourselves in the best light, that they must be carefully discounted when drawing inferences about the value experiences they are supposed to represent. It was Freud who most effectively encouraged skepticism about expressions of feeling, with his theory of "repression" and "reaction formation" in which people try to hide their true feelings, even from themselves.

But we would not take category ratings so seriously if they had no validity at all.

The dangers of inferring value experiences are exceptions that prove the rule: Category ratings are often our most direct and reliable guide to value experiences. Sometimes, we can even infer the true value judgment from category ratings of other events, providing we know enough about the context in which these ratings were made. If we know that a reviewer rates a manuscript primarily on the basis of methodological soundness and we also know how he has rated some that were less sound and also some that were more sound than the one in question, we feel safe in inferring what his rating of it will be; we also believe that this rating, whether actually made or only inferred, is our best guide to his private judgment of the manuscript.

Postulate

The value judgment of any event is determined by the relationship between that event and a context of other events.

This is the essential notion of relativism on which the theory is based. Nothing is valued in itself, only in its relationship to other things. Knowing that certain people are poor does not allow the inference that they therefore must feel deprived—any more than one can infer that the rich feel affluent. Satisfaction with any particular income depends on what it is compared to.

Principles

1. The judgment of any event is determined in part by the proportion of the contextual range that is below that event on the dimension of judgment.

This is a statement of the range principle used for category ratings. It was articulated by Volkmann (1951) and later incorporated as part of range-frequency theory (Parducci, 1965). Algebraically, the range principle can be expressed as follows:

$$R_i = (E_i - E_{min})/(E_{max} - E_{min}), \qquad (1)$$

where R_i, the *range value* of the *i*th event (E_i), represents what the judgment would have been insofar as its value component had been determined simply by the position of that event in the range of its context of related events; E_{min} and E_{max} represent the lowest and highest events in the context for judgment. Initial support for this principle came from research in which subjects rated the numerical magnitudes of numerals printed on a page (Parducci, Calfee, Marshall, & Davidson, 1960). In that research, the range values of the different numerals could be calculated directly from their printed numerical values, for example, if the numeral 400 were being rated in a contextual set varying from 100 to 1000, the range value of 400 would equal the proportion of the contextual range below it: $R_{400} = (400 - 100)/(1000 - 100) = 300/900 = .33$.

With psychophysical materials, the positions of different stimuli in the range must be inferred from empirical ratings, using the other principles of range-frequency theory (Parducci, 1974). As we shall see when we consider practical applications, the inference of range values can be quite conjectural. However, events for which the experienced values are very extreme (e.g., events that would be rated "absolutely terrible" or "perfectly delightful") must be very close to the endpoints of the context in which they are experienced.

2. *The judgment of any event is also determined by the proportion of all contextual events that are below that event (i.e., .01 times the percentile rank of the judged event).*

This is a restatement of the frequency principle of range-frequency theory. Insofar as judgments reflect this frequency principle, the same number of contextual events occur at each level of value experience. This can be expressed algebraically in a form paralleling Equation 1:

$$F_i = (i - 1)/(N - 1), \tag{2}$$

where F_i *is the frequency value* of Event i, i is its rank in the set of contextual events, and N is the total number of contextual events. In the example of rating numerals, the numeral 400 would have a frequency value of .67 if two-thirds of all the numerals were below 400. Frequency values can be calculated a priori in experiments for which the experimenter has control of all stimuli that will be included in the context; however, one can only hazard rough guesses about frequency values for events occurring in the grander contexts of everyday life. When an event estimated to be low in the range nevertheless is experienced as of neutral or average value, then it must have a frequency value above .50, that is, higher than at least half of the events in the context.

3. *The actual value judgment of an event is a weighted average of the range and frequency values of that event, that is, of its positions with respect to the range and frequencies of other events in the context.*

The actual value experience, expressed as a judgment, is thus represented as a compromise between the first two principles of judgment. Algebraically,

$$J_i = wR_i + (1 - w) F_i - .5, \tag{3}$$

where w is the relative weight of the range value, with $0 < w < 1$. The additive constant, $-.5$, places the judgments on a zero-centered scale from $-.5$ to $+.5$ (instead of the 0-to-1 scales of Equations 1 and 2). Again, Equation 3 is taken directly from the equation for the compromise between range and frequency principles developed to account for overt category ratings. The resulting judgment represents the experienced value component of the event it is characterizing, and it in turn could be expressed as an overt category rating. The evidence for this compromise lies in the success of the range-frequency equations in predicting category ratings of psychophysical stimuli presented in various systematically varied contexts (e.g., Parducci, 1983b; Parducci & Perrett, 1971). From these three equations, the following theorem can be derived algebraically.

Theorem

The mean of the value judgments of all events in a context is directly proportional to their degree of skewing, with the relative weighting of position in the range being the constant of proportionality.

This theorem can be stated algebraically:[1]

$$\bar{J} = w(\bar{E} - .5(E_{max} + E_{min}))/(E_{max} - E_{min}). \tag{4}$$

The constant of proportionality, w, is the range weight from Equation 3, and $\bar{E}$ is the mean of all contextual events on the dimension of judgment. The right side of Equation 4 provides a measure of skewing, the difference between the mean and midpoint of contextual events, divided by their range; this measure correlates almost perfectly (but *negatively*), with traditional measures of skewing: The greater the pileup of events near the top of the range, the greater the mean judgment. If happiness is taken as the mean of all judgments (Definition 6a), this theorem states that happiness is proportional to the negative skewing of the distribution of contextual events. Again, the best objective evidence comes from category ratings in experiments in which the skewing of the contextual distribution of stimuli is varied systematically: In such experiments, the mean of all ratings does vary directly with skewing (Parducci, 1983).

This theorem may be deceptively simple; in fact, most applications of the theory follow directly from it. Before taking up these applications, it may be useful to discuss the theorem at a more abstract level. The left panel of Figure 1-1 illustrates two distributions of events that differ in their absolute levels on the dimension of judgment and also in the direction of their skewing, one being skewed positively (+), the other negatively (−). None of the events in the negatively skewed distribution are as high on the dimension of judgment as any of the events in the upper two-thirds of the positively skewed distribution. Thus, if both distributions were in the same context, that is, their component events were being compared, each of these upper events in the positively skewed distribution would be rated higher than any event in the negatively skewed distribution.

But if each distribution constitutes a separate context for judgment, the theorem tells us that the mean of all judgments would be higher for the negatively skewed distribution. Since the mean is always further than the midpoint from the tail of a skewed distribution, the mean must be above the midpoint for the negative context and below it for the positive context. Depending on the value of w, the distribution of judgments reflects the degree of skewing and is always skewed in the same direction as the distribution of contextual events. The right panel of Figure 1-1 shows the two distributions of value judgments, calculated from Equation 3 under the assumption that $w = .5$.

It should be clear that the mean of judgments, according to this theorem, is independent of the absolute levels of the events being judged. What counts are their relative levels, where the events fall in relation to the endpoints of their own contextual range. The closer most events are to the upper endpoint, whatever its absolute value may be, the higher the overall mean of the judgments.

The right panel of Figure 1-1 also shows that the range of judgments is the same for both contexts (as it must be for all contexts). The top events in the negative context,

[1]This derivation can perhaps be appreciated intuitively by considering that dividing the mean of the events by their range puts the mean on a 0-to-1 scale so that it can be substituted for the mean of the range values. Since the mean of the frequency values is .5, it is also the midpoint on this 0-to-1 scale.

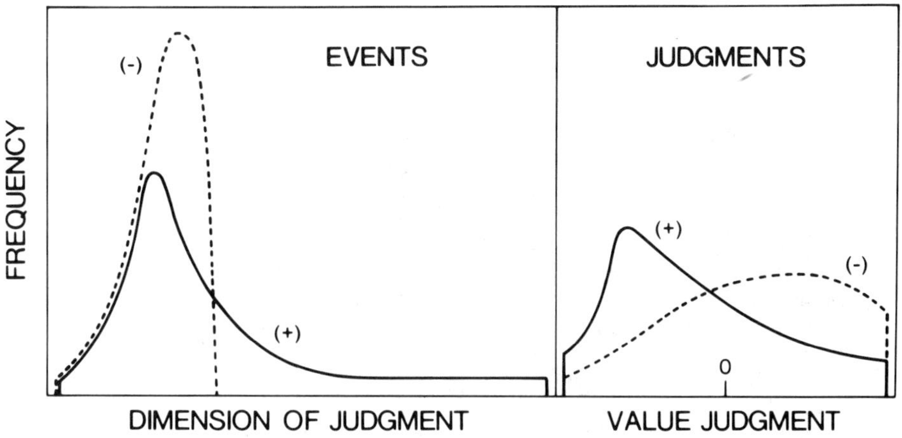

Fig. 1-1. Effects of contextual skewing. Left panel shows two frequency distributions of contextual events. Although events tend to be higher for this example of a positively skewed context (labeled "+"), it is the negatively skewed context of events (labeled "−") that elicits higher judgments—as shown in the right panel. The mean of all judgments, on a scale from −.5 to +.5, approximates +.08 for the negative context, −.08 for the positive context (calculated using Equation 3, with $w = .5$).

in spite of their lower absolute level, elicit the same value judgments as the top events in the positive context—only more of them since the top scores come more frequently in a negatively skewed distribution.

Applications

The remainder of the chapter is an attempt to apply these admittedly abstract and subjective notions to problems of happiness in the real world. The proposed applications are presented as prescriptive generalizations, illustrated by concrete examples.

1. The happiest lives include relatively large proportions of extremely high value judgments.

This claim is suggested by the hedonistic conception of happiness as the balance of satisfaction over dissatisfaction, or in present terms (Definition 6a), as the mean of all value judgments. It is intrinsic to the algebraic concept of the mean that extreme scores have the greatest effect on its value. Thus, an overwhelming pileup of judgments around zero, that is, close to the indifference point, precludes a marked imbalance in the direction of either happiness or unhappiness. Even if mildly positive experiences were much more frequent than mildly negative ones, the overall balance would be fairly even (i.e., their mean would be close to zero). As shown in Figure 1-1, the distribution of judgments is less skewed than the distribution of events.

To achieve the highest possible level of happiness, the highest values must be experienced relatively frequently. Who would not want such a concentration of the best?

Yet most of us are wary of inordinate "highs," fearing that when they occur we are (like Alcibiades) riding for a fall. Ironically, patterning one's life to avoid the extremes (a rule in classic Epicureanism and in many other philosophies) precludes the possibility of an extremely happy life.

One type of "high" that can work against subsequent happiness comes from experiencing a new event better than any that had previously been experienced in the same domain. This new event extends the range upward so that lesser events become less satisfying. Although this makes an immediate positive contribution to the balance of happiness, its long-term effects are harmful unless the new upper endpoint can be experienced with high relative frequency. For example, it would be risky to move temporarily into a much better house if you must subsequently go back to your old one.

The act of advancing to a higher level, whether in housing, work, or play, can itself be an event that defines the upper endpoint of its context. Because advancement cannot be an everyday event, its relative frequency must be low. Given the pyramidical structure of most competitive situations, a level is reached where further advancement is unlikely. Even anticipations of future advancements become much less frequent. Unless this type of upper endpoint is dropped from the context, lesser events will remain unsatisfying.

2. *Happy lives are fuller, in the sense that a higher proportion of their experiences have value components.*

This follows from the conception of happiness as a sum total of value judgments (Definition 6b). A life that was completely devoid of value judgments (Nirvana?) could not be a happy one. The prescription to avoid value judgments or comparisons (besides asking for what is psychologically impossible) seems predicated on a philosophy of pessimism, a philosophy that has abandoned all hope for happiness.

3. *When the best comes rarely, the upper endpoint of the range is too high: it is then that one should settle for less (if one cannot greatly increase the frequency of events near the upper endpoint).*

When the most positive value judgments are extremely infrequent (as for the positively skewed distribution in the left panel of Figure 1-1), then the contextual distribution could be skewed more negatively by dropping the best events from the context (e.g., shifting to the negatively skewed distribution in the same panel). As described by the theorem and Equation 4, this would increase the average value judgment and hence the overall level of happiness.

Consider a concrete example from the domain of material success. Suppose that one rarely experiences a real sense of accomplishment. Suppose that the events one values most in this domain—promotions, awards, testimonials, unusual respect—almost never happen, and that one's regular accomplishments are only mildly satisfying. Is not this a common lot, even among those who are reasonably successful by worldly standards? But if one's regular accomplishments are only mildly satisfying, it is because they are being compared with something better, something that constitutes the upper endpoint of the range for this domain. Perhaps this upper endpoint is an occasional dream or anticipation of future success, a possibility suggested by the achievements of others. The pyramidical structure of most competitive situations encourages setting standards that are unrealistically high. So do our notions about the relationship between high standards and high achievement: Young people are urged to reach for the stars, in the belief that they will accomplish more than if they set more realistic standards. This may be a good prescription for higher absolute levels of success, but the theory suggests that for most people it must be a poor prescription for happiness. With lower standards, regular accomplishments would be much more satisfying.

Consider the domain of love rather than that of success at work. The different kinds of "romantic agony" cherished by certain poets—unrequited love, resignation to perpetual mourning for a lost love, despair over human frailty—all can be subjected to the same kind of analysis. A particular example might be the man who has in his imagination an exalted picture of the ideal woman, a standard that no real-life woman could meet. His occasional imaginary visions of this ideal define the top of his range, insuring a positively skewed (and therefore unhappy) distribution of events in this important domain of his life. For such a romantic, giving up his vision would constitute the most bitter resignation. He cannot give up his dreams because they represent hope, the very best of what he experiences in this domain. However, if he could give them up, if he could drop this upper endpoint from his context, the best of what remained would be valued just as highly as what he has given up had been valued. This new best might even be a real-life woman, with all the faults that previously seemed so grievous when judged by his exalted standards.

Sometimes, there may be a reasonable alternative to settling for less, as when a higher level of success can really be achieved or a woman found who is close to one's romantic ideal. However, the domain will only remain happy if new, higher standards are not generated. This is the tug-of-war between achievement and happiness. The present theory does not solve the apparent conflict, but it does argue for a more realistic appraisal of the possibilities; and it does suggest that if one can truly settle for less, one's happiness is likely to increase.

4. In the happiest contextual domains, the worst events are very much worse than the great bulk of experiences.

The present theory assumes that painful lows occur, at least occasionally, in each of life's contexts. This is because some event must always be the worst in the context. This lower endpoint may be only imaginary, such as a morbid fear of some anticipated misfortune; but being the worst we experience, it is as horrible when we experience it as the worst of real-life misfortunes. Therefore, even the happiest lives cannot escape occasional miseries. What distinguishes happy from unhappy lives is the relative frequency with which the miseries occur.

The ideal distribution is one in which the worst events are so bad that everything else falls close to the top of the range. Although this lower endpoint of the range is really a blessing rather than a misfortune, it cannot be judged as such at the time it is experienced—for then it would not be the lower endpoint. When the worst is really a misfortune is when it is experienced too frequently, that is, more frequently than the bare minimum needed to keep it within the context. The pain of a physical or psychological injury often stays with us: we experience it again and again. This skews the distribution of experiences back in the unhappy direction. The ideal lower endpoint might be a strong electric shock, unbearable but quickly over. The shock would have to be readministered occasionally, whenever it dropped from the context or whenever its memory ceased to be dreadful. Prisoners who have experienced systematic torture might be justifiably skeptical of this example; but in his *One Day in the Life of Ivan Denisovich*, Alexander Solzhenitsyn (1963) made credible the incredible: that even under the worst of conditions, there may still be genuine happiness.

If one thinks of those physical activities in which people are courting pain—backpacking, long-distance running, contact sports such as boxing—it seems that the participants do not dwell on the painful parts. How quickly such people forget the awful pain! The heavily laden climb up the mountain becomes a wonderful memory. For the price of a short period of misery, there may be rewards of much longer duration.

The pain of psychic injuries may be much more enduring. An insult, a rejection, a withdrawal of love—such experiences can grow worse in memory. And when they are experienced again and again, even if only in memory, they can make the overall balance of happiness tip down on the negative side.

The deliberate seeking out of new lower endpoints thus seems a perilous road to happiness. It runs the danger of getting out of hand, resulting in a pileup of misery. That is the trouble with banging your head on the wall—it does not really feel so good when you stop! The pain lingers, just as it does from most misfortunes. We know this from rueful experience—so that we would not seek out the worst even if we could believe, on theoretical grounds, that it might improve the rest of life.

5. Attempts to repeat one's best experiences are often doomed to failure.

The value judgment of any repeated experience shifts systematically. This follows from the tendency for the same number of contextual events to occur at each level of value experience (Principle 2 of the theory). As events pile up in one part of the range, their ratings tend to spread out over neighboring categories. With repetitions, an event at the top of the range evokes progressively lower judgments. For example, an athlete may be ecstatic at winning his first race; but with repeated victories, winning comes to be taken for granted. We all experience this in our pleasures with new possessions. The new acquisition that is so highly valued at first comes to seem ordinary, sometimes even before its polish has worn off. What this suggests is that we are mistaken to think that enduring satisfaction can come from anything so simple as an acquisition.

6. Unhappiness may have to be accepted in one domain to insure happiness in other domains, but the trade-off may be disadvantageous.

People who are unhappy with their work may regard it as a necessary evil that makes possible happy balances in other domains: eating, love, friendship, recreation, health, and so forth. However, if one includes travelling to and from the job, most people spend the majority of their waking moments at work. So if work is an unhappy domain, the positive balances experienced in other domains may not be sufficient, when properly weighted for frequency, to average out to a positive overall balance of happiness.

7. The limits of happiness are much more restricted than is commonly believed. Surveys conducted on representative samples of adult Americans regularly report that their self-avowals of happiness are overwhelmingly positive (e.g., Andrews & Withey, 1976; Cantril, 1965; Freedman, 1978). Using Cantril's ladder of happiness, where the endpoints are defined for the interviewees as the worst and best of the lives they can imagine for themselves, the mean rating approaches 7 on a scale from 0 to 10; on a 7-category scale from "terrible" (1) to "delightful" (7), Andrews and Withey obtained a mean between 5 and 6, with very few self-avowals of unhappiness. Findings from the various major surveys seem to be in agreement: The average person rates his own level of happiness as more than one-third of the way up from the middle of the scale (an even balance) toward the top of the scale (extreme happiness). Approximately the same high level of happiness is reported by different subgroups classified by objective sociometric factors such as income, occupation, age, and sex; none of these objective factors correlate very highly with happiness (Andrews & Withey, 1976; Freedman, 1978).

Can people be telling the truth about their own levels of happiness? The present theory suggests that they are not, that their self-avowals exhibit a strong positive bias. Although the general failure to find systematic differences in happiness associated with differences in objective conditions fits in with the notion, basic to the present theory, that value judgments are relative to their own contexts, the high levels of reported happiness seem inconsistent with the theory.

Two kinds of adaptation place restrictions on how high the overall level of happiness can be. We have already considered the first when discussing Application 5: Adaptation to events near the top of a contextual range reduces the mean of their value judgments. The magnitude of this kind of adaptation depends on w, as described in Equations 3 and 4. The conditions affecting this relative weighting of range and frequency principles are not yet well understood (Parducci, 1982); however, in a variety of psychophysical experiments, w has averaged about .5, that is, equal weighting of range and frequency tendencies. With $w = .5$, the mean of all judgments (our first measure of happiness) cannot be more than halfway up to the top of the scale from 0, that is, from an exactly even balance of negative and positive judgments. For the balance to be even this positive, events would have to pile up at the very top of the range of each of life's important contexts, with only a very occasional lesser event to define the lower endpoint of the range. This most negatively skewed of all possible distributions seems highly unrepresentative of even the happiest lives; we do not seem to be living in this best of all possible worlds. Most or at least many events seem of intermediate value. For the level of happiness reported in the surveys, life's more important domains would have to be more skewed than the ups and downs of everyday life would seem to allow. Even the highly skewed distributions shown in the left panel of Figure 1-1 yield mean overall judgments that are only about one-sixth of the way from neutrality to the most extreme value judgment (about 3.5 or 4.5 on a scale from 1 to 7).

But even if one could arrange events so that the best of them came most frequently, there is a second kind of adaptation that also tends to reduce the degree of positive balance. This is the tendency to extend the range when the best comes relatively often.

Consider, for example, a salesman whose distribution of commissions varies between $0 and $100, with the latter coming most often. Under these conditions, the salesman would come to anticipate commissions greater than $100; he would consider working harder, finding a more lucrative product, improving his sales pitch—all with the effect of extending the upper endpoint of his range. Unless the great bulk of his actual commissions could increase to this anticipated level, his overall satisfaction with his earnings would drop.

The theory does not assert that the range must get extended in this way. However, even in simple psychophysical experiments, the subjective range sometimes extends beyond a frequently presented end-stimulus (Parducci, Knobel, & Thomas, 1976). Do not most of us let our hopes and expectations go beyond the best of what we are experiencing, particularly if this best is relatively frequent?

Each of these two kinds of adaptation suggests that high self-avowals of happiness should be discounted. Indeed, if one defines happiness as a mean or summation across millions of value judgments, it is hard to imagine how people could even attempt to perform such an operation while replying to an interviewer. It seems more likely that their self-avowals of happiness reflect philosophical preconceptions rather than empirical self-assessments. For example, most people may realize that experiences cannot always be positive, that they would quickly adapt to even a marked improvement in their own circumstances; at the same time, they realize how hard it would be to adapt to poorer circumstances. Simple psychophysical experiments demonstrate much more rapid adaptation to extensions than to restrictions of the range (Parducci, 1956), and people may be intuitively aware of a parallel phenomenon in their own lives.

It is also possible that these self-avowals of happiness are really reports of *changes* in material circumstances. Although surveys do not find marked correlations with objective variables such as income, type of work, or place of residence, avowals of happiness are more highly correlated with ratings of change on these variables (Gutek, Allen, Tyler, Lau, & Majchrzak, 1983). This raises the possibility of an ascending sequence of circumstances. If Coue's prayer that "day by day, in every way, life is getting better and better and better" really describes what happens in certain important domains of experience, then there would be a way out of the bitter restrictions we have been considering. This seems, at least superficially, to be the characteristic feature of the successful capitalist in the domain of material success: "Money makes money, and the money money makes makes more money." However, even the most successful capitalists can hardly avoid anticipating future profits so that these seem like losses when they do not match up to expectations.

Still another possibility is that most people have a basic intuitive understanding of the relational nature of their value judgments. They know that life must include both ups and downs, that even the best of circumstances include disappointments and misery. They may conclude, falsely according to the present theory, that the balance must normally be just about even. Therefore, when they experience more good than bad in their own present circumstances, they report that they are very happy. And they *are* more happy than the perfectly even balance that they assume is the norm. But an averaging of their value judgments, moment by moment over some substantial period of their lives (as required by Definition 6), would not yield nearly so favorable a balance as regularly reported in the surveys. A curious finding that seems consistent with this interpretation of positive bias is that the average person reports himself happier than he believes the average person to be (Andrews & Withey, 1976; Freedman, 1978)!

It should be clear that happiness, as defined and described by the present theory, is not to be identified with any objective behavior, not even a self-avowal of happiness. Even a conscious attempt to express a particular value judgment as a category rating may be subject to systematic distortions. If one actually tried to average across untold numbers of value judgments, the result would be subject to distortions of memory and weighting for frequency and also the various misunderstandings such as those we have just been considering.

8. Comparisons between different lives with respect to happiness can be made only by inference, not by directly experiencing the different lives.

This is an old philosophic problem invoked by John Stuart Mill (1863/1961) when he tried to distinguish between different *qualities* of pleasure. Where Bentham had put all pleasures in the same basket, Mill wanted a hierarchy of pleasures: "better to be Socrates dissatisfied than a fool satisfied." Mill proposed that this comparison could be confirmed by people who had led both lives. The present theory suggests that this would be a misleading procedure because the combined context of events experienced only by Socrates and events experienced only by the fool is different from the restricted context experienced by just one or just the other. Perhaps the fool would no longer be so satisfied with his earthly pleasures once he had experienced the joys of contemplative philosophy, but as a fool he does not have Socrates' philosophy to hold up for comparison. And in this respect, what he does not know may not hurt him.

The only sense in which such comparisons seem possible is by inference about the frequency distributions of contextual events. We may conjecture about the distribution of full stomachs and empty ones in the fool's life, the time spent with hangovers versus the time spent drinking himself into oblivion. So too with the intellectual and moral domains of Socrates. If we conclude that the best in Socrates' life, perhaps the contemplation of pure ideas, came relatively often, and that the worst, perhaps an occasional inability to live up to his own lofty ideals, came relatively infrequently, then we may deduce that his life was a happy one, happier even than the fool's. But the hazards of this kind of conjecture are not reduced by direct comparison between drinking and contemplation, even if we have personally done a good deal of each. Just as with interpersonal comparisons, the context for the comparison may be very different from the separate contexts for drinking and for contemplation. This is the problem with any attempt to characterize differences in terms of absolute levels. Because we prefer more money to less does not imply that happiness is correlated with income.

Conclusion

The present emphasis upon the relational character of value judgments suggests a different way of thinking about happiness. It goes beyond commonsense appreciation of judgmental relativism in specifying the kinds of relationships that produce higher or lower average judgments. As with any attempt to apply general principles to complex situations, its usefulness would not be easy to evaluate. But it should be subjectively testable. We should be able to assess, at least occasionally, how our own value judgments shift with shifts in the context in which specific events are experienced. Unfortunately, if a century of scientific psychology has taught us anything, it is to be skeptical of inferences drawn from uncontrolled observations of complex phenomena.

References

Anderson, N. H. (1981). *Foundations of information integration theory*. New York: Academic Press.

Andrews, F. M., & Withey, S. B. (1976). *Social indicators of well-being: Americans' perceptions of life quality*. New York: Plenum.

Beebe-Center, J. G. (1932). *The psychology of pleasantness and unpleasantness*. New York: Van Nostrand.

Bentham, J. (1961). *An introduction to the principles of morals and legislation*. In *The utilitarians*. New York: Dolphin Books. Originally published in 1789.

Brickman, P., & Campbell, D. T. (1971). Hedonic relativism and planning the good society. In M. H. Appley (Ed.), *Adaptation-level theory*. New York: Academic Press.

Campbell, D. T., Hunt, W. A., & Lewis, N. A. (1957). The effects of assimilation and contrast in judgments of clinical materials. *American Journal of Psychology*, *70*, 347-360.

Cantril, H. *The pattern of human concerns*. (1965). New Brunswick, NJ: Rutgers University Press.

Eiser, J. R., & Stroebe, W. (1972). *Categorization and social judgment*. New York: Academic Press.

Freedman, J. L. (1978). *Happy people*. New York: Harcourt Brace Jovanovich.

Green, D. M., & Swets, J. A. (1966). *Signal detection theory and psychophysics*. New York: Wiley.

Gutek, B. A., Allen, H., Tyler, T. R., Lau, R. R., & Majchrzak, A. (1983). The importance of internal referents as determinants of satisfaction. *Journal of Community Psychology*, *11*, 111-120.

Helson, H. (1964). *Adaptation-level theory*. New York: Harper & Row.

Hunt, W. A., & Volkmann, J. (1937). The anchoring of an affective scale. *American Journal of Psychology, 49*, 88-92.

Johnson, D. M. (1944). Generalization of a scale of values by the averaging of practice effects. *Journal of Experimental Psychology, 34*, 425-436.

Johnson, D. M. (1955). *The psychology of thought and judgment*. New York: Harper & Brothers.

Mellers, B. A., & Birnbaum, M. H. (1982). Loci of contextual effects in judgment. *Journal of Experimental Psychology: Human perception and performance, 8*, 582-601.

Mill, J. S. (1961). *Utilitarianism*. In *The utilitarians*. New York: Dolphin Books. Originally published in 1863.

Parducci, A. (1956). Direction of shift in the judgment of single stimuli. *Journal of Experimental Psychology, 51*, 169-178.

Parducci, A. (1965). Category judgment: a range-frequency model. *Psychological Review, 72*, 407-418.

Parducci, A. (1968). The relativism of absolute judgments. *Scientific American, 219*, 84-90.

Parducci, A. (1974). Contextual effects: A range-frequency analysis. In E. C. Carterette & M. P. Freedman (Eds.), *Handbook of perception* (Vol. II). New York: Academic Press.

Parducci, A. (1982). Category ratings: Still more contextual effects! In B. Wegener (Ed.), *Social attitudes and psychophysical measurement*. Hillsdale, NJ: Lawrence Erlbaum.

Parducci, A. (1983a). Category ratings and the relational character of judgment. In H.-G. Geissler, P. Petzold, H. Buffant, & Y. M. Zabrodin (Eds.), *Psychological judgment and the process of perception*. Amsterdam: North-Holland Publishing Co.

Parducci, A. (1983b). Perceptual and judgmental relativity. In V. Sarris & A. Parducci (Eds.), *Perspectives in psychological experimentation: Toward the year 2000.* Hillsdale, NJ: Lawrence Erlbaum.

Parducci, A., Calfee, R. C., Marshall, L. M., & Davidson, L. P. (1960). Context effects in judgment: Adaptation level as a function of the mean, midpoint, and median of the stimuli. *Journal of Experimental Psychology, 60,* 65-77.

Parducci, A., Knobel, S., & Thomas, C. (1976). Independent contexts for category ratings: A range-frequency analysis. *Perception & Psychophysics, 20,* 360-366.

Parducci, A., & Perrett, L. P. (1971). Category rating scales: Effects of relative spacing and frequency of stimulus values. *Journal of Experimental Psychology Monograph, 89,* 427-452.

Riskey, D. R., Parducci, A., & Beauchamp, G. K. (1979). Effects of context in judgments of sweetness and pleasantness. *Perception & Psychophysics, 26,* 171-176.

Sherif, M. (1936). *The psychology of social norms*. New York: Harper & Row.

Skinner, B. F. (1948). *Walden two*. New York: Macmillan.

Skinner, B. F. (1971). *Beyond freedom and dignity*. New York: Knopf.

Solzhenitsyn, A. (1963). *One day in the life of Ivan Denisovich*. New York: Dutton.

Stevenson, C. L. (1944). *Ethics and language*. New Haven: Yale University Press.

Thurstone, L. L. (1927). A law of comparative judgment. *Psychological Review, 34,* 273-286.

Volkmann, J. (1951). Scales of judgment and their implications for social psychology. In J. H. Rohrer & M. Sherif (Eds.), *Social psychology at the crossroads*. New York: Harper & Brothers.

Wever, E. G., & Zener, K. E. (1928). The method of absolute judgment in psychophysics. *Psychological Review, 35*, 466-493.

Zoeke, B., & Sarris, V. (1983). A comparison of "frame of reference" paradigms in human and animal psychophysics. In H.-G. Geissler, P. Petzold, H. Buffant, & Y. M. Zabrodin (Eds.), *Psychological judgment and the process of perception.* Amsterdam: North-Holland Publishing Co.

Chapter 2

Psychological Perspective in Attitude Research

Harry S. Upshaw and Thomas M. Ostrom

The variable perspective approach to social attitudes was inspired by two events that occurred when the present authors worked together as faculty advisor and research assistant. One was a challenge by a granting agency to defend the use of Thurstone's equal-appearing intervals scaling procedure in light of evidence that judges' attitudes affect their judgments of opinion statements (Hovland & Sherif, 1952). The other was a televised interview of retiring President Dwight Eisenhower in which he described his manner of making political decisions. The first event led to a study in which it was demonstrated that judges whose own positions are not included in the range of statements offered for judgment act as though their positions were included, thereby effectively extending the range (Upshaw, 1962). In other words, the perspectives assumed by judges appeared to vary according to the judges' own attitudes when those attitudes were out of the range of a set of items that were judged.

In his interview, Eisenhower claimed a "middle-of-the-road" political philosophy. He described a rule for implementing that philosophy which required that he obtain from his advisors many alternative positions on an issue. Following his rule, he then ordered these positions along a liberal-conservative dimension, and typically selected a middle one. The Eisenhower rule suggested to us a distinction between attitude content and attitude rating (Ostrom, 1970; Ostrom & Upshaw, 1968; Upshaw, 1964). The former president apparently chose a particular content position in order to protect his moderate self-rating.

We speculated that the "Eisenhower rule" could be generalized to include instances in which people are committed to self-judgments of any sort, not just to those of moderation. Furthermore, we reasoned that some people might be more committed to a content position than to a label of any sort. Ostrom (1970) showed experimentally that a shift in the range of what was assumed to be the content alternatives induces an apparent content change for people who are committed to a self-rating, and a rating change for people who are committed to a content position. (A modified interpretation of this experiment is discussed in a later section.) Eisenhower, then, had simply articulated the rule of rating-committed recipients of persuasion.

In all of our work on variable perspectives, we have attempted to apply general principles of judgment to social-psychological phenomena. This effort does not reflect any dedication on our part to a reductionist position. Nor do we believe that psychophysics provides adequate explanations of all, or even most, social-psychological phenomena. On the other hand, many of those phenomena that we want to explain are judgmental (cf. Upshaw, 1974, in press). It seems reasonable to ask whether they can be explained by the same relatively simple cognitive processes that suffice in other areas of judgment. An affirmative answer challenges the need to formulate more complex, ad hoc explanatory principles.

It is not appropriate here to provide a thorough survey of the psychology of judgment. That task has been performed with different degrees of comprehensiveness by authors or several recent volumes (e.g., Carterette & Friedman, 1974; Eiser & Stroebe, 1972; Wegener, 1982; Wyer & Srull, in press). However, one of our goals is to integrate social judgment with the general psychology of judgment. Accordingly, we first describe the variable perspective model of attitude phenomena within the context of the broader psychology of judgment. We do this by stating a set of principles that we think the reader will accept either as axioms or as facts that can be supported by the literature. Following that presentation, we describe some specific methodological problems that are posed by this judgmental theory of attitudes, and we suggest that the same problems are inherent in some other current approaches. Finally, we conclude that solutions exist for the problems we pose, and that the variable perspective theory remains a promising approach for attitude research.

Some Principles of Absolute Judgment

1. In any "absolute" judgment, the judge compares the focal stimulus to a reference set of other stimuli.

2. Any set of stimuli can be ordered (judged) according to many different criteria, but all of the orderings are not the same. For example, attitudinal positions might be ordered according to the extent to which they favor some particular social group, the extent to which they reflect socially desirable views, the extent to which they imply idealism, or the degree of the judge's agreement with them. The exact ordering of the stimuli depends upon the underlying dimension. Thus, it cannot be assumed, in principle, that endorsement-rejection judgments lead to the same ordering of attitude positions that would result from judgments of anti-pro, responsible-irresponsible, and so forth. All of this is to say that it is an attribute of stimuli that one judges, not the stimuli per se. Accordingly, virtually an infinite number of independent judgments is possible for any set of stimuli.

3. It has been demonstrated repeatedly in modern psychophysics (Stevens, 1966, 1974) that the same judgmental information can be conveyed in many different ways. In fact, any sensory dimension can serve as a judgmental language provided only that the judge has control of it. A person could express judgments of, say, heaviness, by matching stimuli to the brightness of lights, the vigor of handgrip, or the grittiness of sandpaper specimens. In the attitude domain, a person might render judgments by volunteering an amount of service to a charity, giving money to it, or (negatively) by urging friends to boycott it (see Upshaw, 1969).

4. In rendering an absolute judgment, a person effectively associates the ordered stimulus set with a limited part of the response dimension, and proceeds to divide that part into unitary segments. This joining of the response dimension to the stimulus set is one form of what is commonly called "anchoring."

5. The anchoring of a response dimension to a stimulus set, as described above, is a major determinant of the absolute judgment of every stimulus within the set. It even "commits" the judge to responses for stimuli that are not salient at the moment, but which qualify for inclusion in the stimulus set.

6. According to this formulation, anchoring results in a response scale that is efficiently described in terms of its origin and unit (cf. Upshaw, 1969). The origin is indicated inversely by the level of the judgments, and the unit is indicated inversely by the dispersion of judgments.

7. It follows from the previous formulation that a change in the stimulus range without an accompanying change in the response range results in a general displacement of all responses in the direction opposite to that in which the stimulus range was expanded. The result is the well-known contrast effect. This effect and its hypothesized cause are illustrated in Figure 2-1.

The functional stimulus range need not coincide with the range presented for judgment. The range might be extended because the judge imagines stimuli that were not included in the stimulus set. For example, Tresselt (1948) compared weight judgments by professional weight lifters and watchmakers. The mean judgments were consistent with the hypothesis that each professional group initially added familiar stimuli to the set that was specified for judgment. In a similar manner, a judge might

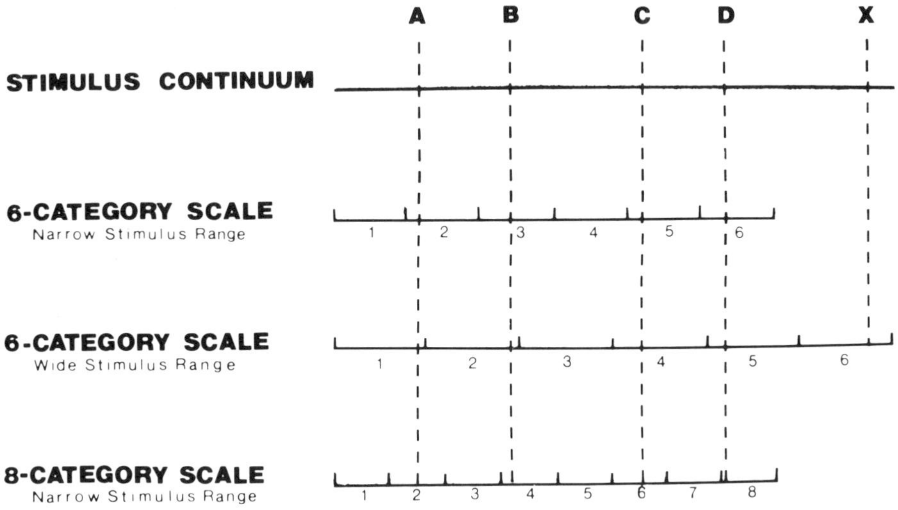

Fig. 2-1. A model of scale anchoring, illustrating contrast following the extension of stimulus range and assimilation following the extension of response range. *Note:* From "Social Influences on Attitudes and on Anchoring of Congeneric Attitude Scales" by H. S. Upshaw, 1978, Journal of Experimental Social Psychology, *14,* 329. Copyright 1982 by Academic Press. Reprinted with permission.

perceive a set of alternative attitude positions as being biased and add to the set his or her position, or any other position that is thought to be relevant. A president's stimulus range might be expanded because an advisor suggests a plausible position that is more extreme than any previously considered, or because social and political developments make more extreme positions salient.

In a study of judgments of attitude statements relating to the social position of blacks, we (Ostrom & Upshaw, 1970) found that white subjects more than black subjects changed their judgments of the Hinckley (1932) scale statements as the American civil rights movement progressed. Furthermore, the changes were in the direction that suggested a perspective expansion by white subjects in the pro-black direction. Ostsrom (1966) asked subjects to write statements expressing the most extreme pro-black position that they took into account when judging the Hinckley items. His data confirmed the interpretation that the white perspective had by that time expanded more in the pro-black direction than had the typical black perspective. Presumably, the expansion of stimulus range in this instance did not result from their imagining their own position. Such an interpretation would require us to conclude that the typical white respondent had become more pro-black than the typical black respondent. It was far more plausible to conclude that the change in white subjects reflected an increased range of positions that had become salient and likely of attainment.

8. If the stimulus range is held constant and the response range is expanded, the result is a shift in the judgment of all items in the direction of the expansion. This result is what has been called "assimilation." Figure 2-1 illustrates both contrast as a result of stimulus range expansion and assimilation following response scale expansion.

The Perspective Model of Attitudes

In applying these judgmental principles to social attitudes, a number of problems arise. Foremost is the problem of defining attitude. The model requires a distinction between a judgment and that which is judged, that is, the stimulus. In our earlier work we referred to the judgmental stimulus as the content of one's attitude and the judgment of that stimulus as the self-rating. We were purposely nonspecific about attitude content, describing it as "a compound . . . made up of many elements, each of which implies a positive or negative evaluation of the attitude object . . . [and to] . . . which beliefs, feelings, and policy orientations all contribute" (Ostrom & Upshaw, 1968, p. 220). Behind this lack of specificity in definition is the concept of attitude content as a latent variable that can only be inferred from its indicators. The rating, on the other hand, is a manifest response that conveys information about both the underlying attitude content and other processes that operate at the response level. Although we used the term "rating," the model applies to any form of quantifiable judgmental response.

The perspective model of attitudes focuses upon the effects of context upon judgments. In terms of the model, context might vary in either of two ways. As indicated earlier, context may vary because different stimuli are judged, or because different response alternatives are available. As a consequence of variation in context, whether that variation is at the stimulus or response level, there might be an effect upon attitude content, rating (judgment), or both. The major challenge of the theory is to identify determinants of differential effects upon content and rating, and to formulate methodological criteria for distinguishing content from judgment.

As we have indicated, the perspective model of attitudes draws a sharp distinction between attitude content and judgments of that content. We equate content with the stimulus that underlies an absolute judgment. We seek an explanation of a particular rating or judgment by reference to the way in which a response scale is anchored to a stimulus (content) dimension. This basic formulation is essentially an application of a commonly assumed model of psychophysical judgment (cf. Guilford, 1954, pp. 312-320). The basic psychophysical model provides a strict accounting for attitude phenomena only when all elements are in place, that is, when the person has a content position and a well-anchored response scale. Within this framework, some of the more vital issues in attitude research concern the adoption and change of content positions, and the adoption and change of reference scales. To address these issues in a meaningful way requires an expansion of the basic psychophysical model. The next two sections describe how we have sought to accomplish this expansion in order to deal with these fundamental issues of attitude research while remaining consistent with the general judgmental model.

Attitude content

The content dimension is equivalent to the stimulus dimension in psychophysical judgment. As such, there are two types of changes that might occur as a consequence of a change in context. On the one hand, the segment of the stimulus continuum that is taken into account at the time of judging might be expanded or contracted. On the other hand, the qualitative nature of the content dimension might be altered. Most past research on the perspective model has focused upon changes that result from expansion or contraction of the range of positions on the stimulus continuum. Indeed, the term "perspective" refers to this stimulus (or content) range. In most of this research the nature of the content dimension has been held constant. However, the study of qualitative changes in the content dimension is in no way incompatible with the theory.

As an aid to understanding change in a person's content position, it is valuable to consider how that position might have been adopted in the first place. It has been suggested (Upshaw, 1975) that people order salient, alternative content positions according to a preference criterion that is, in principle, idiosyncratic. If the object of the attitude is at all complex, then the preference criterion is likely to be a composite of many different attributes. Choosing an attitude position, according to this formulation, is not substantially different from choosing anything else, for example, an apartment, a spouse, or an automobile.

Let us pursue the analogy between choosing a content position and choosing which automobile to purchase. Suppose that the choice criterion for the automobile is a composite of safety, economy, and ease of handling. For present purposes we need not be concerned with the way in which a person puts these considerations together in order to define a preference criterion, that is, the composition rules. However, we can surely imagine that it can be done. When all of the salient choice alternatives are ordered according to the composite criterion, the one that is at the most preferred end of the preference ordering is, except in unusual circumstances, the chosen one (cf. Upshaw, 1975). If, subsequent to the original preference ordering, an alternative becomes salient which has more of the criterion property than does the previously chosen one, then the person would presumably shift his or her preference to the newly added alternative. Hence, discovering a car with the proper combination of economy, safety, and maneuverability could lead the buyer to purchase it instead of the one that had previously been preferred. A similar process probably operates in politics, social policy, and other areas within the domain of social attitudes.

A change in attitude content can, therefore, be produced by an expansion of the set of alternatives at the preferred end of the series. Obviously, the change can also be accomplished by restricting the range at that end of the series. Discovering that a desired mate is pledged to another, that a preferred apartment has already been rented, or that a chosen automobile is no longer available is frustrating, but when fully comprehended, it will lead to a new preference. We hypothesize that coming to believe that events have invalidated a preferred position on a social issue functions in a similar fashion to force a change in one's attitude-content position.

A change in content position might result from an expansion of the set of alternatives or a contraction at the preferred end of the series. A third way by which it might occur is by means of a change in the composition of the preference criterion. In the automobile analogy, suppose that one were to win a lottery and, as a consequence cease to consider economy as important in the purchase of an automobile. Now, the ordering of alternative automobiles will very likely change because the preference criterion has changed. (Most likely, the range of salient alternatives will also increase, producing a confounding of this and the previously described means of content change.) Analogously, persuasive communication might convince a person that some aspect of a policy issue is more important than it was previously considered and, thereby, cause the person to revise the ordering of alternative positions. If the reordering leads to a new preference, then a change in content position will have occurred.

The mechanisms that have been described for producing a change in attitude content all refer to the ordering of salient alternatives on an idiosyncratically defined preference continuum. Any judge is capable of ordering a set of alternatives on a variety of continua other than the one that corresponds to preference. As a matter of fact, the preference ordering, as described above, is a composite of a self-selected set of other orderings.

Judgments of attitude content

A major concern in much attitude research is the evaluative implication of a person's choice of content position, that is, how favorable or unfavorable toward the attitude object the preferred content position is. For example, endorsement of a content position such as "A woman should control her own body" might be the basis for inferring a favorable disposition toward a public policy of abortion on demand. This assumption is the key to attitude measurement by means of a Thurstone scale. It should be noted, however, that Thurstone's (1928) procedures require that a group of judges rate each statement of opinion to express their judgments about the evaluative implications of the opinions. Relative consensus in those judgments determines the confidence with which the implications of any item can be asserted.

Not only did Thurstone provide a criterion of ambiguity for determining confidence in the evaluative status of an opinion statement, he also provided a criterion for determining (somewhat indirectly) whether the evaluative implication of a statement was the reason for subjects' endorsement or rejection of it. This "criterion of irrelevance" assesses the probability of similar reactions (i.e., endorsement or rejection) of each item and every other item, ordered according to scale values of anti-pro sentiments toward the attitude object. Thurstone reasoned that if subjects endorsed or rejected items in order to express their evaluations of an object, they would show an increasing probability of joint endorsement and joint rejection with increasing evaluative similarity of the items. Absence of the relationship was, to Thurstone, evidence that subjects responded to the items on some basis other than their attitudes.

Thurstone's criteria of evaluative ambiguity and irrelevance have substantive as well as methodological importance. The ambiguity criterion calls attention to the fact that the evaluative implication of an attitudinal position (i.e., content) is subject to judgment. Thus, asking subjects to make self-ratings of favorability toward an object is tantamount to asking them to judge their content positions on a pro-anti dimension. Although the researcher may have particular interest in this dimension, from the subjects' point of view these judgments may not differ in any important way from judgments of content along other dimension. Insofar as a self-rating is a judgment of content, rather than content itself, it is possible for the rating to change without implying a corresponding change of content.

Whereas Thurstone's criterion of ambiguity calls attention to the fact that the evaluative implication of a content position is subject to judgment, both by the person who holds the position and by others, his criterion of irrelevance points to the fact that a person may embrace a particular position for many different reasons, including consideration of its judged evaluative implication. In the latter case a change in rating directly signifies a change in content position. However, a rating change, alone, is not diagnostic of the content basis of an attitude because content changes for any reason affect ratings.

A critical implication of the present discussion is that a researcher can seldom be absolutely sure whether a change in rating resulted from a change in content position or whether it resulted from other causes. In a later section of this chapter we address the methodological question of distinguishing these two situations. For present purposes, we focus on those cases in which ratings change as a function of context, but the underlying content positions are unaffected.

The perspective model accounts for the effects of context upon ratings as the result of differences in the parameters of judges' reference scales (Upshaw, 1969). Any sensory continuum, including numbers (see Rule & Curtis, 1982), over which the judge has control can serve as the response language for a reference scale. A scale is essential for any absolute judgment, for it is the unit and origin of the scale that provides the metric, hence the vocabulary for making the judgment. If an experimental manipulation such as a shift in context produces only a change of scale, then it must be true that the distribution of a set of judgments under the various conditions differ only in location, corresponding to a change in scale origin, and/or dispersion, corresponding to a change in scale unit (see Ellis, 1966; Upshaw, 1969). Any nonlinearity in the comparison of two sets of judgments would indicate an effect due to nonscale factors. In the attitude domain, nonlinearity in the comparison of pre- and postexperimental judgments could reflect changes in preference among content positions. Alternatively, it might reflect a qualitative difference in meaning of the underlying scale property.

In research on the perspective model, the only determinants of scale parameters that have been systematically explored are the stimulus and response ranges. According to the model, the judge anchors the endpoints of a segment of the stimulus continuum to the endpoints of a segment of a response continuum. The wider the stimulus range relative to a fixed response range, the larger the judgmental unit is expected to be. The unit, in turn, determines the spacing of the various stimuli in the distribution of judgments. The scale unit is thought to be a function of the difference between the upper and lower perspective anchors and, the origin is thought to be a function of the sum of these two values. The origin is, as described above, a location parameter. Thus, the predicted result of expanding perspective at either the upper or lower end of the stimulus segment is to shift the origin and thereby produce a general displacement of the original judgments in the direction opposite to that of the expansion. The expanded perspective is also expected to result in an enlarged unit that is manifested by reduced differentiation among the stimuli. Results confirming these predictions have been reported in psychophysical research as well as in attitude studies (see, e.g., Hansen, Thomas, & Upshaw, 1962; Murdoch, 1969; Parducci, 1974, 1982; Poulton, 1968; Simpson, Ostrom, & Sloan, 1973; Upshaw, 1978, in press; Volkmann, 1951).

Although a great deal of research has established that manipulations of perspective produce effects that can be interpreted as alterations of origin and unit, the exact causal relationship between scale parameters remains somewhat unclear. In what is apparently the only study in which the independent and dependent variables were interchanged (Upshaw, 1970), manipulation of the judgmental unit led to differences in reported perspectives. A larger unit was associated with estimates of both lower low values and higher high values for a variety of different stimulus dimensions.

According to the theory, any experimental effects upon the reference scale persist when that same scale is utilized in judging stimuli other than those that produced the experimental effects. Steele and Ostrom (1974) established differential perspectives for judgments that referred to a scenario involving a legal case. Their results showed the predicted context effects produced by manipulating the stimulus range. When the same scale was employed to judge a second legal case, the obtained results confirmed predictions based upon perspective theory that the previously established origin and unit were utilized in judging the new case. Similar results were reported by Rehm (1976).

Let us summarize here our conception of content and rating change. The former can be said to occur under two conditions: when the qualitative nature of the content dimension changes, and when the subject judges a new position to be the most preferred among alternatives. In practice, a qualitative change in the content dimension almost certainly produces an inversion in the preference order. If it does not, it may well go undetected by current methods. A rating or judgment change occurs (a) when there is a content change or b) when there is an effect upon the parameters of the reference scale in terms of which the subject describes his or her content position.

Judgments on Congeneric Attitude Scales

Our discussion of the perspective model up to this point has proceeded as though there were in every application a single stimulus dimension and a single associated response dimension. In the previous discussion, we pointed out the arbitrariness of the response dimension, noting that many alternative dimensions are possible for rendering judgments about any stimulus. The most recent developments in perspective theory are concerned with the multiple scales that a judge might associate with a single stimulus set. The multiple scale phenomenon seems especially appropriate in the domain of social attitudes. There are obviously very many ways in which attitudes are expressed: donations of time or money to political or social causes, words of praise or blame, joining picket lines, and so forth. Any of these modes of expression might function as a judgmental medium.[1]

Different scales that are used to convey the same judgmental information about content positions have been called *congeneric attitude scales* (Upshaw, 1978). The terminology, as well as the concept, was borrowed from psychological test theory, particularly the work of Jöreskog (1971). He defined two congeneric tests as measures yielding scores that are both linear functions of the same "true scores." According to this conception, congeneric tests, hence congeneric attitude scales, may differ in mean and standard deviation but not in their factorial composition. Two congeneric measures would be perfectly correlated if it were somehow possible to remove all unreliable variance from both measures.

Lord (1957, 1973), McNemar (1958), Jöreskog (1971), and Kristof (1973), have described statistical tests of whether a correlation coefficient corrected for attentuation is 1.00. The least restrictive of these procedures utilizes linear structural realtions analysis (Jöreskog & Sörbom, 1981). With this technology available to establish whether, indeed, various attitude scales are congeneric, interesting extensions of the perspective model can be studied rigorously.

The concept of congeneric scales invites a close examination of the process called "anchoring." Many writers have commented that anchoring is fundamental in most explanations of absolute judgment phenomena and, at the same time, ill-defined as a concept and poorly understood as a process. In all the various accounts of anchoring there is a basic notion that the process involves establishing a link between a response scale and the stimuli that are judged. The linkage is often achieved in experiments by instructing judges to consider a designated stimulus to be an exemplar of a particular response. Hence, a 14-inch line might be exposed to the judge with the instruction to

[1]We find it difficult to distinguish between attitude and behavior as many have done. Given our conception of attitude content as a latent variable, we view the person as seeking ways to express the latent attitude. Any expression is a behavior, and it is also a judgment. In this sense, one can learn about attitude content only by inference from behavior.

place it into category 6, where the categories range from 1 to 6. In the same way, an experimenter studying attitudes toward abortion-on-demand might instruct the judge to consider a statement such as "a woman should have complete control of her body" as an example of whatever response is considered to be maximally proabortion, whether that response is a number, a descriptive phrase, the strength of grip on a hand dynamometer, or some other sensory or cognitive response dimension.

The process of anchoring obviously occurs outside the laboratory without an experimenter's instructions. In rendering a judgment in a natural setting, no less than in a laboratory, a judge must adopt a rule for converting his or her perceptions and cognitions into a response that can be understood by others. As in the laboratory, anchoring in natural settings determines the context of the judgment. The anchors, hence the context, probably result most often from a kind of linguistic accommodation (cf. Rosenberg & Cohen, 1966; Upshaw, 1974) by which people readily accept suggested anchors in order to converse in a common language with other people. If one's partner in conversation has just remarked about the excellent acoustics in Carnegie Hall, it is not likely that he or she will in that context describe the much poorer acoustics in the new junior high school auditorium as excellent. On the other hand, such a judgment might well be made in a conversation in which the partner decries the absolutely horrible acoustics in the school gymnasium. Absolute judgments are relative in context in the world outside the laboratory, as well as within.

With multiple response scales, there is need to consider not only the linkage between each scale and the underlying continuum, but also the links among scales. In any instance, all scale-to-scale and scale-to-content-continuum anchors are systematically related. Figure 2-2 illustrates two kinds of implicit anchoring. One kind, the implicit anchoring of two response scales to each other, is illustrated by Anchor Stimulus A in the figure. This kind of anchoring results from the explicit anchoring of each scale to the same content continuum. The second type of implicit anchoring is illustrated by Anchor Stimulus B. In this case, Stimulus B serves to anchor explicitly the two scales to each other, and Scale I to the content continuum. Implicitly it also anchors Scale II to the content continuum.

The implications of anchoring with congeneric scales can perhaps best be described by discussing specific examples.

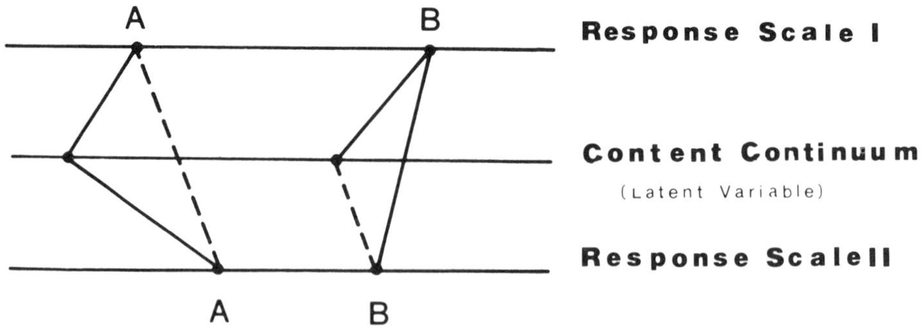

Fig. 2-2. An illustration of implicit and explicit anchoring. (See text for an explanation.)

Case 1. Change in the range of the stimulus series

If the ranges of neither of two congeneric response scales change, expansion of the stimulus range results in a contrast effect on both congeneric scales. Under the same conditions, contraction of the stimulus range produces an opposite effect, which might be described as an assimilation effect. It should be emphasized that these contrast and assimilation effects can be confidently predicted only if the ranges of the response scale remain unchanged. It is also important to recognize that, under the conditions that were specified, manipulations of stimulus range should produce equivalent effects on all congeneric response scales.

Case 2. Change in the range of response options

If there are two congeneric response scales that are anchored to a stimulus continuum, they will convey equivalent judgmental information by virtue of the implicit anchoring that exists between them. If now the range of one of the scales is changed, and there is change in neither the stimulus range nor the range of the other scale, there is likely to be a revised anchoring of the altered scale to the stimulus series. Consequently, there will also be a revision of the implicit anchoring of the two scales. Under these circumstances, responses on the altered scale are expected to show either contrast or assimilation, depending upon whether the scale range was expanded (assimilation) or contracted (contrast). No change is expected on the unaltered scale. This prediction was confirmed by Upshaw (1978) in a study that varied the anchoring of a lenient-stern rating scale to a scale of advocated length of prison sentence. In that study, changing the length of sentence associated with a particular rating of leniency-sternness resulted in an effect only on the sentence scale, and changing the rating associated with a particular sentence affected only the leniency-sternness rating scale. Furthermore, the direction of the effects were as predicted. Expansion of a response range led to assimilation on that scale.

It is not always possible to identify the stimulus (content) dimension and the response dimensions with great confidence. In principle, the judgmental response is the vehicle by which the person conveys information about the stimuli. Hence, donating money may be an alternative to a verbal endorsement as a way of expressing approval of a political cause. A person might on suitable occasions both donate money and verbally endorse the cause. Several interpretations are possible.

According to the self-perception model of attitude described by Bem (1972), the verbal endorsement could be viewed as a consequence of the actor's reflecting upon the attitudinal implications of the prior act of donating (or deciding to donate) money. Some traditional formulations might equate the verbal endorsement with attitude and hypothesize that the donation was a behavior that was caused by holding a favorable attitude toward the political movement. In contrast to both these approaches, the congeneric scale formulation views the endorsement and the donation as two ways of expressing approval (i.e., the latent attitudinal position).

Judgment is a task whereby the judge attempts to realize some goal (cf. Upshaw, in press). Because the perspective theory of attitude is an application of judgment principles to social attitudes, it is particularly appropriate to consider in every instance how the subject defines the attitude judgment task. It is probably often the case that the subjects seeks (or finds it convenient) to express a content position in multiple ways. When that is the case, the criteria that have been discussed for congeneric scales will be satisfied. To recapitulate, these criteria are: (a) a perfect correlation between scales when their correlation coefficient is corrected for attenuation, (b) equivalent effects on all scales when the underlying content position is altered, and (c) effects only on those response scales that are altered when content is unchanged. In the latter case, response scale expansion results in assimilation and scale contraction results in contrast.

If the congeneric scale criteria are not satisfied in a particular instance, the result could arise from any of several circumstances. It may be the case that one of the dimensions is exactly collinear with the content dimension. If that were the case, alteration of that scale could produce a change in perspective (i.e., content change) which would produce a corresponding change in the other response scale. On the other hand, alteration of the noncontent scale might have no effect at all on a scale that is firmly anchored to the content dimension.

Another circumstance that might lead to a failure of the congeneric scale criteria is, of course, that the congeneric hypothesis is not true. Two scales might serve as response mechanisms for different content dimensions. As we indicated earlier, any given set of stimuli can be ordered in virtually an infinite number of ways. Hence, knowing that a person judged the same set of stimuli on different scales provides no assurance whatsoever that the scales are congeneric.

The thrust of this discussion is that any strict test of the perspective theory of attitudes requires a confident identification of the content and response dimensions. In the absence of such a clear distinction, no firm predictions can be made. The hazards of proceeding with inadequate information in this regard is illustrated by ambiguous results that have been reported in several studies.

Some Ambiguous Findings

Early in the development of the theory, before the congeneric scale criteria were formulated, several experimental tests were performed in which, in retrospect, the distinction between content and rating seems to have been made somewhat arbitrarily. In one study (Upshaw, Ostrom, & Ward, 1970) the salient range of opinions regarding the social position of black Americans was manipulated along a pro-to-anti-black continuum. Subjects rated themselves on that continuum, and completed a Thurstone scale as a measure of content. There is, of course, little doubt that the rating measure is an appropriate indicator of the judgment component of our model. To interpret the Thurstone scale as a content measure, however, requires justification.

Thurstone scales assess attitudes as the average of the affective implications of opinion statements that a person endorses. It seems a plausible hypothesis that our respondents based their self-ratings of favorability toward black people upon their opinions. However, given our present recognition that rating versus content involvement leads to different reactions to the alteration of perspective, it was perhaps a design deficiency that we failed to obtain supporting evidence that these respondents based their ratings on logically prior opinions.

As it turned out, the results seem clearly to indicate that our assumption was warranted. This interpretation rests upon confirmation of the hypothesis that the expansion of perspective (i.e., the range of salient opinions) produced a contrast effect on the rating measure and no change in Thurstone scale scores. Were it otherwise, had the respondents selected opinion statements for endorsement in order to express a logically prior self-rating, then the expected results would have been a change in opinion endorsement (assimilation) in response to the expansion of perspective, and no accompanying change in rating. A third possibility in that study would have been that the rating and Thurstone measures served as congeneric attitudes scales, both anchored to a common underlying content dimension. In that case, extending the range of opinions would serve to change the anchoring of the Thurstone scale to the content dimension without affecting the way in which ratings were linked to content. Under both the congeneric scale and rating-involvement hypotheses, expansion of the opinion range is predicted to leave rating unaffected while causing Thurstone scores to change in the direction of the expanded range. That result did not occur.

Content-rating involvement reconsidered

The discussion here of the Upshaw, Ostrom, and Ward study suggests an important reformulation of our earlier work on rating versus content commitment (Ostrom, 1970; Ostrom & Upshaw, 1968). It is obviously logically possible for a judge to adopt as attitude content any stimulus whatsoever, including what we formerly described as ratings. A person who is "rating-involved" is one whose content is his or her preferred self-image as conveyed, for example, by a categorical label such as "pro," "anti," or "middle of the road." On the other hand, a judgment might be rendered by matching one's content position to a magnitude of any dimension over which the judge has control. Thus, what we originally thought of as a content dimension could serve as a response dimension. A person, then, might be committed to a content position, a judgment on any of many alternative response scales, or not committed at all. Application of the model is more complicated than we at first imagined.

In Ostrom's (1970) test of the differential effects of content versus rating commitment, subjects read about a fictitious case of a bomb threat in a hospital. After learning the history of the person who had been found guilty of making the threat, subjects indicated the prison sentence that they believed appropriate in the case. They also rated themselves in terms of leniency-sternness toward the offender. It was assumed that the advocated prison sentence functioned as attitude content, and that the self-rating functioned as a judgment. Subjects wrote essays justifying either their sentence or rating, which served to induce commitment. Perspective was assumed to have been manipulated by disclosing different legal definitions of the presiding judge's discretion in sentencing. At issue in the study was the differential reaction to differences in the sentence range according to whether the respondent was committed to a previously justified sentence or self-rating.

Ostrom's (1970) results were as expected. The manipulation led respondents to change that response to which they were not committed. In light of the reformulation that we now advocate, this result is to be expected under either of two conditions. The advocated sentence may, indeed, have been the content of the respondents' attitudes.

Alternatively, the advocated sentence and the self-rating may have functioned as congeneric attitude scales conveying equivalent information about a latent attitude content. Subsequent work by Upshaw (1978) supported this latter interpretation. In that study, advocated sentence and self-ratings of leniency-sternness were interpreted as congeneric judgments.

Multiple scales in the work of other investigators

A study by Manis. The problem of interpreting multiple scales has posed a challenge for the work of others, as well as for the perspective model. Consider, for example, a recent study by Manis (1982), in which he reported a series of experiments in which subjects rated the degree of psychopathology that characterized the authors of vocabulary definitions and handwriting samples. These indicators of pathology presumably convey evidence concerning the extent to which underlying thought processes are or are not clear and orderly. Manis observed an apparent contrast effect when either a high- or low-pathology series preceded a midscale series, provided that the same indicator was employed for induction and for test. Thus, the common midscale items in the test series were attributed to more pathological authors in the low pathology induction group than in the high pathology group. However, this contrast effect was not found if the indicators changed between the induction and test phases of the study. Switching from handwriting to definitions, or vice versa, typically eliminated the effect.

Manis did not design his study to test our formulation of perspective theory. Accordingly, we can only speculate about some of the critical judgmental processes of his respondents. For example, it seems reasonable to assume that psychopathology corresponds to the content continuum in this case. If that is true, then the manipulation of the degree to which handwriting samples and definitions are bizarre or chaotic does not necessarily constitute a manipulation of the stimulus range. For example, the stimulus continuum might be thought of as containing a set of persons whom the judge holds in mind while making responses. The handwriting samples and definitions can be viewed as symptoms that are manifested by persons on the content dimension. A manipulation of the range of symptoms does not require that judges revise the set of stimulus persons nor their placement on the content dimension.

As indicators of underlying content, these samples of handwriting and definitions might be conceived as equivalent to the judgments that a person might make about the degree of underlying pathology. The task of the respondent was then to interpret these "judgments" by matching each of them both to a hypothetical stimulus within an imagined set that the respondent brought to the experiment, and to the rating scale of psychopathology that was specified in the experimental instructions. What Manis assumed to be a manipulation of stimulus range can be viewed as manipulations of the ranges of the congeneric scales that subjects used to judge pathology during the induction phase: numerical ratings plus either handwriting quality or definitional quality.

The results that Manis reported in the part of the study that we have described are those that are expected under the congeneric scale interpretation. In the induction phase of the experiment the numerical scale was apparently anchored either to the handwriting or definition scale. This was accomplished by supplying extreme samples of handwriting or definitions along with a constant numerical rating scale. Subsequently, midscale handwriting or definition items were presented for judgment in terms of numerical ratings. Manis interpreted the initial presentation of extreme items as a manipulation of the stimulus range. We, on the other hand, suggest that those items established different response ranges which were subsequently extended toward the middle of the scales when, during the test phase, new items were presented that were more moderate than those in the induction phase. We expect an apparent displacement of judgments toward the middle of the scale, but only on the manipulated scales. That was found.

In another experiment that was part of Manis' study, paired comparison judgments were obtained for the implied pathology of handwriting samples and definitions under conditions in which the range of one indicator had been altered. The results were again those that the congeneric scale model anticipates. A given definition was judged more or less frequently to surpass a given handwriting sample in pathology in just those conditions in which the indicator scale had been expanded. Manis suggested that this result indicates that context effects are representational, as opposed to judgmental in nature. We, on the other hand, interpret the same data as evidence that context effects are reference scale phenomena.

Although the results of the Manis study conform to predictions based upon the perspective model, we confess to some uneasiness in pressing that interpretation. That model applied to the experiment treats handwriting samples and definitions as though they were no different from strength of grip, brightness of a light, or any of the other judgmental dimensions that have been employed in psychophysical studies. The fact is that the dimensions that Manis used can be viewed as symptoms of the content dimension (psychopathology). For that reason, the range manipulations might have altered the content range. It does not appear to us that it did. However, we cannot decisively rule out that possibility.

Eiser's work on accentuation theory. In recent years, Eiser and his associates have developed an approach to social judgment that is similar in many respects to the congeneric scale version of the perspective model. Their approach, which is known as *accentuation theory,* focuses on a situation in which stimuli are judged on two or more scales that differ only in their evaluative connotations (Eiser & Mower White, 1974, 1975; Eiser & Osmon, 1978; Eiser & van der Pligt, 1982). In the published research, scale connotations have typically been manipulated by the social desirability of labels that designate the extremes of numerical or linear rating scales. Eiser and his associates have recognized some of the common concerns of accentuation and perspective theories, and they have tried to test the theories differentially (see, particularly, the study by Eiser & van der Pligt, 1982).

A critical distinction in accentuation theory is that between the denotative and connotative meanings of language. This distinction is commonly used in two somewhat different ways (Fowler, 1926). In one sense, a word denotes all of the objects that have the attributes that it connotes, and a word connotes all of the attributes that are shared by the objects that it denotes. According to this usage, adjectives such as those that have been used as rating scale labels by Eiser and his associates denote characteristic objects that are presumably made salient by the judging task. Thus, scales that differ in connotative meaning necessarily refer to different stimulus (content) sets. Hence, this definition of the terms implies that denotations and connotations of sets of content sets cannot be independently manipulated. Accordingly, it would not be possible to meet the requirements of congeneric scales. Each connotatively different scale would entail a different content set. If this distinction is what is intended in accentuation theory, it precludes comparison with perspective theory.

The second sense in which denotations are distinguished from connotations construes denotation as the essential referent of a word, and nothing more. Connotation, within this meaning of the distinction, refers to all attributes that are associated with the denoted referent. Thus, a "disobedient child" denotes a nonadult who typically does not act as he or she is commanded to act. On the other hand, the phrase connotes immaturity, hostility, negativism, and so on. This distinction between the correlated concepts does appear to permit independent manipulations of the two types of meanings. However, such manipulations imply that connotative meanings of response scales can be studied only when the denotative meanings are controlled, and vice versa. These conditions are clearly those that characterize congeneric scales. Hence, this meaning of denotation-connotation not only renders accentuation theory comparable to perspective theory, it suggests that the two theories may be essentially the same.

Conclusions

The variable perspective model of attitudes was inspired by a notion that it would be worthwhile to distinguish between how a person describes his or her attitude and what that attitude truly is. The full conceptual and methodological implications of that distinction were not immediately obvious. Fortunately, there are solutions to the problems that we have isolated. The approach by means of the analysis of congeneric scales appears to solve the methodological problems of our original formulation. In addition, it sheds new light on other research in the literature, and it holds promise for future work on perspective theory.

In assessing the present status of perspective theory, we are led to the conclusion that its most critical deficiency is a lack of principles by which to account for the range of content positions that a person considers in forming, changing, and judging an attitudinal position. Surely, information from external sources is a major determinant of this variable within the theory. However, there are certainly processes within the person that interact with external information to produce the effect. With the apparent solution to the difficult methodological problems of distinguishing content from response scale changes. Progress can now be made in supplying this needed addition to the theory.

References

Bem, D. J. (1972). Self-perception theory. In L. Berkowitz (Ed.), *Advances in experimental social psychology* (Vol. 6). New York: Academic Press.

Carterette, E. C., & Friedman, M. P. (Eds.). (1974). *Handbook of perception* (Vol. 2). New York: Academic Press.

Eiser, J. R., & Mower White, C. J. (1974). Evaluative consistency and social judgment. *Journal of Personality and Social Psychology, 30,* 349-359.

Eiser, J. R., & Mower White, C. J. (1975). Categorization and congruity in attitudinal judgment. *Journal of Personality and Social Psychology, 31,* 769-775.

Eiser, J. R., & Osmon, B. E. (1978). Judgmental perspective and value connotations of response scale labels. *Journal of Personality and Social Psychology, 36,* 491-497.

Eiser, J. R., & Stroebe, W. (1972). *Categorization and social judgment.* London: Academic Press.

Eiser, J. R., & van der Pligt, J. (1982). Accentuation and perspective in attitudinal judgment. *Journal of Personality and Social Psychology, 42,* 224-238.

Ellis, B. (1966). *Basic concepts of measurement.* London: Cambridge University Press.

Fowler, H. W. (1926). *A dictionary of modern English usage.* Oxford: Oxford University Press.

Guilford, J. P. (1954). *Psychometric methods* (2nd ed.). New York: McGraw-Hill.

Hansen, A. C., Thomas, D. B., & Upshaw, H. S. (1962). Judgment of priorities for home visits. *Nursing Outlook, 10,* 385-389.

Hinckley, E. D. (1932). The influence of individual opinion on construction of an attitude scale. *Journal of Social Psychology, 3,* 283-296.

Hovland, C. I., & Sherif, M. (1952). Judgmental phenomena and scales of attitude measurement: Item displacement in Thurstone scales. *Journal of Abnormal and Social Psychology, 47,* 822-832.

Jöreskog, K. G. (1971). Statistical analysis of sets of congeneric tests. *Psychometrika, 36,* 109-133.

Jöreskog, K. G., & Sörbom, P. D. (1981). *LISREL V, analysis of linear structural relationships by maximum likelihood and least squares methods, User's guide.* Uppsala, Sweden: University of Uppsala, Department of Statistics.

Kristof, W. (1973). Testing a linear relationship between true scores of two measures. *Psychometrika, 38,* 101-111.

Lord, F. M. (1957). A significance test for the hypothesis that two variables measure the same trait except for errors of measurement. *Psychometrika, 22,* 207-220.

Lord, F. M. (1973). Testing if two measuring procedures measure the same dimension. *Psychological Bulletin, 79,* 71-72.

Manis, M. (1982). *Judging psychopathology.* Paper presented at the Symposium on Social Perception in Clinical and Counseling Psychology, Texas Technological University.

McNemar, Q. (1958). Attenuation and interaction. *Psychometrika, 23,* 259-266.

Murdoch, P. (1969). Effects of perspective and payment on reference scale formation. *Journal of Experimental Research in Personality, 3,* 301-310.

Ostrom, T. M. (1966). Perspective as an intervening construct in the judgment of attitude statements. *Journal of Personality and Social Psychology, 3,* 135-144.

Ostrom, T. M. (1970). Perspective as a determinant of attitude change. *Journal of Experimental Social Psychology, 6,* 280-292.

Ostrom, T. M., & Upshaw, H. S. (1968). Psychological perspective and attitude change. In A. G. Greenwald, T. C. Brock, & T. M. Ostrom (Eds.), *Psychological foundations of attitudes.* New York: Academic Press.

Ostrom, T. M., & Upshaw, H. S. (1970). Race differences in the judgment of attitude statements over a 35 year period. *Journal of Personality, 38,* 235-248.

Parducci, A. (1974). Contextual effects: A range-frequency analysis. In E. C. Carterette & M. P. Friedman (Eds.), *Handbook of perception* (Vol. 2). New York: Academic Press.

Parducci, A. (1982). Category ratings: Still more contextual effects! In B. Wegener (Ed.), *Social attitudes and psychophysical measurement.* Hillsdale, NJ: Lawrence Erlbaum.

Poulton, E. C. (1968). The new psychophysics: Six models for magnitude estimation. *Psychological Bulletin, 69,* 1-19.

Rehm, H. H. (1976). *A social psychophysical approach to reference scale principles.* Unpublished doctoral dissertation, University of Illinois at Chicago Circle.

Rosenberg, S., & Cohen, B. D. (1966). Referential process of speakers and listeners. *Psychological Review, 73,* 208-231.

Rule, S. J., & Curtis, D. W. (1982). Levels of sensory and judgmental processing: Strategies for the evaluation of a model. In B. Wegener (Ed.), *Social attitudes and psychophysical measurement.* Hillsdale, NJ: Lawrence Erlbaum.

Simpson, D. D., Ostrom, T. M., & Sloan, L. R. (1973). Anchoring effects of trait range in impression formation. *Bulletin of the Psychonomic Society, 2,* 383-384.

Steele, C. M., & Ostrom, T. M. (1974). Perspective-mediated attitude change: When is indirect persuasion more effective than direct persuasion? *Journal of Personality and Social Psychology, 29,* 737-741.

Stevens, S. S. (1966). On the operation known as judgment. *American Scientist, 54,* 385-401.

Stevens, S. S. (1974). Perceptual magnitude and its measurement. In E. C. Carterette & M. P. Friedman (Eds.), *Handbook of perception* (Vol. 2). New York: Academic Press.

Thurstone, L. L. (1928). Attitudes can be measured. *American Journal of Sociology, 33,* 529-554.

Tresselt, M. E. (1948). The effect of experience of contrasted groups upon the formation of a new scale. *Journal of Social Psychology, 27,* 209-216.

Upshaw, H. S. (1962). Own attitude as an anchor in equal-appearing intervals. *Journal of Abnormal and Social Psychology, 64,* 85-96.

Upshaw, H. S. (1964). *Opinion change vs reference scale change in the study of attitudes.* Paper delivered at the 72nd Annual Convention of the American Psychological Association, Los Angeles.

Upshaw, H. S. (1969). The personal reference scale: An approach to social judgment. In L. Berkowitz (Ed.), *Advances in experimental social psychology* (Vol. 4). New York: Academic Press.

Upshaw, H. S. (1970). The effect of unit size on the range of the reference scale. *Journal of Experimental Social Psychology, 6,* 129-139.

Upshaw, H. S. (1974). Personality and social effects in judgment. In E. C. Carterette & M. P. Friedman (Eds.), *Handbook of perception* (Vol. 2). New York: Academic Press.

Upshaw, H. S. (1975). Judgment and decision processes in the formation and change of social attitudes. In M. F. Kaplan & S. Schwartz (Eds.), *Human judgment and decision processes.* New York: Academic Press.

Upshaw, H. S. (1978). Social influences on attitudes and on anchoring of congeneric attitude scales. *Journal of Experimental Social Psychology, 14,* 327-339.

Upshaw, H. S. (in press). Output processes in judgment. In R. S. Wyer & T. K. Srull (Eds.), *Handbook of social cognition.* Hillsdale, NJ: Lawrence Erlbaum.

Upshaw, H. S., Ostrom, T. M., & Ward, C. D. (1970). Content versus self-rating in attitude research. *Journal of Experimental Social Psychology, 6,* 272-279.

Volkmann, J. (1951). Scales of judgment and their implications for social psychology. In J. R. Rohrer & M. Sherif (Eds.), *Social psychology at the crossroads.* New York: Harper.

Wegener, B. (Ed.). (1982). *Social attitudes and psychophysical measurement.* Hillsdale, NJ: Lawrence Erlbaum.

Wyer, R. S., & Srull, T. K. (Eds.). (in press). *Handbook of social cognition.* Hillsdale, NJ: Lawrence Erlbaum.

Chapter 3

Accentuation Theory, Polarization, and the Judgment of Attitude Statements

J. Richard Eiser and Joop van der Pligt

In this chapter we shall be considering what at first sight may seem a phenomenon of limited importance—the tendency of people to make extreme rather than moderate differentiations between statements that express varying viewpoints on an issue. In attempting to explain this tendency, however, we shall mention a number of principles of far wider interest and applicability. Two such principles are of particular importance. The first—*accentuation*—concerns the tendency of people to group objects of judgment into separate categories, with the effect that the subjective differences between categories are accentuated relative to the differences within them. The second concerns the distinction between the *evaluative and descriptive functions of language.* The essential idea is that words often do not have single meanings but may fulfill a number of separate functions simultaneously. The same adjective, for instance, can both describe an attribute and communicate approval of the attribute described. These two principles are combined to form an approach that we have identified by the term *accentuation theory.*

Judgment of Attitude Statements and the Effect of Judges Attitudes

The starting point for the development of this approach was a consideration of the manner in which attitude statements are rated depending on the attitudes of the individuals who are doing the rating. From a historical point of view, the primary focus was that of the methodology of attitude scale construction. Thurstone's method of equal-appearing intervals (Thurstone & Chave, 1929) was designed to provide unidimensional measures of attitude interpretable as interval scores. To this end, considerable attention was paid to the question of how statements or "items" should be selected for inclusion in an attitude scale. A crucial stage involves presenting a large number of items to a group of independent "judges" whose task it is to judge the extent to which each item expresses a more-or-less favorable position on the issue with which the scale is concerned. From these judgments, scale values for the items are derived.

According to Thurstone's standard procedure, these judgments involve placing the items into 11 different response categories (originally by means of sorting, more recently through the use of rating scales). Typically, the extreme response categories are labeled "extremely unfavorable" and "extremely favorable" with the intermediate categories left unlabeled. Note that the judges' task is to say whether the *items* express a favorable or unfavorable viewpoint, *not* whether they personally find these items acceptable or unacceptable. Indeed Thurstone and Chave (1929, p. 92) put themselves rather on the line by declaring that "if the scale value is to be regarded as valid, the scale values of the statements should not be affected by the opinion of the people who help to construct it." In other words, the items should be rated the same, and hence obtain the same scale values, regardless of whether the judges themselves happen to hold pro or anti attitudes on the issue.

There is by now a considerable amount of research that demonstrates that Thurstone's original assumption was incorrect (cf. Eiser & Stroebe, 1972). The turning point was the study by Hovland and Sherif (1952) who took a scale designed by Hinckley (1932) to measure attitudes "toward the social position of the Negro" and found that judges differed considerably in their ratings as a function of their own attitude. This left two broad questions to be resolved. The first was methodological: In view of such findings, can Thurstone scales still be regarded as valid? The most reasonable conclusion seems to be that drawn by Upshaw (1962, 1965): Thurstone and Chave (1929) were correct in assuming that the validity of scale values as *absolute* measures of item favorability would be negated by systematic effects of judges' own attitudes. However, such effects would not destroy the validity of scale values as *relative* measures. Furthermore, since high linear correlations may be observed between sets of scale values obtained from different judges, such relative measures may still be treated as interval scores. The second question was more theoretical: How is the influence of judges' attitudes to be explained?

Anchoring and Contrast

A powerful assumption in most attempts to answer this question is that the judgment of attitude statements is likely to obey many of the same principles as the judgment of other objects or stimuli. Probably the most influential example of this is the notion that judges use their own position on the issue—the degree to which they themselves approve or disapprove of racial segregation or whatever—as a reference point or *anchor* against which to compare the items which they have to judge. The term anchor is taken from the literature on psychophysical judgment, where subjects may be presented with a series of stimuli varying in magnitude, alternating with a standard anchor stimulus of constant magnitude.

The appeal of this notion is that it leads directly to a prediction about how people with different opinions should judge the favorability of attitude statements. In a psychophysical judgment task involving, say, lifted weights, one's dependent variable would be the judged heaviness of the weights in the stimulus series, and one's independent variable would be the weight of the anchor stimulus. A very highly replicable effect is that judgments of the stimulus series depend on the magnitude of the anchor. When the anchor is relatively heavy, the stimuli are judged as relatively light; when the anchor is relatively light, the stimuli are judged as relatively heavy. This phenomenon is termed *contrast.*

In the context of attitudinal judgment, the prediction is that judges whose own position is more favorable will judge a given item series as relatively more unfavorable on the issue, whereas judges whose own position is more unfavorable should rate the items as relatively favorable. There is a fair amount of evidence that this is indeed what occurs. When Hovland and Sherif (1952) compared the ratings from different subject groups, they found that their group of anti-Negro whites produced scale values not too dissimilar from those obtained by Hinckley (1932). However, pro-Negro whites and black judges rated a large proportion of the statements as being close to the unfavorable extreme.

Interpretations of the Contrast Effect

Demonstrating the contrast effect is easier than explaining it. In psychophysics, the predominant interpretation of contrast effects has been in terms of adaptation. Helson (1964) proposed his adaptation level (AL) theory, which states that all stimuli are experienced relative to the prevailing level of adaptation of the organism. AL is conceived of as a psychological neutral point, with stimuli that fall above it being seen as more intense (larger, heavier, louder, brighter, hotter, etc.) and those that fall below it being seen as less intense (smaller, lighter, quieter, dimmer, colder, etc.). According to Helson, AL varies as a direct function (in fact, a weighted mean) of the organism's past and present levels of stimulation. Thus, a person judging lifted weights in the presence of a heavy anchor stimulus will have a higher (heavier) AL, and will therefore judge the weights, on average, as lighter than a person judging the same weights in the presence of a light anchor stimulus.

Applying this to attitudinal judgment, one could explain contrast effects by saying that someone who was extremely pro on some issue would have a more pro AL for judgment of attitudes on that issue than someone who was extremely anti. This might be because judges subjectively include their own position in the series or because they might be assumed to have more experience of viewpoints similar to their own. An indirect test of this latter assumption is to vary the stimulus series so that it includes more or fewer pro or anti items. The prediction is that common items should be rated more anti in the context of a predominantly pro series than in the context of a predominantly anti series. This is supported in studies by Fehrer (1952), Segall (1959), and Upshaw (1962), although not precisely in the form AL theory would predict (cf. Eiser & Stroebe, 1972, pp. 110-114).

For years there has been a debate about whether contrast effects reflect "true perceptual shifts," resulting for instance from physiological adaptation, or whether they reflect "semantic" effects due to judges redefining the terms of the judgment scale to suit the stimuli presented to them. Do judges rate different weights as "heavy" in a given condition because they perceive the weights differently, or because they have learned that different weights are the "heavy ones" in their condition?

There is no universal answer to this perceptual versus semantic controversy. Although Helson himself was clearly in the "perceptual" camp, many of his own studies could be interpreted as evidence of semantic shifts. Often one does not *need* to assume perceptual shifts to explain judgmental contrast. Contrast effects can also occur with stimuli for which an explanation in terms of physiological adaptation is implausible. On the other hand, adaptation-like perceptual changes certainly do occur with some kinds of stimuli, and such changes are likely to affect judgment. What can be said for certain is that Helson underestimated the importance of semantic factors in the judgment of many kinds of stimuli.

Also damaging to his original conception of AL is research that shows that subjects do more than simply compute an "average" to represent the pooled efect of previously stimulation. They also take account of the dispersion of stimulus values around that "average." The two most influential approaches that are based on this observation are represented in the two preceding chapters. Parducci's (1963, 1974) "range-frequency compromise" states that judgments reflect both the range of stimulus values presented, and the distribution (e.g., skewing) of values within that range.

Similarly, the "variable perspective model" (Ostrom, 1970; Upshaw, 1962, 1969) assumes that people judge stimuli relative to a subjective range or "perspective." While Upshaw and Ostrom do not pay the same attention as Parducci to the question of how stimulus values are distributed within a given range, they make the assumption that, in the specific context of judgment of attitude statements, judges will include their own position within their perspective. According to Upshaw (1962), when none of the items in a series is as extreme as the position held by the judge, the judge's perspective will be extended to include that position. Since judgmental shifts are presumed to occur as a result of such changes in perspective, this leads to the assumption that judges' attitudes should only influence ratings when they fall *outside* the range of items presented for judgment. This specific prediction has received only mixed support.

Assimilation and Polarization

In spite of the attention paid to contrast effects and their importance in psychophysical judgment, it could be that Hovland and Sherif (1952) were in fact observing part of a very different kind of judgmental effect. Let us emphasize one very important feature of contrast effects of the kind observed by Helson and others—they apply to the stimulus series *as a whole.* The *whole* stimulus series is judged heavier or lighter as the case may be. Now, it so happens that this is *not* what Hovland and Sherif found. Although *most* of their items were judged as more unfavorable by blacks and pro-Negro whites, a few of their items showed an apparent displacement in the direction of greater favorability.

Although Hovland and Sherif (1952) originally paid less attention to this latter part of the effect, nine years later (Sherif & Hovland, 1961) they had recognized its importance, and termed it *assimilation.* There are two important characteristics of the items that show assimilation in their study: There are fewer of them and they tend to be the most favorable items in the series. Sherif and Hovland (1961) therefore proposed their *assimilation-contrast model,* which states that judges compare statements with their own position (the anchoring assumption) and assimilate statements that are already quite close to their position, but contrast those which are further away.

A number of other constructs come into play at this point. First, there is the distinction among *latitudes of acceptance, rejection,* and *noncommitment.* These refer, respectively, to the regions of the dimension of favorability-unfavorability, which include statements a person finds acceptable, unacceptable, or about which he or she feels neutral or undecided. The simplest version of their position is that statements within a person's latitude of acceptance will be assimilated, whereas those in the other two latitudes will be contrasted. This would be compatible with the pattern of more items showing contrast than assimilation. Also relevant, though, is the idea that such judgmental shifts reflect differences in the perceived implication of the statements—in other words, a "perceptual" rather than "semantic" effect—that Sherif and Hovland consider should be stronger for more "ambiguous" items, which presumably are those that are less extreme on the favorability dimension.

Next comes the very important concept of ego-involvement which is developed further in the Sherifs' later work (e.g., Sherif, Sherif, & Nebergall, 1965). Two assumptions are relevant here: first, that individuals who are highly ego-involved in an issue should show more judgmental shifts (since their perceptions are more likely to be "biased" by their attitudes); and second, that more highly involved individuals should have narrower latitudes of acceptance and wider latitudes of rejection. It is an empirical fact, too, that individuals who are more highly involved tend also to be more extreme in terms of their own position on an issue. (See Chapter 4 for a discussion of involvement in terms of the effects of "affective intensity.")

But how compatible is the assimilation-contrast model with the more general judgmental principles so far described? Sherif and Hovland (1961) interpret assimilation-contrast effects in terms of the *anchoring* effects of judges' own attitudes, but what evidence is there that anchors can produce assimilation, and not just contrast? About the only evidence comes from a study on lifted weights by Sherif, Taub, and Hovland (1958) showing that anchors that lie just outside the range of the stimulus series (in terms of magnitude) produce assimilation, whereas more distant anchors produce contrast. There are two problems, however. First, the Sherif et al. (1958) experiment has been criticized by Parducci and Marshall (1962) who show that the assimilation effects found by Sherif et al. were not generalizable when more orthodox instructions and procedures were employed. Second, even if the Sherif et al. data were replicable, their relevance is not explained. The attitudinal judgment effect is that the same judges *both* assimilate some items *and* contrast others *within the same series.* The psychophysical judgment effect shown by Sherif et al. is that, depending on the condition, the stimulus series *as a whole* will be *either* assimilated *or* contrasted.

There are other ambiguities about the attitudinal judgment effect. Sherif and Hovland build quite a lot of theoretical work on the fact that more items are contrasted than assimilated, but might not this be just a function of the item series used? Remember that the items in their study were from a standard scale that was already 20 years old, and what might have been a "pro-Negro" statement in 1932 might have seemed less so in 1952. In fact, if one looks at the wording of the items, this possibility strikes one very forcefully. An example of an item close to the favorable extreme and showing assimilation in the Hovland and Sherif (1952) study is "The Negro should be given the same educational advantages as the white man." An example of a statement only somewhat less favorable in terms of its original (1932) scale value espouses a straight segregationist position: "The Negro should have the advantage of all social benefits of the white man but be limited to his own race in the practice thereof." This is rated as definitely unfavorable by Hovland and Sherif's black and pro-Negro white students—an example of contrast. Such statements may be compared with those originally included to represent (and even, it is frightening to remember, to *discriminate*) attitudes at the anti-Negro extreme—for instance, "No Negro has the slightest right to resent, or even question, the illegal killing of one of his race." In view of such comparisons, it is at least an open question whether Hovland and Sherif would have found stronger assimilation effects if their item series had included more statements acceptable to pro-Negros.

Because of this, it seems to us to be highly dangerous to place much weight theoretically on the difference in strength of assimilation and contrast effects. Rather than attempting to find separate explanations for each effect, therefore, we prefer to treat both together as part of a more general phenomenon, which we shall term *polarization*. By polarization of judgment we mean the tendency to make ratings in the more extreme categories at *both* ends of the judgment scale, in other words the *bilateral* extremity of a set of ratings. Both assimilation *and* contrast contribute to polarization.

Viewed in this way, what Sherif and Hovland's (1961) assimilation-contrast model predicts is that certain judges will give more polarized ratings than others. Specifically, pro judges should give more polarized ratings than neutral judges because they should assimilate pro items to the favorable extreme and contrast anti (and neutral) items toward the unfavorable extreme. Similarly, anti judges should give more polarized ratings than neutral judges because they should assimilate anti items to the unfavorable extreme and contrast pro (and neutral) items to the favorable extreme.

Unfortunately for Sherif and Hovland, this does not happen. At least, in a series of studies using the issue of attitudes towards blacks (the most commonly used issue during that period), pro-Negro judges polarized more than neutral judges, but anti-Negro judges, if anything, polarized *less* than neutral judges (Selltiz, Edrich, & Cook, 1965; Upshaw, 1965; Zavalloni & Cook, 1965). So, not only is it doubtful whether Sherif and Hovland (1961) derive their hypothesis from an appropriate theoretical principle, it is also doubtful whether their model is adequate at a predictive level. The accentuation theory approach that we shall now present starts from an attempt to correct these shortcomings in previous work.

Accentuation Theory—Basic Principles

The first question we may ask is: Are there other general principles of judgment, apart from anchoring and assimilation-contrast, that enable one to predict that judgments of any stimuli will be more polarized in some conditions than others? The answer is that there is a fair amount of research on processes of accentuation and categorization that leads directly to such predictions.

The basic requirement for accentuation or categorization effects is that the stimuli being judged should vary not only along the dimension of judgment, but also in terms of some other attribute. Following Eiser and Stroebe's (1972) analysis, we may term the judged dimension the *focal* dimension. Other unjudged attributes may be termed *peripheral.* What is crucial is the relationship between focal and peripheral variation. Where there is a simple predictable relationship between the different dimensions or attributes, judgments tend to be more polarized.

The basic principles of accentuation theory were laid down in the early work of Tajfel. The starting point was a consideration of the effects of value on judgments of physical magnitude. Previous research appeared to show simply that valued stimuli (e.g., coins) were overestimated relative to valueless stimuli of the same size (e.g., Bruner & Goodman, 1947). Tajfel's (1957) interpretation was that subjects accentuate the differences between larger and smaller value stimuli, provided the stimuli are of a kind where value and size are correlated (i.e., where there is a correlation between the focal dimension of size and the peripheral dimension of value). This interpretation was developed into a more general theoretical statement by Tajfel (1959a, 1959b). The effects of value are a special case of the influence of peripheral cues on judgment.

A simple, but important, case of a peripheral cue influencing judgment is where stimuli fall into one of two categories in terms of some superimposed classification. A demonstration of this is the experiment by Tajfel and Wilkes (1963), in which subjects estimated the length of a series of eight lines presented singly. In the experimental condition, the four shorter lines were labeled A and the four longer lines were labeled B (or vice versa). In the control condition, the lines were presented without labels. Compared with the control condition, judgments of the lines were more polarized in the experimental condition. In other words, there was an *accentuation of interclass differences*, that is, of the differences between the class of shorter lines and the class of longer lines.

Tajfel uses such results obtained with physical stimuli as the springboard for theorizing about social judgments in the context of divisions between social groups. In a paper that anticipates much of the current discussion of schematic processing in social stereotypes, Tajfel (1969) argues that a target person's group membership can function as a peripheral cue, analogous to the *A*s and *B*s in the Tajfel and Wilkes (1963) study, and thus influence judgments by others of that person's position on attributes *assumed* to be correlated with group membership. Tajfel specifically predicts that stereotypes arise from both an accentuation of perceived interclass differences and a reduction of perceived intraclass differences. In other words, blacks may not only be seen as more different from whites on some attribute, but also more like one another. He also assumes that the more "salient" or personally relevant a judgment is for particular individuals, the stronger these effects should be. Tajfel's concept of "salience" seems to have a great deal in common with Sherif and Hovland's (1961) concept of ego-involvement. (See also Chapter 8.)

Two features of this research are worth noting briefly. First, the superimposed or peripheral cue does not have to be discontinuous or dichotomous for it to produce increased polarization of judgment. (Witness, for instance, the early work on value and size of coins.) Second, although there is good evidence for reduction of intraclass differences in judgments of *people* (e.g. Tajfel & Wilkes, 1964), the evidence for such effects is less reliable in the context of judgments of physical stimuli. Overall, accentuation of interclass differences appears a more robust effect than reduction of intraclass differences, although the mediating factors may not be fully understood.

Applying Accentuation Theory to the Judgment of Attitude Statements

In attempting to apply such principles to problems of attitudinal judgment, two main questions have to be answered. The first is whether superimposed classifications can lead to accentuation of interclass differences in the judgment of attitude statements in a manner analogous to that found in psychophysical judgment by Tajfel and Wilkes (1963). This issue can be resolved quite quickly. Eiser (1971b) obtained ratings of a series of 64 statements concerned with the nonmedical use of drugs, on a scale labeled "extremely permissive" to "extremely restrictive." The crucial manipulation depended on the distinction between a control condition, in which judges were simply told that all the statements were (supposedly) "drawn from newspapers," and an experimental condition, in which judges were informed that the statements all came from just two newspapers. Furthermore, for these latter judges, the statements were presented in the form of quotations, with a fictitious name of a newspaper printed underneath. It was explained that fictitious names had been substituted for the real names of the newspapers to control for possible bias. In fact, the 32 items attributed to one newspaper were all those in the more "permissive" half of the series, whereas those attributed to the other "newspaper" were the 32 more "restrictive" items in the series. The mean difference between the ratings of these two item groups was significantly greater in the experimental than the control condition—a straightforward accentuation effect.

The second question to be answered is whether this kind of principle can, in fact, account for the effects of judges' attitudes. This is more difficult to resolve. However, it seems reasonable to assume that judges may discriminate between items not only in terms of the positions of the items on the (focal) dimension of favorability toward the issue, but also in terms of their positions on the (peripheral) dimension of personal acceptability. Other things being equal, judges with more extreme positions should experience a stronger correlation between the two dimensions of favorability and acceptability than those with more neutral attitudes. This correlation should be positive for pro judges and negative for anti judges, but *both* should show an accentuation effect, that is, give more polarized judgments than neutral judges.

It is worth pausing to note that, in broad terms, this is the same prediction as that derived from the assimilation-contrast model. Indeed it is remarkable how close Sherif and Sherif came to this kind of interpretation without ever quite endorsing it. In their conceptualization of latitudes of acceptance, noncommitment and rejection (Sherif & Hovland, 1961) and the "own categories" procedure (Sherif et al., 1965), it is clear that they assumed, as we do, that judges subjectively categorize items on the basis of personal acceptabaility. However, when it came to interpreting the effects of this subjective categorization, Sherif and Sherif did *not* invoke any accentuation principle, but instead derived their predictions from an anchoring principle. Part of the reason for this must have been their interest in the role of communication discrepancy in attitude change, which they saw as related to distance between own position and item positions in judgment tasks. Such discrepancy was assumed to interact with the anchoring properties of judges' own attitudes.

However, an alternative derivation of assimilation-contrast predictions is of limited use if it cannot account for the *observed* relationship between judges' attitudes and polarization of judgment. One still has to explain why only pro judges (in the American studies on attitudes toward blacks) showed the predicted polarization effects, whereas anti judges did not. A similar asymmetry was found by Eiser (1971b) when judges were divided on the basis of their own attitudes on the drug issue. More "permissive" judges gave significantly more polarized rating than more "restrictive" judges. This study was not designed to distinguish extreme from neutral judges, but there is no evidence that even the most extremely "restrictive" judges showed any increase in polarization over those with attitudes closer to the center of the distribution.

Connotations of Judgmental Language—A Neglected Variable

It should be remembered that the historical background for research on judgment of attitude statements was a concern with the validity of a *unidimensional* measure of attitude. Items were selected to vary in terms of *favorability-unfavorability,* and the dimension of judgment was not considered as a variable to be manipulated. However, as we shall argue, it can make a crucial difference how the judgment scale is labeled. If the principles we have been considering are to apply in their simple form, we need to be able to say that the judgment scale is directly analogous to scales of psychophysical judgment such as heavy-light, long-short, and so on. In other words, we have to be able to say that favorability judgments are descriptions *and nothing more.* If we cannot say this, we must adapt our hypotheses accordingly.

If favorability judgments were more than description pure and simple, what else could they be? A real possibility is that they also involve some element of *evaluation.* In other words, within a given social context, describing an attitude or a communicator as pro-X or anti-Y might be seen as implying more approval than describing the attitude or communicator as anti-X or pro-Y. Let X equal "peace" and Y equal "war" and the implication becomes clear. Could this have been a factor in previous research? We cannot say for sure, since no attempt was made to build in controls against such a possibility. Nonetheless, it appears intuitively plausible that in the studies of attitudes towards blacks, to apply a label such as "extremely unfavorable toward Negroes" might be recognized as implying a negative evaluation, even among some segregationists.

How might this influence judgments? Suppose we take the issue of nuclear disarmament. Opponents of unilateral disarmament may object to unilateralists calling themselves the "peace movement," on the grounds that it implies that multilateralists do not want peace, and *not* to want peace is a very bad thing indeed. At the same time, unilateralists would object to any attempt to describe their position as "naive" or "endangering security," or, even more extremely, as "treasonable." We can see such contests for the ownership of words going on in the outside world, but how might it produce effects in the more esoteric world of our experiments? Well, suppose we presented unilateralists and others with a series of statements for and against unilateral disarmament, and had these rated alternatively on scales labeled "pro-peace/anti-peace" and "naive-realistic." It seems difficult to avoid the conclusion that, relatively speaking, the unilateralists would "prefer" to use the first scale to discriminate between the statements, and that their opponents would prefer the second (assuming that there is consensus about the *ordinal* positions of the statements on each scale, which might not be the case).

What this means is that the way the judgment scale is labeled might *interact* with judges' attitudes. We can express this interaction more formally in two alternative, but compatible, ways. The first is to propose a general tendency for individuals to prefer to attach evaluatively positive labels (e.g., pro-peace, realistic) to positions, people, or attributes of which they approve, and evaluatively negative labels (e.g., anti-peace, naive) to positions, people, or attributes of which they disapprove. The broader implications of this argument will be explored more fully in Chapter 8. In the context of judging attitude statements, what it means is that unilateralists will be happy to describe their own views as "pro-peace" but not as "naive," and their opponents will be more happy to describe their own views as "realistic" than as "anti-peace." Unless either group simply reverses the scales (so as to always see themselves as more pro-peace and realistic than their opponent, regardless of whether or not they are unilateralists), this will have the effect that *judges will give more polarized judgments on scales* where their "own end" is marked by an *evaluatively positive label.*

The alternative way of expressing this is to think of the value connotations of the judgment scale labels as a further peripheral cue superimposed on the focal dimension of favorability. Polarization of judgment then depends on the relationship between this peripheral cue and the other peripheral cue, namely the acceptability of the items to the judges. If the two sets of cues are evaluatively inconsistent, polarization should be diminished. In other words, the accentuation effects that should be produced by judges categorizing items subjectively on the basis of personal acceptability are dependent on the *evaluative consistency* between such acceptability and the language in terms of which the ratings are expressed.

The simple test of this hypothesis is to compare ratings given by different attitude groups of the same items *in terms of different rating scales.* When this procedure is adopted, it has been repeatedly shown that polarization of judgment depends on an interaction between judges' attitudes and the wording of the rating scales. This has been found with issues such as drug use (Eiser, 1973; Eiser & Ledger, 1983; Eiser & van der Pligt, 1982; van der Pligt & van Dijk, 1979), adult authority over adolescents (Eiser & Mower White, 1974, 1975), risk-taking in choice dilemmas (Eiser, 1976), and people's perceptions of their own attitudes (van der Pligt & Eiser, 1983). Mostly, judgmental language has been manipulated as a "within subjects" variable, that is, judges each use more than one rating scale. However, this is not a critical feature since comparable results are found when different rating scales are given to different groups of judges (Eiser & Ledger, 1983; van der Pligt & van Dijk, 1979).

As an example of the form of this interaction, consider the study by Eiser and Mower White (1974). Subjects were 14-15-year-old students who judged 10 short communications concerning the issue of adult authority. These communications were supposedly drawn from interviews with other young people, and half were chosen to represent relatively pro-authority positions and half, relatively anti-authority positions (see Eiser & Stroebe, 1972, pp. 159-160). Subjects were split into groups that were relatively pro, neutral, and anti on the basis of their own agreement with the statements.

All subjects rated the statements on 10 separate scales. Five of these, which we shall term P^+ scales), were chosen so that the anti-authority term would be seen as evaluatively negative, and the pro-authority term evaluatively positive (e.g., disobedient-obedient). The remaining (A^+) scales were chosen so that the anti-authority term would be seen as evaluatively positive and the pro-authority term would be seen as evaluatively negative (e.g., adventurous-unadventurous). The task was presented as one of trying to imagine the kind of person who would have made each of the statements.

If we focus on the mean difference between the ratings given to the pro and anti items, the result is a clear-cut tendency for pro judges to polarize more than neutral and anti judges on P^+ scales, but for anti judges to polarize more than neutral or pro judges on A^+ scales. This effect was replicated with a somewhat different selection of scales by Eiser and Mower White (1975), and the mean scores are shown in Figure 3-1.

A number of other features of these experiments bear noting. To start with, differences in polarization, while striking, are not the only effects that can be observed. There is *some* evidence for overall contrast effects when ratings of items are averaged over different scales. That is, one can observe, often but not always, a tendency for pro judges to rate more items as anti, over and above differences due to the judgment scale. This tendency is not large in absolute terms, and not that reliable statistically, but it allows grounds for the suggestion that simple contrast processes due to the anchoring effects of judges' own position still play some part. We do not seek to deny this possibility. Another effect, which we shall refer to more specifically in the following, is a *positivity effect,* consisting of a tendency for judges, irrespective of their own attitude, to give more ratings toward the evaluatively positive extreme of each scale.

Also, a number of manipulation checks are included (in the main experiments and/or studies), mainly to confirm how judges perceive the value connotations of the judgment scale labels. It seems, at least for the issues studied, that it is not too difficult to select labels so that there is (a) reasonable consensus about which labels are relatively pro and anti from a descriptive point of view, and (b) reasonable consensus about which labels are relatively positive and negative from an evaluative point of view. However, while the relative differences tend to be perceived as required by the design of the experiments, judges' attitudes still influence the absolute ratings given in ways that are interpretable in terms of evaluative consistency—labels seen as applicable to one's own position tend also to be seen as somewhat more positive or less negative.

How might this apply to the interpretation of previous studies that have used only

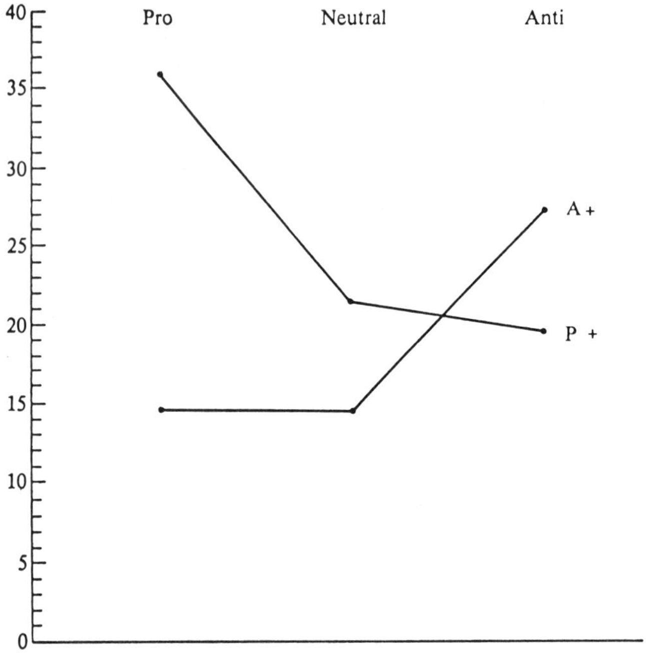

Fig. 3-1. Mean item group differences (polarization of judgment) as a function of judges' attitudes (pro, neutral, anti) and value connotations of scales (P^+ scales: pro end positive, vs. A^+ scales: anti end positive). Data are from Eiser and Mower White (1975). Ratings of items scored from 0 (anti end) to 100 (pro end). *Note.* From *Cognitive Social Psychology: A Guidebook to Theory and Research* (p. 85) by J. R. Eiser, 1980, London: McGraw-Hill. Copyright 1980 by McGraw-Hill. Adapted with permission.

one response scale? The implication is that the relationship between attitudes and polarization found in such studies was simply one-half of a potential interaction. With different response scales the relationship could have been reversed. The Eiser (1971b) study on attitudes toward drug use is nonproblematic from this point of view. As supported by the Eiser study (1973), it seems that the term "permissive" carried more positive value connotations than the term "restrictive"; consequently, the more permissive subjects were using a scale more evaluatively consistent with their own acceptance-rejection of the statements.

The major part of the literature, however, involves the issue of attitudes toward blacks. The finding to be explained is that pro-blacks give more polarized ratings than anti-blacks. This can be reconciled with accentuation theory so long as we assume that a term such as "favorable toward Negroes," in the context of its use, carries more positive connotations than its opposite. To put it differently, no one (or hardly anyone) wants to admit that they are racially prejudiced.

Now, of course, we cannot prove this assumption to be correct retrospectively, and because of this a confusion has arisen. It has more than once been suggested to us that what accentuation theory predicts is simply that pros should polarize more than antis, because the "pro" end of the scale is the more evaluatively positive. This is a serious misconception. The pro end of any attitude continuum is not *necessarily* positive or negative in value connotation—it depends simply on the words used to label the ends of the scale. The whole point is that pro judges may polarize *less* than anti judges on certain scales. The search for effects due to manipulation of judgmental language, however, was originally stimulated by the intuitive appeal (at least to us) of the idea that, *in the context of this specific issue* (attitudes toward blacks), the "favorable" label was more positive in connotation than its opposite.

Nonetheless, it has to be said that the effect could still be due, in part at least, to other factors. There is the unexciting, but perhaps more than negligible, possibility of simple semantic confusion between saying a statement is "favorable" and finding oneself "in favor" of the position it advocates. Anti judges should have "unfavorable" reactions to "favorable" items, and might tend therefore to be more confused over how to respond than pro judges. Also quite real may be the possibility that people prefer to say that they are *for* something than *against* its opposite. Obviously, a label like "pro-war" is not going to be evaluatively positive (at least let us hope not), but it is still interesting how groups and movements may relabel themselves in ways that are not only evaluatively but also grammatically positive—for example, anti-abortionists declaring themselves to be "pro-life." For such reasons, it is important to distinguish between the accentuation theory *reinterpretation* of previous studies, which rests ultimately on an intuitive assumption, and the accentuation theory *predictions* that have been supported in subsequent empirical findings.

An important recent study by Romer (1983) reinforces this point. Romer argues that experiments such as those by Eiser and Mower White (1974, 1975) have manipulated judgmental language by comparing scales with "connotatively stable meanings." Experiments that have followed the Thurstone rating procedure more closely, on the other hand, have used scales such as pro-anti or favorable-unfavorable, where the labels may have "connotatively unstable meanings." Romer does not deny that labels such as favorable-unfavorable may carry value connotations, but he disputes the idea that these connotations will be broadly stable or consistent across different attitude groups (e.g., that both pro and anti judges think that it is bad to be anti-Negro).

Romer presents data from two experiments on the issue of abortion, paying particular attention to different patterns of individual responding that underlie group means, and to the varying degrees to which judges appear to understand standard experimental instructions. Among those who understood the instructions, neutral judges gave less-polarized ratings than *both* pro and anti judges. This is what accentuation theory would predict for scales with value connotations that are unstable across attitude groups. The sample of anti judges, however, tended to include a higher proportion who misinterpreted the instructions as requiring a rating of their *own* attitude toward the statements, leading to them rating anti statements as pro, and vice versa.

This calls to mind an earlier study by Ward (1966) on the issue of attitudes toward blacks, in which a large proportion of anti judges were excluded for apparent confusion of the ends of the response scale. Elsewhere (Eiser, 1971a) we have argued that Ward's criterion may have been overexclusive, raising doubts over the conclusions from his analysis. Nonetheless, one cannot entirely dismiss the argument that the standard instructions for rating statements can give rise to confusion, with some judges thinking that they have to say whether they personally agree or disagree with the items (no doubt because this is how they normally have to respond to questionnaires). In most of our own experiments, we have circumvented this difficulty by evoking a "person perception" set, instructing our subjects to "imagine the kind of person" who could have made each of the statements. This, however, is another methodological departure that might invite caution over our reinterpretation of previous studies.

Categorization, Congruity, and Appropriateness

The assumptions we have made concerning the interactions between judges' attitudes and the response language go beyond the principles that can be derived from work on psychophysical judgment. If we interpret the effects of judges' attitudes as those of a superimposed peripheral cue, we have to make the additional assumption that

> polarization of judgment depends both on the correlation between the focal and peripheral continua and on the degree of congruity between the peripheral cues and the response scale labels. (Eiser & Mower White, 1975, p. 770)

So far in this chapter we have only looked at the effects of congruity in terms of *evaluative* consistency, but other bases of congruity are possible. As mentioned, Eiser and Mower White (1975) used the issue of adolescents' attitudes towards adult authority. In two of three conditions, the statements were presented in the context of a peripheral classification, specifically the sex of the supposed authors of each statement. In the *direct* condition, five male and five female names were attached to the 10 statements, so that the more anti-authority statements were all attributed to boys and the more pro-authority statements to girls. In the *reverse* condition, the pro statements were shown as coming from boys and the anti statements from girls. Finally, a control condition was included, without any names attached to the statements.

These statements were then rated by all judges on eight scales. Four were A^+ and four P^+, as previously explained, but independently of value connotation, half the scales were chosen so that the terms would also differ on the basis of their perceived appropriateness as descriptions of males and females. These four (*marked*) scales all took the form of an antiauthority term seen as more applicable to boys (e.g., bold) and a proauthority term seen as more applicable to girls (e.g., timid). (It says something about the stability of sex-role stereotypes that the pilot data used to select these labels revealed *no* suitable pairs of labels where the gender connotations were reversed, i.e., where the anti term was the more feminine and the pro term the more masculine.) The remaining four (*unmarked*) scales showed no reliable gender connotations, that is, the pro term was not seen as more applicable to girls than the anti term.

If the connotations of the response language were irrelevant to the accentuation effects produced by a superimposed classification, the prediction would be that polarization should be greater in both the *direct* and the *reverse* conditions than in the control condition across all scales. However, on the basis of the hypothesis that accentuation depends on the congruity between peripheral cues and the response language, a rather complex interaction was predicted. On the *unmarked* scales, the question of incongruity should not arise; both *direct* and *reverse* conditions should therfore show more polarization than the control condition. On the *marked* scales, the superimposed classification would be congruent with the response language in terms of gender connotations for judges in the *direct* condition; consequently, these judges should polarize more than those in the control condition. However, for judges in the *reverse* condition, the superimposed classification would be incongruent with the gender connotations of the *marked* scales, and consequently these judges should *not* polarize more than control judges on these scales. The data are shown in Figure 3-2.

While an unpredicted main effect is also evident (there being more polarization on *marked* than *unmarked* scales), the interaction is as predicted. This gives strong support to the argument that the highly replicable tendency for people to describe their own positions in positive terms is not just an effect *sui generis*, but is a special case of a more general judgmental principle: Peripheral cues correlated with differences between stimuli on the focal dimension will produce accentuation effects, but only if the judgmental language is appropriate for expressing such distinctions on the peripheral dimension.

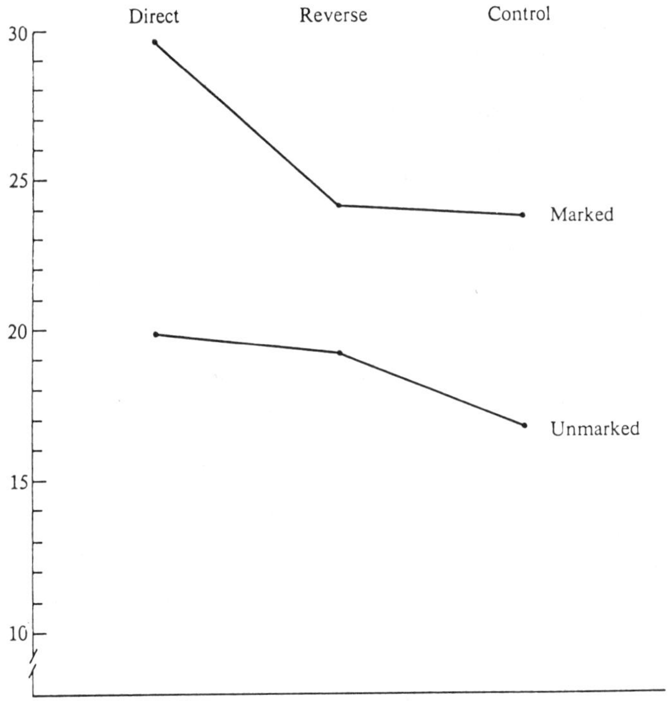

Fig. 3-2. Mean item group differences (polarization of judgment) as a function of superimposed classification (direct, reverse, control) and congruency of scales with classification (marked vs. unmarked scales). Data are from Eiser and Mower White (1975). *Note.* From *Cognitive Social Psychology: A Guidebook to Theory and Research* (p. 86) by J. R. Eiser, 1980, London: McGraw-Hill. Copyright 1980 by McGraw-Hill. Reprinted with permission.

This question of whether the judgmental language is appropriate for the expression of distinctions between items is quite crucial. It may also be tackled from another point of view, by considering simply distinctions on the focal dimension of favorability. As mentioned, a powerful effect in most of the studies that have manipulated the value connotations of the judgmental language is an overall positivity effect, that is, a tendency for items to be judged closer to the positively labeled extreme of each scale. In other words the overall mean judgment of all items tends to be more anti on A^+ scales and more pro on P^+ scales. (The exception is the Eiser and Ledger 1983 study, which found the opposite effect, but this seems attributable to most of the items being unacceptable to most of the judges.)

One interpretation rests on the assumption that positive and negative terms differ in their applicability to moderate and extreme positions. There is, in fact, quite a tradition of research that points to positive terms being used more typically to describe moderate positions on a given continuum, and negative terms to describe extreme positions (e.g., Peabody, 1967; see also Chapter 8). According to this view, an A^+ scale would be more applicable to distinctions ranging from moderate anti to extremely pro, and a P^+ more applicable to distinctions from extremely anti to moderately pro (see Eiser & Osmon, 1978). If this is so, it leads directly to the prediction of a positivity effect. Anti items can be relatively moderate and still be rated as extremely anti on an A^+ scale, whereas pro items can be relatively moderate and still be rated as extremely pro on a P^+ scale. Put differently, an adolescent can be called "adventurous" without being sufficiently anti-authority to be called "disobedient." Similarly, an adolescent can be called "obedient" without being sufficiently pro-authority to be called "unadventurous." This has interesting implications for the variable perspective model (see Chapter 2) since it suggests that perspective must be at least partly a function of how the rating scale is labeled.

If A^+ and P^+ scales are therefore more applicable to different ranges of positions on the anti-pro continuum, does this have implications for polarization? This possibility was explored by Eiser and van der Pligt (1982). The idea behind this study was the notion that judges discriminate and hence polarize more readily on scales labeled in a way which they consider "appropriate." This feeling that a scale is "appropriate" can be damaged by a mismatch between judges' own evaluations of the items and the value connotations of the rating scale, as when pro judges are required to use A^+ scales or anti judges, P^+ scales. However, it might also be damaged by a mismatch between the *range* of items presented and the range of positions, moderate or extreme, on the anti-pro continuum to which a particular scale is most appropriate. Such a mismatch would occur when an item range from extremely anti to moderately pro is rated on an A^+ scale or one from moderately anti to extremely pro is rated on a P^+ scale.

The relevant part of the Eiser and van der Pligt (1982) study involved comparisons of ratings of items concerning the nonmedical use of drugs on an A^+ scale (responsible-irresponsible) and a P^+ scale (unadventurous-adventurous). Judges (school and university students) were divided by median splits according to attitude. In addition, the range of items presented was manipulated in a way analogous to that used by Upshaw (1962). In the *whole-range* condition, the items ranged from anti to pro. In the *short-pro* condition, the items ranged from neutral to pro, and in the *short-anti* condition from anti to neutral.

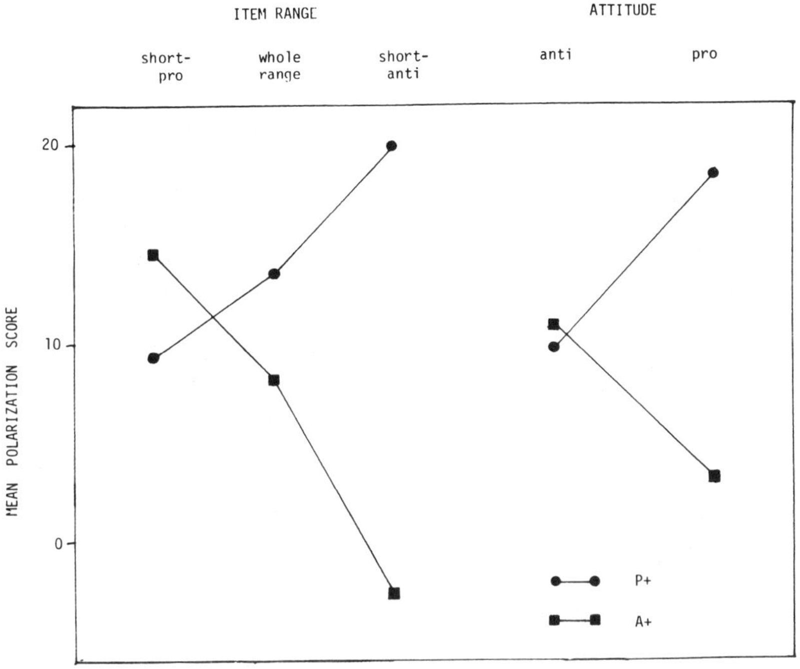

Fig. 3-3. Mean polarization scores on P^+ (pro end positive) and A^+ (anti end positive) scales as a function of item range and of attitude. *Note.* From "Accentuation and Perspective in Attitudinal Judgment" by J. R. Eiser and J. van der Pligt, 1982, Journal of Personality and Social Psychology, *42,* p. 232. Copyright 1982 by the American Psychological Association. Reprinted with permission.

Figure 3-3 shows the mean polarization scores (calculated on the basis of item group differences) on the A^+ and P^+ scales in the three conditions and as a function of judges' attitude. The interaction between attitude and scale (on the right of the figure) replicates previous findings. The novel finding is the range by scale interaction. This clearly supports the prediction that polarization should be greater on scales that are seen as more appropriate to the range of items presented.

Conclusions

If one were to ask how social psychologists have typically defined the concept of "attitude," an obvious starting point would be to see how attitudes have traditionally been measured. Traditional measures, such as those derived by Thurstone scaling, assume an underlying continuum of favorability-unfavorability on which any given item and hence any given respondent can, in principle, be located.

This assumption has invited a close liaison between work on attitude scaling and work in other areas of the psychology of judgment. To derive measures of the scale values of attitude statements (so as to represent where each statement falls on the underlying continuum) one needs to obtain *judgments* of the position of each statement. But how are such judgments made? Far from making attitude measurement simpler, the liaison with judgment research has raised a host of conceptual issues that have yet to be answered satisfactorily.

Judgments are relative, and depend on context (see Chapters 1 and 2). Even if we accept the assumption of an underlying continuum of favorability-unfavorability, we cannot know the *absolute* position of any item or person on that continuum. Indeed, we have to say that there are *no* absolute positions, only relative differences between different items or people, depending on the context. This invites the inference that we cannot measure attitudes absolutely, but only comparatively and in context. If we accept this, can attitudes ever have any meaning, except within a context?

This is not the end to the uncertainties. Ratings imply a dimension of judgment, but how can we be sure that the dimension implied by a particular set of ratings is truly the underlying continuum we are trying to measure? As Upshaw and Ostrom (Chapter 2) make clear in their discussion of congeneric scales, *any* response scale must be assumed to be an imperfect measurement, subject to its own specific influences and biases. Even ratings of statements on a scale labeled "extremely unfavorable/extremely favorable toward X" cannot be assumed to be a *true* measure of the positions of the statements on the underlying continuum.

In this chapter we have examined in some detail the effects on judgment of one kind of difference between alternative response scales—the extent to which the response scale labels carry positive or negative value connotations. It has long been known that judges with different attitudes toward an issue will rate the positions of attitude statements differently—in particular, they will differ in the extent to which their responses are polarized toward the two ends of the response scale. We have shown that the relationship between judges' attitudes and polarization of judgment depends on the values implied by the scale labels. Broadly, judges will be more likely to polarize their ratings on scales where the extreme more acceptable to them is marked by a label with positive value connotations.

In discussing this effect of response language, we have put forward an interpretation based on the following view of what judges are doing in such studies. Judges formulate their own hypotheses about the relevant distinctions that they are required to make among objects of judgment presented to them. If they are provided with only a single response scale, they define this scale so as to represent appropriately the distinctions they wish to make. If more than one scale is provided, they will make more extreme discriminations in their ratings on those scales that are seen as more appropriate representations of the relevant distinctions.

This view of what is going on when judges represent their discriminations in terms of responses on a scale is part of a broader conception of the process of judgment itself. Behind our more specific hypotheses is the more general assumption that judgment (both inside and outside the laboratory) involves *selective processing* of stimulus attributes. This selective processing is shaped by implicit hypotheses or schemata concerning the distribution of objects of judgment and the categories into which they fall. Accentuation theory starts from a concern with people's reliance on superimposed or subjective category systems for the achievement of cognitive economy. Applied to attitudinal judgment, it raises the question of how far attitudes themselves should be thought of as category systems, rather than as points along a continuum.

References

Bruner, J. S., & Goodman, C. C. (1947). Value and need as organizing factors in perception. *Journal of Abnormal and Social Psychology, 42,* 33-44.

Eiser, J. R. (1971a). Comment on Ward's "Attitude and involvement in the absolute judgment of attitude statements." *Journal of Personality and Social Psychology, 17,* 81-83.

Eiser, J. R. (1971b). Enhancement of contrast in the absolute judgment of attitude statements. *Journal of Personality and Social Psychology, 17,* 1-10.

Eiser, J. R. (1973). Judgement of attitude statements as a function of judges' attitudes and the judgemental dimension. *British Journal of Social and Clinical Psychology, 12,* 231-240.

Eiser, J. R. (1976). Evaluation of choice-dilemma alternatives: Utility, morality and social judgement. *British Journal of Social and Clinical Psychology, 15,* 51-60.

Eiser, J. R., & Ledger, C. (1983). Accentuation theory and the judgment of attitudes: Exploring possible limiting conditions. *Canadian Journal of Behavioural Science, 15,* 248-258.

Eiser, J. R., & Mower White, C. J. (1974). Evaluative consistency and social judgment. *Journal of Personality and Social Psychology, 30,* 349-359.

Eiser, J. R., & Mower White, C. J. (1975). Categorization and congruity in attitudinal judgment. *Journal of Personality and Social Psychology, 31,* 769-775.

Eiser, J. R., & Osmon, B. E. (1978). Judgmental perspective and the value connotations of response scale labels. *Journal of Personality and Social Psychology, 36,* 491-497.

Eiser, J. R., & Stroebe, W. (1972). *Categorization and social judgement.* London: Academic Press.

Eiser, J. R., & van der Pligt, J. (1982). Accentuation and perspective in attitudinal judgment. *Journal of Personality and Social Psychology, 42,* 224-238.

Fehrer, E. (1952). Shifts in scale values of attitude statements as a function of the composition of the scale. *Journal of Experimental Psychology, 44,* 179-188.

Helson, H. (1964). *Adaptation-level theory.* New York: Harper & Row.

Hinckley, E. D. (1932). The influence of individual opinion on construction of an attitude scale. *Journal of Social Psychology, 3,* 283-296.

Hovland, C. I., & Sherif, M. (1952). Judgmental phenomena and scales of attitude measurement: Item displacement in Thurstone Scales. *Journal of Abnormal and Social Psychology, 47,* 822-832.

Ostrom, T. M. (1970). Perspective as a determinant of attitude change. *Journal of Experimental Social Psychology, 6,* 280-292.

Parducci, A. (1963). Range-frequency compromise in judgment. *Psychological Monographs, 77* (2, Whole No. 565).

Parducci, A. (1974). Contextual effects: A range-frequency analysis. In E. C. Carterette & M. P. Friedman (Eds.), *Handbook of perception* (Vol. 2). New York: Academic Press.

Parducci, A., & Marshall, L. M. (1962). Assimilation versus contrast in the anchoring of perceptual judgment of weight. *Journal of Experimental Psychology, 63,* 426-437.

Peabody, D. (1967). Trait inferences: Evaluative and descriptive aspects. *Journal of Personality and Social Psychology, 7* (2, Pt. 2, Whole No. 642).

Romer, D. (1983). Effects of own attitude on polarization of judgment. *Journal of Personality and Social Psychology, 44,* 273-284.

Segall, M. H. (1959). The effect of attitude and experience on judgments of controversial statements. *Journal of Abnormal and Social Psychology, 58,* 366-372.

Selltiz, C., Edrich, H., & Cook, S. W. (1965). Ratings of favorableness about a social group as an indication of attitude toward the group. *Journal of Personality and Social Psychology, 2,* 408-415.

Sherif, C. W., Sherif, M., & Nebergall, R. E. (1965). *Attitude and attitude change: The social judgment-involvement approach.* Philadelphia: Saunders.

Sherif, M., & Hovland, C. I. (1961). *Social judgment: Assimilation and contrast effects in communication and attitude change.* New Haven, CT: Yale University Press.

Sherif, M., Taub, D., & Hovland, C. I. (1958). Assimilation and contrast effects of anchoring stimuli on judgment. *Journal of Experimental Psychology, 55,* 150-155.

Tajfel, H. (1957). Value and the perceptual judgment of magnitude. *Psychological Review, 64,* 192-204.

Tajfel, H. (1959a). Quantitative judgement in social perception. *British Journal of Psychology, 50,* 16-29.

Tajfel, H. (1959b). The anchoring effects of value in a scale of judgements. *British Journal of Psychology, 50,* 294-304.

Tajfel, H. (1969). Cognitive aspects of prejudice. *Journal of Social Issues, 25,* 79-97.

Tajfel, H., & Wilkes, A. L. (1963). Classification and quantitative judgement. *British Journal of Psychology, 54,* 101-114.

Tajfel, H., & Wilkes, A. L. (1964). Salience of attributes and commitment to extreme judgements in the perception of people. *British Journal of Social and Clinical Psychology, 3,* 40-49.

Thurstone, L. L., & Chave, E. J. (1929). *The measurement of attitude.* Chicago: University of Chicago Press.

Upshaw, H. S. (1962). Own attitude as an anchor in equal-appearing intervals. *Journal of Abnormal and Social Psychology, 64,* 85-96.

Upshaw, H. S. (1965). The effect of variable perspectives on judgments of opinion statements for Thurstone scales: Equal-appearing intervals. *Journal of Personality and Social Psychology, 2,* 60-69.

Upshaw, H. S. (1969). The personal reference scale: An approach to social judgment. In L. Berkowitz (Ed.), *Advances in experimental social psychology* (Vol. 4). New York: Academic Press.

van der Pligt, J., & Eiser, J. R. (1983). Value connotations, perspective and self-perception. *European Journal of Social Psychology, 13,* 129-142.

van der Pligt, J., & van Dijk, J. A. (1979). Polarization of judgment and preference for judgmental labels. *European Journal of Social Psychology, 9,* 233-242.

Ward, C. D. (1966). Attitude and involvement in the absolute judgment of attitude statements. *Journal of Personality and Social Psychology, 4,* 465-476.

Zavalloni, M., & Cook, S. W. (1965). Influence of judges' attitudes on ratings of favorableness of statements about a social group. *Journal of Personality and Social Psychology, 1,* 43-54.

Chapter 4

The Polarizing Effects of Affective Intensity

Charles M. Judd and Joel T. Johnson

The relation between cognition and affect has recently reemerged as a central concern in social and cognitive psychology (e.g., Fiske, 1981; Mandler, 1975; Zajonc, 1980). The purpose of this chapter is to explore one particular aspect of this relation: how the intensity of affective reactions to a particular class of stimuli may affect the way in which information about those stimuli is judged, processed, and retained. The particular stimuli that constitute the focus of this chapter are social and political issues. Thus, in more traditional terms for social psychology, this chapter explores how the intensity of attitudes on political and social issues affects the way in which information concerning those issues is handled.

The chapter is divided into three sections. The first section briefly provides some definitions that are necessary for the rest of the chapter. In the second section, we present our hypotheses and supporting data concerning the effects of affective intensity on a set of cognitive tasks. In the third and concluding section, we show some relationships between our research and the work of others who have explored the links between affect and cognition. We close the chapter with some general speculations on the role of affect in information encoding and retention.

Affect and Attitudes

Within social psychology, a currently popular view of attitudes is that they consist of three components: affective, cognitive, and behavioral (Himmelfarb & Eagly, 1974; Katz & Stotland, 1959). Although each of these components is seen as important, the *affective component* is particularly crucial in the definition of attitudes, since that is what differentiates attitudes from beliefs and other cognitions. Indeed, the affective component occasionally emerges as the sole defining component of attitudes (Fishbein & Ajzen, 1975). This component is thought to consist of two variables: the direction or valence of the affect elicited by the attitude object and the intensity of the elicited affect. The direction or valence of affect is determined by whether one's evaluation of the attitude object is positive or negative, or in the words of Thurstone (1931), whether the "affect is for or against a psychological object." The intensity variable concerns the strength of the affective reaction (either positive or negative) elicited by the attitude object.

Operationally, most attitude self-rating scales assess both the valence and intensity of attitudinal affect (Scott, 1968). For instance, suppose a subject is asked to rate his or her attitude toward the issue of abortion on a pro-anti 7-point scale. The direction of the affective component is determined by whether the rating is above or below the scale midpoint. The intensity of the affect is indicated by the deviation or extremity of the self-rating from the midpoint, regardless of its direction.

The other two components of attitudes are of less concern for our purposes. Briefly defined, however, the *cognitive component* consists of the beliefs about the attributes possessed by the attitude object. These beliefs tend to be evaluatively consistent with the valence of the affective component (Rosenberg, 1960), and may at times be responsible for the affect in the first place (Fishbein & Ajzen, 1975). The *behavioral component* is defined as the predisposition to action either toward or away from the attitude object, again, in a direction that is consistent with the attitudinal affect.

This conceptualization of the two variables constituting the affective component is consistent with theory on affect and emotion outside of the attitude domain. The literature on affect and emotions is voluminous (see Strongman, 1978, for a review). Nevertheless, it is useful to connect our discussion of attitudinal affect with work on affect more generally, particularly because in the third section of the chapter we wish to show how our work on attitudinal affect relates to the work of others on the relation between affect and cognition.

In discussing the affective component of attitudes in relation to more general work on affect and emotions, the first distinction that needs to be made concerns the specificity of the object that elicits or is the focus of the affect. Clearly, in the case of attitudes, there exists a relatively specific eliciting object, that is, the attitude object. In this way, the affective component of attitudes can be differentiated from more general emotions or moods. This distinction defines one of the differences between our work and the recent work on the relations between mood and memory (Bower, 1981; Clark & Isen, 1982).

The second point to be made in relating research on attitudinal affect to general theories of emotion is that in nearly all of the attitudinal research the direction or valence of affect is conceptualized as lying along a single dimension: positive versus negative evaluation or, alternatively, approach versus avoidance. The more general study of emotions or affect, however, is full of attempts to invoke more richly defined distinctions (e.g., Arnold, 1970; Izard, 1977; Tomkins, 1965). Within the field of emotion, the controversy concerning the utility of a simple pleasantness or evaluative dimension versus more finely differentiated emotions has occurred on a number of different levels: physiological, phenomenological, and psychological. Without attempting to resolve whether multiple dimensions are necessary in a complete theory of emotions, we submit that attitude researchers have learned a great deal by simply treating valence as a unidimensional construct. For our part, we will not attempt further to differentiate valence (e.g., discriminating between attitudes when the object elicits disgust and when it elicits anger).

Effects of Affective Intensity

Now that we have discussed what we mean by affect in attitude research, we will present the results of various studies exploring the effect of affective intensity on judgment, information processing, and retention. This presentation is divided into three subsections. In the first we discuss intensity effects upon the judgment of attitude position statements; in the second, effects on the judgment of consensus and diagnosticity; and finally, we will focus on intensity effects on information encoding and retention.

Judgments of attitude position statements

Our research in this area started with an attitude judgment effect that has been well-documented over the course of 30 years: the contrast effect (Hovland & Sherif, 1952). In developing attitude-measurement procedures, Thurstone and Chave (1929) had argued that subjects espousing different attitudes on an issue show no differences in how they judge statements advocating various positions on the issue. Hovland and Sherif (1952), and many others since, have argued that Thurstone's conclusion is not correct, but rather, judges with fairly extreme attitudes on an issue tend to "contrast" positions that are discrepant from their own. That is, they tend to judge discrepant positions as even more discrepant from the judges' own point of view than they in fact are. In addition, the more extreme a judge's own position, or, in the words of Sherif and Hovland (1961), the more the judge is "ego-involved" in the attitude, the larger the judgmental contrast effect.

A variety of explanations for judgmental contrast that borrow extensively from the literature on psychophysical judgment (e.g., Ostrom & Upshaw, 1968; Sherif & Hovland, 1961) have been offered (see also Chapters 1 and 2). One such explanation has been offered recently by Eiser and his colleagues (Eiser & Stroebe, 1972; see also Chapter 3), based on the work of Tajfel (Tajfel & Wilkes, 1963). According to Tajfel, judges *accentuate* the differences among stimuli on a judgmental rating scale if those stimuli differ not only on the dimension being rated (the *focal* dimension) but also on some other correlated dimension (the *peripheral* dimension).

To apply this to the attitude-contrast effect, we need to assume that, when rating position statements, a judge is likely to see each position statement as either agreeable or disagreeable—that is, each position statement is associated with either positive or negative affect. The more intense the affective component of the attitude on the issue in general, the more intense the affective reaction to individual position statements is likely to be. Hence, when judging the positions advocated by statements on a pro-anti dimension (i.e., the focal dimension), judges with relatively intense attitudes on the issue are likely to see the statements as differing also on an agreeable-disagreeable peripheral dimension.

As we have stated previously, and as has been repeatedly demonstrated empirically (Cantril, 1945; Judd & Krosnick, 1982; Suchman, 1950), subjects with intense attitudes tend to espouse extreme positions on an issue. As affective intensity increases, subjects self-ratings on a pro-anti scale diverge from the scale midpoint. Hence, those judges who spontaneously tend to see position statements differing on an agreeable-disagreeable peripheral dimension will also tend to espouse extreme positions. Hence, for them, the peripheral and the focal dimensions will tend to be correlated. Subjects with extremely pro attitudes will see statements espousing pro positions as agreeable and statements espousing anti positions as disagreeable. For subjects with extremely anti attitudes, the agreeable-disagreeable dimension will simply be reversed.

As a result of the salience of the agreeable-disagreeable peripheral dimension and as a result of the correlation between the peripheral and focal dimensions, subjects with extreme attitudes, and hence intense affect on some issue, will tend to accentuate the differences among position statements in their judgments relative to subjects with less extreme attitudes. This accentuation results in an apparent contrast effect: Extreme judges view discrepant position statements as more extreme, and more discrepant with their own position than do less extreme judges.

By now, there is a fairly large body of evidence supporting the accentuation explanation for contrast effects (e.g., Eiser, 1973; Eiser & Mower White, 1974; Judd & Harackiewicz, 1980). As an example of this supporting research, consider a study reported by Judd and Harackiewicz (1980) that manipulated the salience of the agreeable-disagreeable peripheral dimension. In this study, subjects who were feminists were recruited to participate in a study concerning the "process of discussion." Subjects were told that they would be discussing the women's rights issue with another subject. Half of the subjects were randomly assigned to a condition in which they anticipated a discussion concerning the extent to which they agreed or disagreed with each other. The other half were assigned to a condition in which they were told the discussion would focus on the economic and political factors affecting the women's rights issue. This manipulation was intended to affect the salience of the agreeable-disagreeable peripheral dimension. Subjects were then told to write down two or three of their ideas on the issue that they might want to talk about during the discussion. For the ostensible reason of speeding up the discussion, subjects were then told they would exchange what they had written. In fact, at this point all subjects received the same three sentences that had supposedly been written by their discussion partner. These three sentences were all moderately anti-women's rights, as determined by pretesting, and they all made some mention of economic or political factors that affected the issue. Subjects were then asked to rate the three sentences on 9-point pro-anti rating scales. The experiment was then terminated.

The mean ratings of the three sentences in each of the two conditions are presented in Figure 4-1. As predicted, when the peripheral agreeable-disagreeable dimension was made salient to subjects, the three sentences were judged to espouse a significantly more anti position than when this peripheral dimension was not as salient ($F(1,37) = 6.72, p < .05$). To be sure that subjects in the two conditions did not differ in the extremity of their attitude positions, their positions were measured both at the start and conclusion of the study using two different procedures. At neither time did the difference between conditions approach significance.

Judgments of consensus and diagnosticity

In light of these data, and in light of other data suggesting that subjects with more intense attitudes on an issue spontaneously invoke an agreeable-disagreeable judg-

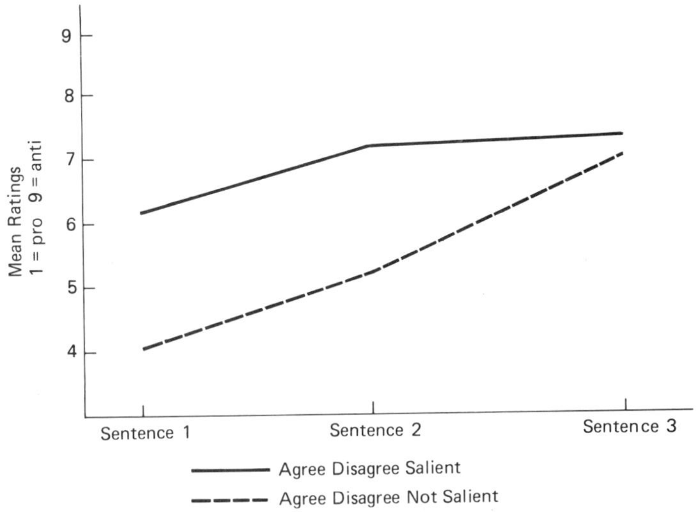

Fig. 4-1. Mean ratings of stimulus sentences at different levels of agree/disagree salience.

mental dimension (Judd & Harackiewicz, 1980, Study 1), it seemed likely that affective intensity might have other judgmental effects as well. For instance, it seemed likely that if subjects were asked to describe the frequency distribution of public opinion on some political issue, subjects with more intense affect on the issue should tend to show a polarized frequency distribution relative to subjects with less intense affect on the issue. Relative to other subjects, subjects with intense affect should overestimate the extent to which others adopt either a very extreme pro position on the issue or a very extreme anti position. This hypothesis follows from the same accentuation hypothesis that suggests that judgments of position statements should be relatively polarized by judges with intense affect on an issue: In judging positions of others on a pro-anti scale, subjects with intense affect should invoke an agreeable-disagreeable peripheral dimension that will be highly correlated with the focal dimension.

Estimations concerning the choices, positions, and behaviors of others have been of interest to attribution researchers for quite some time, since perceived consensus is known to be a key variable in the attribution process (Kelley, 1967). Likewise, sociologists interested in social comparison processes (e.g., Fields & Schuman, 1976) have also been interested in how one estimates the positions and choices of others. A review of the literature in both the attribution and social comparison areas, however, revealed little support for the polarization hypothesis that we had derived from accentuation effects. Instead, both literatures independently reach the conclusion that judges relatively overestimate the degree of consensus concerning their own choices and behaviors but relatively underestimate the degree of consensus concerning different choices and behaviors. In the attribution literature this effect is labeled a "false consensus" effect (Ross, Greene, & House, 1977), while the sociologists have called it the "looking glass" effect (Fields & Schuman, 1976).

While the evidence for the false consensus or looking glass effect is quite persuasive, we discovered two quite plausible reasons why research investigating the effect had not uncovered the polarization of consensus estimates that we hypothesize.

First, in the studies of false consensus conducted by Ross and his colleagues (Ross et al. 1977), subjects were asked to describe the frequency distribution for a dichotomous behavioral choice variable. That is, subjects were asked to indicate the percentage of the population that would perform a given behavior and the percentage that would not. With a dichotomous choice variable, it is not possible to find polarized consensus—that is, simultaneous overestimation of both the agreeable and disagreeable choices. At the very least, three choice alternatives into which others might be categorized are necessary. The second reason for the lack of evidence in prior research for the polarization of consensus estimates that we hypothesize is that choices that involve a great deal of affective intensity for the subjects have not been examined. When at least three choice alternatives are allowed, we predict relative polarization of consensus estimates only by subjects for whom the choices involve considerable affective intensity. If the issue is uninvolving for all subjects, no relative polarization should be apparent.

To determine whether subjects with high affective intensity on an issue would show polarized consensus estimates relative to less involved subjects, two studies were conducted: one focusing on the issue of feminism and the other focusing on the issue of nuclear power. Both studies used similar procedures and yielded highly consistent results. For brevity's sake we will here discuss only the results of the feminism study (Judd & Johnson, 1981).

To make certain that subjects in this study differed in affective intensity on the women's rights issue, we recruited two groups of female subjects in two different ways. A group of extreme feminists was recruited by using a network approach. A few feminists who were known to the experimenters identified other feminists who were then contacted and recruited for the study. To recruit subjects with less affective intensity on the issue, two sign-up sheets for research participation were placed next to each other in the lobby of the psychology building. The first sheet asked for subjects to sign up for a study on the comprehension of written text. The second sheet explicitly recruited feminist subjects for a study of political attitudes. Women who signed the first sheet but not the second were then contacted for the study.

To be sure that the two groups of subjects differed in affective intensity, we administered a set of questions on their attitudes and involvement in the women's rights issue. The differences between groups in responses to these questions were all highly significant. The attitudes of the feminist group were significantly more extreme than those of the nonfeminists. Likewise, the feminists reported a much higher degree of involvement in the issue and were also much more likely to report behavior consistent with their attitude (e.g., participating in demonstrations in support of the Equal Rights Amendment). These differences between the two groups of subjects were differences in affective intensity rather than in affective valence, since all subjects were generally pro-women's rights, regardless of how they were recruited. One group was simply more extreme in their sentiment than the other.

To assess whether affective intensity leads to relative polarization of consensus estimates, all subjects were asked to indicate the prevalence in various population groups of the following three positions on the women's rights issue: "generally pro-women's rights," "generally neither pro- nor anti-women's rights," and "generally anti-women's rights." Subjects were told to be sure that the percentages assigned to the three positions summed to 100%. The mean consensus estimates given by each group of subjects for "all adults in the U.S." are presented in Figure 4-2. These data show two primary effects. First, both groups of subjects believed the pro position to be more prevalent than the other two positions. Since all of our subjects espoused pro positions themselves, this result is consistent with the false consensus or looking glass effect.[1] The second significant effect that is clearly visible in Figure 4-2 is the relative polarization of consensus estimates by the extreme feminist subjects. Relative to the group of subjects with less intense affect on the issue, the extreme feminists overestimated the prevalence of *both* the pro and anti positions and underestimated the neutral position. The polarized consensus effect was also replicated in estimates of the prevalence of both pro- and anti-feminist positions among four different groups of women who might stereotypically be expected to differ form one another in their attitudes: Southern housewives, single women in California, divorced women in the East, and nurses in the Midwest. In sum, subjects with intense affect on the issue consistently showed relatively polarized consensus estimates.

One of the reasons why consensus extimates have been of interest to social psychology is because the degree of perceived consensus associated with some behavior or choice has been hypothesized to be a factor affecting attributions about the causes of that behavior (Kelley, 1967). That is, if a behavior is seen as relatively

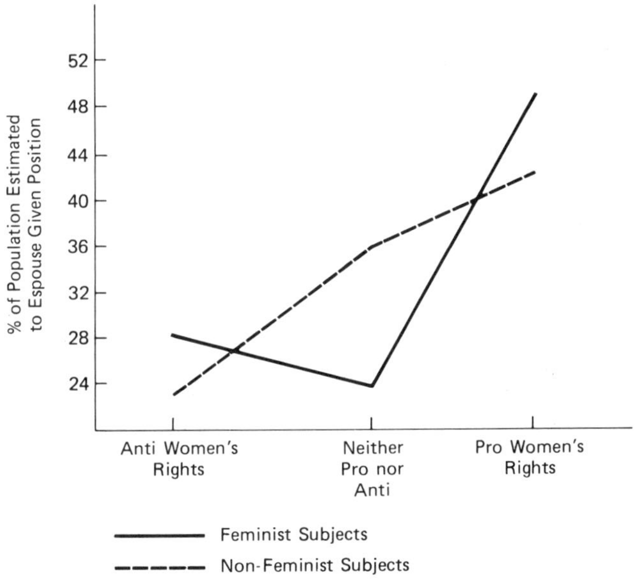

Fig. 4-2. Mean consensus estimates for "all adults in the U.S." by feminist and nonfeminist subjects.

[1] Although this result is consistent with the false consensus effect, it may be due to other factors as well. Strictly speaking the false consensus effects consists of *relative* displacement of consensus estimates towards one's own choice. Since all of our subjects were pro-women's rights, such relative displacement cannot be demonstrated.

common, it tends not to be diagnostic concerning the dispositions or characteristics of the actor. On the other hand, uncommon behaviors should be more diagnostic or revealing of the actor's dispositions. Research on the false consensus effect (Ross et al., 1977) has demonstrated this effect. Since subjects relatively overestimate the prevalence of their own behavioral choices, they tend to underestimate the diagnosticity of those choices relative to subjects who make different choices.

In connection with our research on polarized consensus estimates, we wanted to see whether the negative relationship between perceived consensus and the perceived diagnosticity of a behavior would hold in the domain of affectively charged attitudes. According to the attribution hypothesis concerning the use of consensus information, subjects who show polarized consensus, that is, who overestimate the prevalence of pro and anti positions, should find such positions relatively less diagnostic of personal characteristics than subjects who indicate that such positions are less prevalent. We suspected, however, that this prediction might not apply to the present case.

Subjects for whom the issue elicits intense affect might engage in relatively little of the active reasoning process implied by attribution theory. Rather, since such subjects find the issue to be a central concern, we suspected they would see it as central in how to respond to others. In other words, such subjects would be more likely to infer the characteristics of others from the position they espoused on the women's rights issue than subjects for whom the issue elicits less intense affect. In fact, this turned out to be the case. Contrary to the prediction from attribution theory, feminist subjects, who judged pro and anti positions to be more prevalent, also found those positions to be *more* diagnostic of personality qualities than subjects who were less extreme on the issue. Again, our point is not that the prediction from attribution theory is generally wrong; rather, we believe that it simply is not relevant in the present case. Put another way, differences in perceived consensus are not always negatively associated with differences in perceived diagnosticity.

Information encoding and retention

The discussion and research so far suggest that as the intensity of affect elicited by an issue increases, subjects tend to invoke an agreeable-disagreeable judgmental dimension in evaluating others and their positions on the issue. As affective intensity increases, judgments and evaluations seem to become more polarized—that is, organized around highly agreeable and highly disagreeable positions or poles. In essence, the subject who feels intensely about an issue has expectations that others and their positions are relatively polarized. This line of argument suggests that perhaps underlying the polarized judgments and expectations is a cognitive processing apparatus or schema (Taylor & Crocker, 1981) that is increasingly utilized as affective intensity increases. The research evidence suggests that, if such a schematic apparatus exists, it should be bipolar in form such that information that is either quite agreeable or disagreeable is more easily accommodated and processed. This line of reasoning encouraged us to look for schema-related effects of attitudes on information processing and retention (Judd & Kulik, 1980). Specifically we sought evidence for two related hypotheses:

1. Position statements that are either quite agreeable or quite disagreeable should be more easily encoded than position statements that elicit less affect.
2. Position statements that are either quite agreeable or quite disagreeable should be more likely to be remembered than position statements that elicit less affect.

The first of these hypotheses we examined by gathering data on judgmental decision or reaction times to determine if agreeable or disagreeable positions are judged more easily than other positions. The second hypothesis was explored by examining recall for the position statements that had previously been judged. Interestingly, in combination, these two hypotheses suggest that those statements that can be judged more quickly (i.e., less time spent examining them to determine what they say) will be retained more easily.

To test the first hypothesis, subjects made judgments about positions advocated by statements on three different issues: women's rights, capital punishment, and majority rule in South Africa. These three issues were chosen because a preexperimental survey established that they elicited fairly strong affect. On each issue, subjects judged 18 different one-sentence position statements. These 18 statements were spread across the full spectrum of possible attitude positions on each issue, as established by their Thurstone scale values. Examples of the statements are: (a) "The Equal Rights amendment should be supported by all who believe that discrimination is wrong"; (b) "Only for the very most serious crimes should capital punishment even be considered"; and (c) "Majority rule would only complicate the lives of most South Africans."

Subjects made two sets of judgments. First they rated the degree to which they agreed or disagreed with each of the 54 position statements (18 statements on each of three issues). These ratings were done on a 7-point scale. Subjects then made judgments about the positions advocated by the statements on a 7-point pro-anti rating scale.

For both judgment tasks, statements were shown for a 12-second interval and subjects made their judgments by pressing one of seven keys that were arranged in a semicircle around their hand. The judgments themselves and the judgmental decision times, in hundredths of seconds, were automatically recorded.

To examine whether statements that elicited extreme agree-disagree judgments were rated more quickly, judgmental decision times from both pro-anti and agree-disagree judgments were regressed on the extremity of agree-disagree ratings (i.e., the absolute value of the difference between the agree-disagree rating given and the scale midpoint) controlling for the number of words in the statement. Consistent with the first of our two hypotheses, both agree-disagree and pro-anti judgments were made significantly more quickly as agree-disagree ratings increased in extremity.

Although these results are consistent with our hypothesis, there is an alternative explanation based upon statement ambiguity that had to be eliminated. Statements differ in their ambiguity vis-à-vis particular judgment dimensions, and it is likely that less ambiguous statements are judged more easily—that is, processed more rapidly—along these dimensions than less ambiguous ones. Furthermore, ambiguity along the pro-anti dimension is likely to be related to extremity along that dimension; statements that advocate extreme pro-anti positions are likely to be less ambiguous than moderate ones. It might also be that extremity of agreement-disagreement ratings is highly correlated with extremity of pro-anti ratings. If so, the effect of the former variable on the reaction time of pro-anti ratings may have been due not to the affect accompanying strong agreement or disagreement, but to the fact that these items may have been less ambiguous along the pro-anti dimension. To eliminate this alternative explanation, we need to control for item ambiguity in determining whether statements that elicit stronger affect are judged more easily.

Controlling for statement ambiguity was done in two ways. First, we examined whether judgments on a pro-anti rating scale were done more quickly for statements that had been rated extremely on our agree-disagree rating scale, while controlling for the extremity of ratings on the pro-anti scale. Second, we conducted separate analyses within statements, to determine whether subjects who agreed or disagreed strongly with a statement judged it more quickly on the pro-anti rating scale than subjects who felt less strongly about that same statement. Each of these two analysis strategies is explained in more detail in the following.

The first analysis involved regressing pro-anti judgment times on the extremity of both pro-anti ratings and agree-disagree ratings. We expected the first predictor to exert a significant effect upon rating speed since we believed that items rated extremely on a scale are less ambiguous relative to that scale. The second predictor, agree-disagree rating extremity, was also expected to affect pro-anti judgment time, following the schematic hypothesis that we were testing. Also included in the regression equation were three other predictors: the number of words in the statement judged, the actual agree-disagree rating (*not* its extremity), and the actual pro-anti rating (*not* its extremity). These last two predictors were included in order to examine the possibility that attitude schematic effects are unipolar rather than bipolar. While we predicted that both agreeable and disagreeable statements should be more easily judged than more moderate ones, it is possible as well that more agreeable ones are more easily judged than less agreeable ones.

The results of this regression analysis are presented in Table 4-1. In this regression equation, the dependent variable is the pro-anti judgment times in hundredths of

Table 4-1. Results from Regression of Pro-Anti Rating Time on Pro-Anti and Agree-Disagree Ratings and Statement Length

Predictor	Unstandardized regression coefficient	t	p
Pro-anti rating[a]	−5.12	1.86	$<.10$
Agree-disagree rating[b]	−1.05	.40	$>.5$
Pro-anti rating extremity[c]	−54.17	9.83	$<.001$
Agree-disagree rating extremity[c]	−15.46	2.73	$<.01$
Statement length[d]	8.46	5.42	$<.001$

Note. Multiple correlation coefficient = .344, $F(5,1201) = 31.79$, $p < .001$. Rating times are in hundredths of seconds.

[a]High = more pro ratings.
[b]High = more disagree ratings.
[c]High = more extreme ratings.
[d]Coded as number of words in statement.

seconds. The unstandardized regression coefficients that are reported in the table can then be quite simply interpreted as the decrease (or increase) in rating time (in hundredths of seconds) associated with a one-unit change in the relevant predictor.

The following conclusions are supported by the results in Table 4-1: (a) Statements that were rated extremely on the pro-anti scale were rated substantially more quickly on that scale. On average, a statement that was rated at the pro-anti scale midpoint was rated 2 seconds more slowly than one rated either a "1" or a "7" on the scale. This effect is due, we believe, to differences in statement ambiguity. (b) Over and above the fact that statements rated more extremely on the pro-anti scale were judged more quickly on that scale, statements with which there was strong agreement or disagreement were rated more quickly on the pro-anti scale than statements that evoked less intense affect. This result supports our hypothesis concerning the bipolar schematic effects of attitudes. (c) There is no evidence that statements with which people agree are rated more quickly than statements with which people disagree. There is, however, a tendency for pro ratings to be made more quickly than anti ratings.

While this analysis partially solves the statement ambiguity problem, at least insofar as statements differ in their ambiguity relative to the pro-anti rating dimension, it is still likely that statements differ in ambiguity even when they receive the same pro-anti rating. These differences in ambiguity may be systematically related to the extremity of agreement-disagreement with the statements. To eliminate this further ambiguity threat, analyses were done for each statement separately, to determine whether someone who agreed or disagreed strongly with a particular statement rated it more quickly on the pro-anti scale than someone for whom that *same* statement elicited less affect. Averaging across the 54 separate regression equations (one for each of the statements), the results were entirely consistent in significance and effect size with those from the overall analysis reported in Table 4-1: On the average, subjects who agreed or disagreed strongly with an item judged its position on the pro-anti dimension more quickly than those who felt less strongly about that *same* item.

The second schematic effect of attitude intensity we hypothesized concerned memory for attitude position statements. Consistent with the judgmental time data, we expected statements with which people agreed or disagreed strongly to be more easily recalled than statements that elicited less affect. To explore this hypothesis, subjects returned the day after they had judged the 54 statements and attempted to recall as many of them as possible. Recalled statements were then matched by four independent judges to the original statements that subjects had seen. Our analysis then explored whether the probability of recall was a function of the extremity of the agree-disagree rating given a statement on the previous day.

In the case of memory for attitude position statements, there exists quite a bit of past research that is relevant to our hypothesis. Most of this literature has explored whether or not position statements with which people agree are more easily retained than position statement with which people disagree. In other words, this literature has examined the hypothesis that the probability of recall of position statements is a linear function of one's agreement or disagreement with those statements. Early research in this tradition (e.g., Jones & Kohler, 1958; Levine & Murphy, 1943) supported the hypothesis; more recently, however, attempts to demonstrate linear effects of agreement upon recall have not been successful (Greenwald & Sakumura, 1967; Waly & Cook, 1966).

Our schematic hypothesis suggests that the probability of recall should be a nonlinear function of agreement rather than a linear one. That is, as agreement-disagreement ratings are more extreme, as the affective reaction to a statement becomes more intense, the probability of recall should increase. In the research we conducted on this hypothesis, we were able to let the traditional linear hypothesis and our schematic nonlinear hypothesis compete against each other. We did this by regressing whether or not a position statement was recalled by a subject both on his or her agreement-disagreement rating of that statement from the previous day and on the extremity of his or her agreement-disagreement rating (i.e., absolute value of rating minus scale midpoint). The traditional linear hypothesis suggests that recall should vary with the first variable. Our schematic hypothesis suggests it should vary with the second.

In addition to these hypotheses about the linear and nonlinear effects of agreement ratings on recall, we suspected that statements that advocate more extreme positions (on the pro-anti dimension) would also be more likely to be recalled since they are more distinctive or novel than statements advocating less extreme positions. In order to unconfound this effect from our schematic hypothesis, we also included the extremity of subjects' ratings of the statements on the pro-anti rating scale as a predictor in the regression equation. The fourth and final predictor in the equation was the statement's rating on the pro-anti rating scale. Thus, in total, whether or not a statement was recalled by a subject was regressed on the agree-disagree rating of the statement given by the subject, the extremity of that rating, the pro-anti rating of the statement given by the subject, and the extremity of that rating.[2]

The results of this analysis are presented in Table 4-2. These results support the following conclusions: (a) Statements that receive more extreme pro-anti ratings are more likely to be recalled than statements that receive less extreme ratings on that dimension. A possible explanation for this effect is that statements that espouse extreme positions on an issue are relatively distinctive. (b) Over and above this effect, our schematic hypothesis received support. Statements that are rated more extremely on the agree-disagree scale are more likely to be recalled than statements rated less extremely on that scale. (c) There is no evidence to support the hypothesis that the probability of recall is a linear function of the agreeableness of the position statements. (d) Finally, statements that are rated as more anti, that is as more opposed to women's rights, capital punishment, and majority rule in South Africa, are more likely to be recalled than more pro statements. This result is consistent with other research showing that negative information is generally accorded more attention and weight in judgmental tasks than more positive information (Fiske, 1981; Kanouse & Hanson, 1971). It is also consistent with research showing that political positions that are relatively unpopular in the general public are more distinctive and hence more memorable (Greenwald & Sakurmura, 1967; Johnson & Judd, 1983).

As in the judgmental decision time data, it was important in the recall data to demonstrate that the hypothesized schematic effects of agreement-disagreement extremity were not due to differences between position statements in their ambiguity or distinctiveness. To do this, analyses were conducted within statements, exploring whether

[2]Statement length was not included as a predictor in this equation since it was found to be uncorrelated with recall.

Table 4-2. Results from Regression of Recall on Pro-Anti on Agree-Disagree Ratings

Predictor	Unstandardized regression coefficient	t	p
Pro-anti rating[a]	−.018	2.44	$<.05$
Agree-disagree rating[b]	−.006	.86	$>.5$
Pro-anti rating extremity[c]	.033	2.28	$<.05$
Agree-disagree rating extremity[c]	.035	2.38	$<.05$

Note. Multiple correlation coefficient = .130 F (5,1101) = 3.79, $p < .01$. Dependent variable: 1 = recalled; 0 = not recalled.

[a]High = more pro ratings.
[b]High = more disagree ratings.
[c]High = more extreme ratings.

subjects who agreed or disagreed extremely with a given statement were more likely to remember it than subjects who agreed or disagreed less extremely with that same statement. The results of these within-statement analyses were entirely consistent in both significance and magnitude of effects with the overall analysis reported in Table 4-2. Thus, even when we remove all variation between statements from the analysis, extreme agree-disagree ratings are associated with a higher probability of recall. Affective intensity thus is an element in the organization of information in memory. Stimuli that elicit more intense affect, regardless of the valence of that affect, are more memorable.

The absence of a linear effect for agree-disagree ratings on memory, in combination with our schematic nonlinear effects, suggests a reason why earlier research was inconsistent in its findings concerning a linear effect on memory. Most of the studies that have explored this linear hypothesis have presented subjects with only two types of attitude statements or information: very agreeable statements on the one hand and very disagreeable ones on the other. Clearly, if the relationship between statement agreeableness and retention is curvilinear, as we have shown, studies using statements at only two points along the agree-disagree dimension will find different results depending on the relative location of the two points. If the agreeable statements are more extremely agreeable than the disagreeable statements are extremely disagreeable, then the linear hypothesis that agreeableness enhances retention will seemingly (and falsely) be supported. The inconsistency of results on the linearity hypothesis is due, we believe, to the fact that the effect of attitudes on retention of relevant information is an effect of affective intensity rather than valence. In searching for valence effects, investigators have not adequately controlled for the intensity of the affect aroused by position statements.

Implications for the Study of Affect and Cognition

Having described our hypotheses and supporting data, we would like to discuss briefly some of our findings in relation to other research. We will conclude with some speculations on the variables mediating the influence of affect upon cognition and on the complexities of the affect-cognition relationship.

The research that we have reviewed in the previous section of this chapter demonstrates some fairly robust links between the intensity of an affective reaction to attitudinal stimuli and typical cognitive process and outcome variables such as decision time, recall, and judgments. More specifically, we have argued that as the affective intensity of an attitude on a social or political issue increases, judgments of position statements and judgments of the positions espoused by various populations tend to polarize. Underlying this polarization phenomenon is the fact that the stimuli to be judged, whether statements or the attitudinal positions of others, elicit intense affect to the extent that the issue in general elicits intense affect. The affect elicited by these stimuli serves as an additional dimension that accentuates judgemental differences on the dimension along which judgments are made. In addition, the intensity of affective reaction to stimuli seems to serve an organizing function in processing and retaining those stimuli. Stimuli that elicit more intense affect, regardless of the valence of that affect, are judged more quickly and recalled more easily than stimuli that elicit less intense affect.

All of this research is consistent with the general notion that affective responses to stimuli influence the organization and storage of information by the social perceiver. This general notion is consistent with the conclusions of other researchers who have explored the links between general mood states and memory (Bower, 1981; Clark & Isen, 1982). However, while we have focused on the intensity of affective responses to stimuli, these researchers have focused on the direction or valence of one's affective responses. Thus, for instance, Clark and Isen (1982) argue that the feeling tone of an event may be stored along with the event and may be later used to access the event from long-term memory. If one is in a pleasant mood, it may be easier to think of pleasant events from the past than if one if rather depressed.

We do not construe our research as in any way inconsistent with these findings or with the proposition that valence may influence both memory and judgment. Our studies indicate, however, that under some conditions the effect of affect is one of intensity rather than valence—that affective reactions of opposite valence will, if similar in intensity, yield similar outcomes in memory and judgment.

Judd and Kulik (1980), for example found superior retention of both extremely agreeable and extremely disagreeable items, but no effect for agreeability of item. This result indicates that the effects of attitude on memory, usually attributed to valence, might at least under some circumstances be more precisely ascribed to affective intensity. Similarly, Judd and Johnson (1981) demonstrated that the false consensus effect, a phenomenon potentially attributable to a motivation to exaggerate the prevalence of subjects' preferred (hence positively valenced) choices, may in reality reflect only one facet of a general tendency toward polarization. Here again, the crucial mediator seems to be intensity rather than valence, for the relative overestimation by committed subjects of agreeable attitudes was echoed by their relative overestimation of disagreeable attitudes as well. Finally, the diagnosticity results of Judd and Johnson (1981), revealed effects for both intensity and valence. Here, the valence effect was manifest in that subjects who were actively involved in the feminist movement viewed stance on feminism as highly diagnostic of personality traits—pro-feminist individuals were perceived as having generally more positively valenced characteristics and anti-feminist individuals as having generally negatively valenced characteristics.

But while this dichotomy in estimated traits reflected a valence effect, there were indications that the judgmental processes of our subjects were mediated by attitude intensity. Only committed feminists viewed the position of another on feminism as highly diagnostic of personality traits. The fact that noninvolved but generally profeminist subjects saw relatively little overall personality differences between pro- and anti-feminist others indicates that perceived diagnosticity is not the product of valence alone.

It is here that we should emphasize an important distinction between our research and the earlier work on accentuation effects in psychophysical judgment (e.g., Tajfel & Wilkes, 1963). In the area of attitudinal judgment, the mere imposition of a categorization along a peripheral dimension (for example, the characterization of the target as either pro- or anti-feminist) may not by itself be sufficient to accentuate judgments along another dimension, even when the categories along the peripheral dimension are differentially valenced. Rather, accentuation may occur only when a threshold level of affective intensity—that is the strong affect associated with deep commitment to the feminist movement—has been reached.

In light of these indications of a strong relationship between affective intensity and cognition, there are obvious questions remaining as to the precise factors influencing that relationship. Given the link between affect and memory on the one hand and affect and judgment accentuation on the other, we may ask whether memory effects are mediated by accentuated judgments or accentuation of judgments is mediated by memory effects. In fact it seems likely that both mediation chains operate. Memory effects of intensity may well arise from judgmental effects. Likewise, the judgmental effects may be induced by differential availability in memory. The Judd and Kulik (1980) finding of superior retention of both extremely agreeable and extremely disagreeable statements is wholly consistent with the polarization phenomenon identified by Judd and Johnson (1981). The greater memorability of affectively charged material may be the key factor inducing this polarization. For involved subjects, statements expressing both pro and anti viewpoints are laden with relatively heavy affect. Consequently, involved subjects may retain more instances of both pro and anti views, and may, because of this superior retention, overestimate the prevalence of both. It also seems certain, however, that accentuated judgments may mediate the effect of affect on memory, particularly by biasing the perceiver toward selective encoding and retention of instances that confirm prior judgments (Taylor & Crocker, 1981; also Chapter 10).

But if judgment and memory are reciprocal mediators of affect, the relationship between affect and general cognitive processes must surely be described as one of reciprocal causality. While this chapter has discussed the influence of affect upon cognition, a number of recent experiments have treated cognition as the independent variable and affect as the dependent measure. For example, Hamilton and Gifford (1976) have demonstrated how negative affect toward minority groups may have a genesis in a systematic tendency to associate infrequent behaviors with relatively small groups. Similarly, Ross, Amabile, and Steinmetz (1977) have demonstrated how insensitivity to situational influence might strengthen prejudice against the socially disadvantaged. Important as these results are in delineating the social ramifications of basic cognitive tendencies, we believe that there is yet much to be gained from research which, treating cognition as the dependent variable, further examines the influence of emotions on perceptions of the social world.

Acknowledgments. The research reported in this chapter was supported in part by grants to the first author from the National Institute of Mental Health and the National Science Foundation.

References

Arnold, M. B. (1970). Perennial problems in the field of emotion. In M. B. Arnold (Ed.), *Feelings and emotions: The Loyola Symposium.* New York: Academic Press.

Bower, G. H. (1981). Mood and memory. *American Psychologist, 36,* 129-148.

Cantril, H. (1945). The intensity of an attitude. *Journal of Abnormal and Social Psychology, 41,* 129-135.

Clark, M. S., & Isen, A. M. (1982). Toward understanding the relationship between feeling states and social behavior. In A. Hastorf & A. M. Isen (Eds.), *Cognitive social psychology.* New York: Elsevier.

Eiser, J. R. (1973). Judgment of attitude statements as a function of judges' attitudes and the judgmental dimension. *British Journal of Social and Clinical Psychology, 12,* 231-240.

Eiser, J. R., & Mower White, C. J. (1974). Evaluative consistency and social judgment. *Journal of Personality and Social Psychology, 30,* 349-359.

Eiser, J. R., & Stroebe, W. (1972). *Categorization and social judgment.* New York: Academic Press.

Fields, J. M., & Schuman, H. (1976). Public beliefs about the beliefs of the public. *Public Opinion Quarterly, 40,* 427-448.

Fishbein, M., & Ajzen, I. (1975). *Belief, attitude, intention, and behavior.* Reading, MA: Addison-Wesley.

Fiske, S. T. (1981). Social cognition and affect. In J. H. Harvey (Ed.), *Cognition, social behavior and the environment.* Hillsdale, NJ: Lawrence Erlbaum.

Greenwald, A. G., & Sakumura, J. S. (1967). Attitude and selective learning: Where are the phenomena of yesteryear? *Journal of Personality and Social Psychology, 7,* 378-397.

Hamilton, D. L., & Gifford, R. K. (1976). Illusory correlation in interpersonal perception: A cognitive basis of stereotypic judgments. *Journal of Experimental Social Psychology, 12,* 392-407.

Himmelfarb, S., & Eagly, A. H. (1974). *Readings in attitude change.* New York: Wiley.

Hovland, C. I., & Sherif, M. (1952). Judgmental phenomena and scales of attitude measurement: Item displacement in Thurstone scales. *Journal of Abnormal and Social Psychology, 47,* 822-832.

Izard, C. E. (1977). *Human emotions.* New York: Plenum.

Johnson, J. T., & Judd, C. M. (1983). Overlooking the incongruent: Categorization biases in the identification of political statements. *Journal of Personality and Social Psychology, 45.*

Jones, E. E., & Kohler, R. (1958). The effects of plausibility on the learning on controversial statements. *Journal of Abnormal and Social Psychology, 47,* 315-320.

Judd, C. M., & Harackiewicz, J. M. (1980). Contrast effects in attitude judgment. An examination of the accentuation hypothesis. *Journal of Personality and Social Psychology, 38,* 390-398.

Judd, C. M., & Johnson, J. T. (1981). Attitudes, polarization, and diagnosticity. *Journal of Personality and Social Psychology, 41,* 26-36.

Judd, C. M., & Krosnick, J. A. (1980). Attitude centrality, organization, and measurement. *Journal of Personality and Social Psychology, 42,* 436-447.

Judd, C. M., & Kulik, J. A. (1980). Schematic effects of social attitudes on information processing and recall. *Journal of Personality and Social Psychology, 38,* 569-578.

Kanouse, D. E., & Hanson, L. R. (1971). Negativity in evaluations. In E. E. Jones, D. E. Kanouse, H. H. Kelley, R. E. Nisbett, S. Valins, & B. Weiner (Eds.), *Attribution: Perceiving the causes of behavior.* Morristown, NJ: General Learning Press.

Katz, D., & Stotland, E. (1959). A preliminary statement to a theory of attitude structure and change. In S. Koch (Ed.), *Psychology: A study of a science.* New York: McGraw-Hill.

Kelley, H. H. (1967). Attribution theory in social psychology. In D. Levine (Ed.), *Nebraska symposium on motivation.* Lincoln, NE: University of Nebraska Press.

Levine, J. M., & Murphy, G. (1943). The learning and forgetting of controversial material. *Journal of Abnormal and Social Psychology, 38,* 507-517.

Mandler, G. (1975). *Mind and emotion.* New York: Wiley.

Ostrom, T. M., & Upshaw, H. S. (1968). Psychological perspective and attitude change. In A. G. Greenwald, T. C. Brock, & T. M. Ostrom (Eds.), *Psychological foundations of attitudes.* New York: Academic Press.

Rosenberg, M. J. (1960). An analysis of affective-cognitive consistency. In M. J. Rosenberg, C. I. Hovland, W. J. McGuire, R. P. Abelson, & J. W. Brehm. *Attitude organization and change.* New Haven, CT: Yale University Press.

Ross, L. D., Amabile, T. M., & Steinmetz, J. L. (1977). Social roles, social control, and biases in social-perception processes. *Journal of Personality and Social Psychology, 35,* 485-494.

Ross, L., Greene, D., & House, P. (1977). The "false consensus effect": An egocentric bias in social perception and attribution processes. *Journal of Experimental Social Psychology, 13,* 279-301.

Scott, W. A. (1968). Attitude measurement. In G. Lindzey & E. Aronson (Eds.), *Handbook of social psychology.* Reading, MA: Addison-Wesley.

Sherif, M., & Hovland, C. I. (1961). *Social judgment: Assimilation and contrast effects in communication and attitude change.* New Haven, CT: Yale University Press.

Strongman, K. T. (1978). *The psychology of emotion.* New York: Wiley.

Suchman, E. A. (1950). The intensity component in attitude and opinion research. In S. A. Stouffer (Ed.), *Studies in social psychology in World War II.* Princeton, NJ: Princeton University Press.

Tajfel, H., & Wilkes, A. L. (1963). Classification and quantitative judgment. *British Journal of Psychology, 54,* 101-114.

Taylor, S. E., & Crocker, J. (1981). Schematic bases of social information processing. In E. T. Higgins, P. Herman, & M. Zanna (Eds.), *Social cognition.* Hillsdale, NJ: Lawrence Erlbaum.

Thurstone, L. L. (1931). The measurement of attitudes. *Journal of Abnormal and Social Psychology, 26,* 249-269.

Thurstone, L. L., & Chave, E. J. (1929). *The measurement of attitude.* Chicago: University of Chicago Press.

Tomkins, S. S. (1965). Affect and the psychology of knowledge. In S. Tomkins & C. E. Izard (Eds.), *Affect, cognition, and personality.* New York: Springer.

Waly, P., & Cook, S. W. (1966). Attitude as a determinant of learning and memory: A failure to confirm. *Journal of Personality and Social Psychology, 4,* 280-288.

Zajonc, R. B. (1980). Feeling and thinking: Preferences need no inferences. *American Psychologist, 35,* 151-175.

Part II
Intergroup Attitudes

Chapter 5

Attributing Attitudes to Members of Groups

Donald Granberg

> I don't really know what you niggers want . . . We have a high percentage of blacks in my company, and they are as good as the next soldier. We have to work together . . . but when I have any free time I want to get as far away from a nigger as I can get. *The other whites feel the same way. We hope the niggers feel the same way about us . . . we whites do not wish to associate with niggers and we want them to feel the same towards us.* For your information and future guidance I am *sure that at least 98% of whites* (north and south) (and I am from the north) *feel the same way.* Just a Yankee giving you the straight poop. (Letter to Tommy Smith, Olympic Gold Medalist Sprinter at 200 meters in 1968, quoted by Edwards, 1969, p. 48 [emphasis added])

Stripped of the pejoratives and viewed analytically, this letter may reflect and reveal tendencies of how humans form and express their impressions of the climate of opinion in intergroup relations. The letter writer is sure of an in-group consensus agreeing with his personal preference for segregation. He is also hopeful, though perhaps less confident, that members of the out-group also prefer segregation.

Only a few years ago, the Prime Minister of then white-ruled Rhodesia stated

> The question of quick majority rule is a facile, superficial argument . . . I want to assure you that not only the Whites but the majority of Blacks in Rhodesia oppose that sort of thing. (Smith, 1976, p. 7)

On what basis Ian Smith made these attributions was not specified, but it is probable that he was showing a tendency similar to that of the letter writer. It is quite possible that both were showing what may be a very pervasive human tendency to make an unwarranted assumption of similarity to self (Granberg, 1972). This tendency has recently been referred to as the *false consensus phenomenon* or egocentric bias (Ross, 1977; Ross, Greene, & House, 1977).

Anecdotal evidence may point to the everyday occurrence of the attribution process, and may contain clues for the formulation of systematic hypotheses. However, if we are to build a framework for a scientific understanding of how people attribute attitudes to members of a group, we must state abstract and general theoretical propositions and assess them in relation to evidence. This chapter does that by using balance theory and an extension of the functional theory of attitudes. The empirical data to be reported relate to preferences and attributions of people in the United States pertaining to racial segregation-desegregation, as expressed in four national representative surveys conducted between 1964 and 1976. We also consider attributions to the public made by members of two opposing social movement organizations. An attempt then is made to show how certain attributional tendencies could be consequential in influencing the course and sequence of intergroup relations. In doing so, a speculative theory is given that pertains to the process in which members of a social movement organization decide how to allocate the resources that have been accumulating within their group.

Balance and Functional Theories

When a person experiences disagreement with a liked other, or agreement with a disliked other, the cognitive condition is said to be imbalanced and motivation is generated to alter the cognitive dialectic. In Heider's (1958) *P-O-X* model, a person could move toward the generally preferred state of cognitive balance by changing *P*'s attitude toward *O* (the other person), *P*'s attitude toward *X* (the object, issue, or question at hand), or *P*'s impression of *O*'s attitude toward *X* (the attributional element). If there is ambiguity or uncertainty about *O*'s attitude toward X, then an available avenue to achieving cognitive balance would be for *P* to alter or distort when making the attribution of *O*'s attitude toward *X*. If the actual difference between *P*'s and *O*'s attitudes becomes underestimated in the attribution process, *assimilation* has occurred, and if the actual difference is overestimated or exaggerated, *contrast* has occurred. It is a straightforward application of Heider's theory to expect that people will tend to engage in assimilation when attributing views to a liked other and contrast when attributing views to a disliked other (Granberg & Brent, 1974; Sherif & Hovland, 1961; Sherif, Sherif, & Nebergall, 1965). There is substantial evidence that these processes occur when individuals attribute policy positions to political candidates. However, an asymmetry has been reported in which the tendency to assimilate a preferred candidate is more robust and pervasive than the tendency to contrast a nonpreferred candidate (Brent & Granberg, 1982; Granberg & Brent, 1980).

For the present problem, only a slight extension is required. *P* is still the person, but *O* becomes some group of people, and *X* remains some issue. Balance theory implies that people would be motivated to stress, highlight, and exaggerate the similarities between their own attitudes and the predominant view within their in-group (assimilation) and to exaggerate the differences between their attitudes and the predominant view in an out-group (contrast). More specifically, it was predicted that *attitude* and *attribution* on a segregation-desegregation scale would be positively correlated when attributing views to members of an in-group but negatively correlated when attributing views to members of an out-group. This assumes that people have a positive attitude toward the in-group and a negative attitude toward the out-group, an assumption that may be generally, but not always, correct. A more refined analysis would take into account both membership and reference group ties, or, in Heider's terms, unit and sentiment relations. When this was done, however, at least in the area of race relations, membership group appeared to dominate in the attribution of attitudes to groups (Granberg, Jefferson, Brent, & King, 1981).

Another dubious assumption here involves the unquestioning application of the logic of balance theory. There may be special situations where a literal interpretation of balance theory may be inappropriate. If an anticommunist were told that communists preferred low speed limits, fried chicken, and gender equality, must the anticommunist necessarily be expected to depart from these positions in order to create or maintain attitudinal distance from an out-group? Indeed, there is evidence that people find disagreement per se to be unpleasant, independent of the degree of balance (Insko, Songer, & McGarvey, 1974; Price, Harburg, & Newcomb, 1966). Perceiving that members of an out-group share one's preference not to associate (segregation) may be a special case in which the logic of balance theory might *not* apply. Perhaps an assumption of hedonic consistency (McGuire, 1980, 1981) may be more relevant here than the assumption of cognitive consistency. Nonetheless, because of its seeming relevance and prior related usage, balance theory is used here as one theoretical point of departure.

The functional theory of attitudes holds that people develop, retain, and alter attitudes for value-expressive, ego-defensive, knowledge, and social adjustment purposes. To change a person's attitude, it is important to know the function of the attitude for that person (Katz, 1960).

It is only a small step to suppose that the impression people form of where others stand on a given issue can also serve a social adjustment or instrumental function. Denying that blacks in Zimbabwe (or South Africa) prefer a one-person, one-vote situation may serve the short-term political purposes of a member of the dominant group. It was often observed on a casual basis that many Southern whites in the United States in the 1950s claimed that the blacks in their area liked things the way they were. (Similar claims were made about the attitudes of slaves in an earlier era.) Thus, the pressure for racial integration could be attributed to outside agitators, the implications being that the injustice was not so severe and that the case for urgency or necessity of social change had not been made. The presumption is that people may, in certain circumstances, attribute views to an out-group that are similar to their own attitudes. This may be especially true in relation to the matter of how closely, and under what circumstances, members of two groups ought to associate. Assimilating the views of an out-group on the matter of segregation-desegregation may have the instrumental or adjustment function of rationalizing or buttressing one's preference in regard to changing or maintaining the status quo. It is, of course, easier to anticipate that people will tend to assimilate, that is, assume more agreement with themselves than the situation actually warrants, when the attitudes of members of the in-group are being considered. Thus, the functional view leads to the prediction that on the matter of segregation-desegregation and association in intergroup relations, people making attributions assimilate in their estimates of the views of members of both the in-group and (perhaps to a lesser extent) the out-group.

Some Data Analyses

In national surveys conducted in the United States by the Survey Research Center/ Center for Political Studies of the University of Michigan in 1964, 1968, 1972, and 1976, adults were asked the following questions:

A. "In general, how many of the Negroes in this area would you say are in favor of *desegregation*—all of them, most of them, about half, less than half of them, or none of them?"
B. "How about the white people in this area? How many would you say are in favor of *strict segregation* of the races—all of them, most of them, about half, less than half of them or none of them?"
C. "What about you? Are you in favor of desegregation, strict segregation or something in between?"

Item C measures the person's attitudinal preference and items A and B involve attributing attitudes to members of two racial groups. There are certain features of these questions that should be noted. First, while a 3-point scale is used for the attitude question (C), 5-point scales are used for the attribution questions. Also, people were asked to estimate the degree of pro-*desegregation* consensus among blacks and the degree of pro-*segregation* consensus among whites. Thus when we interrelate attitude and attribution in this analysis, it is appropriate to use analysis of variance and correlation but not measures of agreement (Brent & Granberg, 1982). While these questions are not ideal, there is the advantage that they were asked, in the same order and with the same wording, of large representative samples of adults in four different surveys over a 12-year period during which substantial social change occurred. And these surveys include an ample number of people in each of the racial and regional groups that are used in the analysis.

Dividing each sample according to racial membership group was obvious. Given the history of race relations in the United States, it also made sense to divide the sample into two regions, the deep South, in which slavery and de jure segregation had been prevalent, and the non-South. (Preliminary analysis suggested that subdividing the latter category was not productive.) The regional division also was prompted by the use of the "in this area" phrase in the attribution questions.

Attitudinal responses

The overall distribution of responses to the attitude question is summarized in Table 5-1. In addition, certain statistical comparisons were made in each year. The attitudes of blacks and whites were compared within the South and non-South regions. And the attitudes of people in the South and non-South regions were compared within each racial group. These comparisons can be summarized as follows:

1. In each year, blacks expressed a significantly stronger preference for desegregation than whites.
2. As expected, in each year the interracial difference in attitudes was larger in the South than in the non-South.
3. In each year, there was a larger regional difference among whites than among

Table 5-1. Percentage of Blacks and Whites in the United States Preferring Desegregation, Segregation, or Something In-Between in 1964, 1968, 1972, and 1976.

Category of respondents	Percentage preferring											
	Desegregation				Something in-between				Strict segregation			
	1964	1968	1972	1976	1964	1968	1972	1976	1964	1968	1972	1976
All	32	40	42	41	45	45	45	50	23	15	13	9
Blacks	73	79	68	73	21	18	30	25	6	4	2	2
Whites	27	33	39	37	48	50	47	53	25	17	14	10
Non-Southern blacks	81	81	71	71	14	17	29	27	5	2	0	2
Non-Southern whites	32	37	42	39	49	50	47	52	19	13	11	9
Southern blacks	65	77	65	79	27	18	31	21	8	5	4	0
Southern whites	10	17	25	23	42	52	49	59	48	31	26	18

Note. The percentages in this table are based only on the people who gave one of the three answers above. Those who said ''don't know'' or who gave some uncodeable answer were excluded from this analysis. The exact wording of the question is given in the text as item C.

blacks in attitudes toward desegregation. That is, the Southern whites differed more from non-Southern whites than Southern blacks differed from non-Southern blacks.

4. The difference in attitudes toward desegregation between Southern blacks and non-Southern blacks was slight and not significant statistically in three of the four years (1964 being the exception).
5. The difference in preference for segregation-desegregation between Southern whites and non-Southern whites diminished during the years 1964-1976.
6. Of the four racial-regional categories, Southern whites were least likely to favor desegregation and the most likely to favor segregation in each year. It was also Southern whites who showed the most change in attitudes during these years with a substantial decrease in the percentage who favored segregation.

These comparisons are not theoretically interesting, but they help to provide a context for the analyses that follow.

Overall attributions

When we consider the attributions to blacks by the four racial-regional groups in each of the four years, there appears to be a general recognition that blacks lean toward preferring desegregation. However, among Southern whites, the attribution in 1964 was that less than half of the blacks in their area preferred desegregation. This was clearly an underestimate (see Table 5-1). Overall, in each year, whites attributed less pro-desegregation sentiments to blacks than did blacks. In each year except 1976, this difference was significant.

When we consider attributions to whites by the four racial-regional groups, one striking difference is that Southern whites attributed significantly more pro-segregation sentiments to whites than did Southern blacks. The difference between non-Southern whites and non-Southern blacks was in the same direction but not so pronounced. The trend across years suggests that Southern whites did have a general sense of diminishing support for segregation among whites.

The results at the aggregate level can be summarized as follows: Blacks expressed a greater preference for desegregation than did whites; blacks attributed more pro-desegregation sentiments to blacks than did whites; and whites attributed more pro-segregation sentiments to whites than did blacks. Thus, blacks estimated more support for the social change they tended to desire both within their own group and in the out-group than did whites. Finally, although the different wording of the attitude and attribution questions makes this observation more tenuous, it appears that both blacks and whites underestimated the amount of support for desegregation among blacks and overestimated the amount of support for segregation among whites. Or to state things more abstractly, both blacks and whites tended to overestimate the preference for the status quo (ante) and to underestimate the attitudinal base of support for social change.

The attitude-attribution relationship

Our primary interest is in the relationship between attitude and attribution. The correlations between a person's attitude and the attributions made to blacks and whites are given for each of the four racial-regional groups in each of the four years in Table 5-2.

Overall, whites tended to assimilate in their attributions to both whites and blacks in each of the four years. This tendency was significant at less than the .001 level in each instance. Also, in each year, whites assimilated in their estimates of the attitudes of whites to a slightly greater degree than in their estimates of the attitudes of blacks.

Figure 5-1 shows graphically the nature of these assimilative tendencies in each year for white respondents. In attributing views to whites, the relationship between attitude and attribution appears linear in each year. However, in attributing views to blacks, the relationship is linear only in 1964. In the three succeeding surveys, the relationship departs from linearity among the whites who themselves prefer segregation.

In each year, blacks showed a significant tendency to assimilate when estimating the attitudes of blacks. In attributing views to whites, however, blacks showed a significant tendency toward neither assimilation nor contrast. In three of the four years, blacks showed a nonsignificant tendency toward contrast in their attributions to whites. As can be seen in Table 5-1, blacks show less variance in their attitudes and this relative lack of variance can limit the degree to which the attitudinal variable can be correlated with another variable. But the lack of attitudinal variance cannot be used to explain completely why whites assimilate in their attributions to blacks, while blacks do not assimilate in their attributions to whites. Blacks did have enough variance in their attitudes to allow assimilation to occur in their attributions to blacks.

Table 5-2. Correlation Between Own Attitude and Position Attributed to Blacks and Whites on the Segregation-Desegregration Issue in 1964, 1968, 1972, and 1976.

	Correlation between own attitude and that attributed to							
	Blacks				Whites			
Category of respondents	1964	1968	1972	1976	1964	1968	1972	1976
All	.40[a]	.35[a]	.20[a]	.24[a]	.47[a]	.35[a]	.32[a]	.36[a]
Blacks	.47[a]	.36[a]	.29[a]	.21[b]	-.04[d]	.09[d]	-.02[d]	-.01[d]
Whites	.36[a]	.30[a]	.17[a]	.24[a]	.49[a]	.38[a]	.34[a]	.38[a]
Non-Southern blacks	.55[a]	.39[a]	.19[c]	.18[c]	-.01[d]	.18[c]	-.01[d]	-.01[d]
Non-Southern whites	.29[a]	.29[a]	.18[a]	.24[a]	.47[a]	.34[a]	.32[a]	.40[a]
Southern blacks	.39[a]	.34[a]	.39[a]	.30[c]	-.08[d]	-.01[d]	-.04[d]	-.06[d]
Southern whites	.22[b]	.19[b]	.08[c]	.22[b]	.38[a]	.42[a]	.34[a]	.21[b]

Note. The wording of the attitude and attribution questions are given in the text. The correlations reported in this table are based only on people who answered the attitude and attribution question by one of the designated alternatives. People who said "don't know" or who gave some other uncodeable answer to either or both of the attitude and attribution questions involved in the correlation were excluded from this analysis. The variables are coded in a way that a positive correlation indicates assimilation (the greater the preference for desegregation, the greater the preference for desegregation attributed to the group) while a negative correlation indicates contrast (the greater the preference for desegregation, the greater the preference for segregation attributed to the group).

[a] $p<.001$.
[b] $p<.01$.
[c] $p<.05$.
[d] $p>.05$.

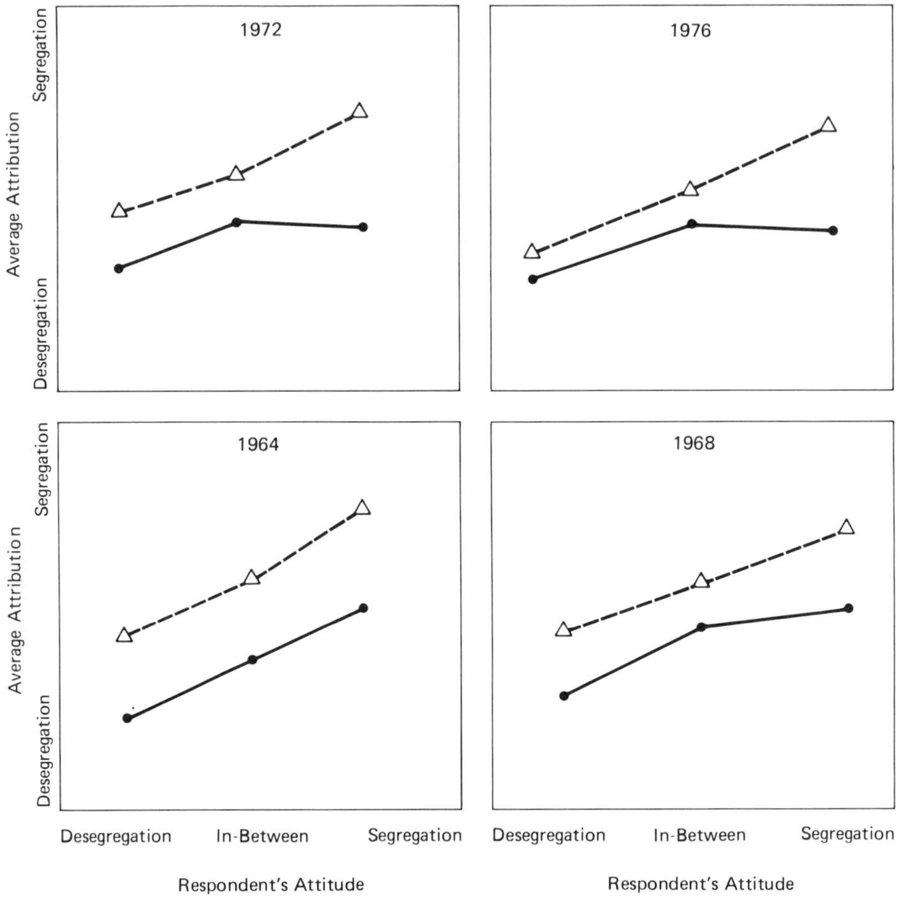

Fig. 5-1. Average attribution to blacks (solid line-circle) and to whites (broken line-triangle) on desegregation-segregation scale *by white respondents*, as a function of their own attitudinal preference regarding segregation-desegregation in four surveys. See the text for the wording of the attribution and attitude questions.

Southern whites and non-Southern whites appear to show a similar pattern. Each group tended to assimilate the views of whites and to also assimilate (albeit to a lesser degree) the views of blacks.

Southern blacks showed no tendency to assimilate in their estimates of whites in their area regarding segregation. In fact, in each year they showed a nonsignificant trend toward contrast. In relation to the in-group, Southern blacks showed a moderately strong and quite consistent trend toward assimilation in estimating the views of blacks in their area.

Non-Southern blacks showed a marginally significant tendency to assimilate in attributing views to whites on the segregation issue in 1968. But in the other three years, this group evinced a nonsignificant trend in the opposite direction, that is, toward contrast. Thus, the tendency of non-Southern blacks to assimilate the attitudes of whites in their area was neither strong nor reliable. Non-Southern blacks did show a significant tendency to assimilate in estimating the views of blacks in their area. But the strength of this relationship diminished to some degree across years.

Differential attrition in response

There is a qualification to the preceding analyses, pertaining to the number of people involved in the various correlations. By the standards of behavioral science, the number of people is adequate for each correlation in Table 5-2 and each average in Figure 5-1. However, at times there was a rather dramatic falloff or attrition from the initial number available in a given group to the number of people involved in the analysis. As the notes in Tables 5-1 and 5-2 indicate, the analyses up to this point are based entirely on those people who answer the questions under consideration by using one of the designated and provided alternatives. In order to see whether anything systematic or consistent was occurring in this area, the percentage of people answering by using one of the structured alternatives was calculated for each question. These percentages are given in Table 5-3 for blacks and whites separately. Certain consistencies in Table 5-3 are striking. People were much more willing to indicate their attitudes than they were to make the requested attributions. Also, they were more willing to attribute attitudes to the in-group than the out-group. Across years, actually less than half of the whites made the attribution estimates of the attitudes of blacks. It was as if many of the whites implicitly said "How should I know?" when asked to estimate how blacks felt about desegregation. Finally, another curious consistency was that blacks were more likely to make the requested attribution of attitudes to whites than whites were to attribute attitudes to blacks. What effect these differences in the amount of missing data would have on the preceding results is hard to say, but the results in Table 5-3 should be kept in mind when interpreting the results in Table 5-2 and Figure 5-1.

Table 5-3. Percentage of Blacks and Whites Willing to Express Their Own Attitudes, Attributions to Blacks, and Attributions to Whites on the Segregation-Desegregation Issue in 1964, 1968, 1972, and 1976.

	1964	1968	1972	1976	Average
	Percentage expressing own attitudes toward desegregation				
Blacks	98	95	98	92	96
Whites	97	95	97	95	96
	Percentage expressing attribution of attitudes to blacks				
Blacks	75	92	94	80	85
Whites	38	53	52	48	48
	Percentage expressing attribution of attitudes to whites				
Blacks	67	81	81	68	74
Whites	60	88	87	81	79

Note. The percentages in this table are based on the number of people in a racial grouping giving a codeable answer within the designated range to a given question divided by the total number of people in that racial group in that sample survey.

Interpretation

Overall, the results offer more support for functional theory than for balance theory as described earlier. Both theories implied that people would assimilate when attributing attitudes to members of the in-group, and this prediction was consistently sustained. But while balance theory predicted people would contrast in estimating views of the out-group, functional theory predicted at least a mild assimilation in that situation. The results were that, in estimating the views of members of an out-group, members of the dominant majority racial group tended to show assimilation, while members of the minority racial group showed neither assimilation nor contrast to a significant extent.

One rather striking finding in Table 5-2 was the complete lack of significant negative correlations between attitude and attribution, that is, contrast. This is similar to findings reported elsewhere concerning the attribution of attitudes to groups (Fields & Schuman, 1977; Korte, 1972; O'Gorman, 1975, 1979; O'Gorman & Garry, 1977; Travers, 1941; Wallen, 1943). Granberg et al. (1981, Tables 5-2 and 5-5) reported no significant negative correlations in their analyses of racial and age groupings. However, one difference between the findings of Granberg et al. and those reported here is in the attribution to whites by blacks. Averaging across five social issues, Granberg et al. found that blacks actually assimilated in their estimates of the views of whites (.22) to a greater extent than whites assimilated in their estimates of blacks (.10). Both blacks (.48) and whites (.42) assimilated more in their estimates of the views of the in-group than in their attributions to the out-group.

Here we should note that the lack of contrast in attributing attitudes to groups is *not* necessarily incompatible with the finding of contrast in placement judgments of individual statements (Eiser, 1971; Hovland & Sherif, 1952; Romer, 1983; Upshaw, 1962). Indeed, the two processes might support each other. One might easily imagine a segregationist saying that most blacks like things the way they are, *and* it is only extremists who want things to change. Thus, it could be quite consistent for a segregationist to think that most blacks favor segregation and, at the same time, rate a moderately anti-segregationist statement as *extremely* anti-segregation. The former would indicate assimilation in the attribution of attitudes to an out-group, and the latter contrast in the rating of a particular attitude statement.

The lack of significant contrast in the attributions to groups has a parallel in studies of the perception of policy positions of political candidates. An initial finding in that area was assimilation of a preferred candidate with no significant contrast of the nonpreferred candidate (Granberg & Brent, 1974; Granberg & Seidel, 1976). Subsequent research has found some significant contrast effects. When contrast occurs, it tends to involve placement judgments of a nonpreferred candidate who is the incumbent (Nixon in 1972, Ford in 1976, or Carter in 1980) rather than the challenger (McGovern in 1972, Carter in 1976, or Reagan in 1980). But the asymmetry still prevails in that assimilation effects tend to be more reliable, robust, and ubiquitous than contrast effects in that context (Brent & Granberg, 1982; Granberg & Jenks, 1977; Kinder, 1978; King, 1978).

It has recently been suggested that this alleged asymmetry in political perception may, as a consequence of methodological artifacts and misspecifications, be more apparent than real (Judd, Kenny, & Krosnick, 1983; Shaffer, 1981). This is not the place to pursue this matter in great depth. Briefly, Judd et al. noted three "misspecifications" in this line of research that may have led to an unwarranted conclusion regarding asymmetry. They were the failure to deal with the possibility of reciprocal causation, not knowing the candidate's real or "true position," and the problem of correlated error in measurement. After correcting for the two latter problems, there was still substantial asymmetry in their analyses. It was only by positing an asymmetrical persuasion effect, which probably does not exist (Markus, 1982), and for which there was no evidence in this context, that the asymmetry could be wiped out completely. Overall, one can say that correlating own attitude and the position attributed to another person or group may be an acceptable though certainly imperfect way of inferring the occurrence of assimilation and contrast. It does give part of the picture and some useful information about what is going on in the attribution process (Jones & Harris, 1967; Jones, Worchel, Goethals, & Grumet, 1971).

One study that did report substantial and pervasive contrast effects using the correlational procedure dealt with judgments by people as to what the current policy of the federal government in Washington, D.C. was (Granberg & Robertson, 1982). The respondents were adults in the United States, and the data were gathered in 1980. That the government was the stimulus that evoked significant contrast is certainly a matter of interest. In common usage, the federal government in Washington had, for many, become a pejorative label for a wasteful, abstract, and generally ineffective bureaucracy. In an era of good feelings in which people have a positive relationship to their government, one would not expect such contrast effects to occur in estimations of governmental policy. If the federal government is considered to be a group or formal organization, then this finding of Granberg and Robertson would also have to be incorporated into a theory of attributions to groups.

To summarize this section, a set of propositions is offered which appears to be generally consistent with existing data:

1. People are more ready and willing to express attitudes on a social issue than to make estimates of the distribution of attitudes within a group.
2. People are more ready and willing to make estimates of attitudes of members of the in-group than they are to make estimates of the attitudes of members of the out-group.
3. Members of a minority group are more willing to estimate the attitudes of members of the dominant majority group than members of the dominant group are willing to estimate the attitudes of members of the minority group.
4. People tend to underestimate the amount of support for social change in the specific area of racial desegregation.
5. People tend to assimilate when making estimates of the attitudes of members of the in-group.
6. On the matter of association (e.g., segregation-desegregation), members of the dominant group tend toward assimilation when making attributions to the out-group, while members of the minority group do not show a corresponding tendency toward assimilation when making attributions to the dominant group.
7. Even when people assimilate in estimating the views of members of the out-group, the tendency is weaker than the assimilation effect that occurs when the same people estimate the views of members of the in-group.

Overall, perhaps the strongest and most notable finding is the strong tendency for people to assimilate in attributing attitudes to members of their own group. This tendency has been observed elsewhere and has been referred to variously as projection, the pro-us illusion, the assumption of similarity to self, the egocentric bias, and the false consensus phenomenon (Granberg, 1972; Ross et al., 1977; White, 1970). It may be more parsimonious to subsume these various labels, which refer to similar if not identical phenomena, under one concept from social judgment theory, namely assimilation. The analysis used representative sample surveys of adults, and this has the advantage that the findings are broadly generalizable rather than peculiar to some group. In the next section, an extension is reported that involves attributions to the public made by active members of competing social movement organizations. The tendency of these people to assimilate in their attributions to the public will then be used as a base to weave a somewhat more speculative theory.

Attributing Preferences to the Public

It is a small extension from the previous section to anticipate that when people are asked to estimate the amount of support for their own point of view within their own society, the tendency will be to overestimate or to assimilate. This framework was used recently to interpret results pertaining to the link between preference and expectation in election research (Granberg & Brent, 1983). In 1980, about 80% of the people who preferred Reagan for president expected that Reagan would win, but 84% of the people who preferred Carter thought Carter would win. Across 10 presidential elections in the United States, with relatively little variation from year to year, people tended to predict that their preferred candidate would win. The ratio of optimists to pessimists in this regard was about 4:1, and the correlation averaged .60. Support for using balance theory to interpret this finding was provided by additional analyses, which showed that this tendency to predict a preferred outcome increased as one's attitude toward one's preferred candidate became more favorable. Also, in panel analyses, people with a balanced set of cognitions (preferring and expecting the same candidate) were more stable than people with an unbalanced set of cognitions.

The presumption in that analysis was that an underlying attributional process was occurring. *P* prefers candidate *X*, and tends to assume that other people comprising the electorate (toward whom *P* tends to have a generally favorable view) also prefer (or will come to prefer by election day) candidate *X*. The prediction that, when preference and expectation were variables, they would be positively correlated, was sustained at a very high level of reliability.

In another research project, two competing social movement organizations were studied over a period of two years. Their newsletters and public pronouncements were scrutinized, their meetings and conventions were attended and numerous informal interviews with leaders and rank-and-file members were conducted. Special attention was given to instances in which people made assertions about what other people preferred, and such instances were numerous. The two organizations were the National Right to Life Committee (NRLC), the largest anti-abortion or "pro-life" group in the United States and the National Abortion Rights Action League

(NARAL), the largest pro-abortion or "pro-choice" group in the United States. In 1980, the author conducted a systematic compositional study of the members of these two organizations in the form of a mailed questionnaire. Details of the method and results of this survey are available elsewhere (Granberg, 1981; Granberg & Denney, 1982). What has not been published previously are data related to the attribution process. Both theoretical considerations and casual observations led the author to include a section in which members of these social movement organizations (SMOs) were asked to estimate the climate of opinion within the society in relation to the issue most pertinent to the organization. The basic assimilation hypothesis was stated two ways:

Hypothesis 1: In their attributions to the public, members of an SMO overestimate the amount of support for their preferred position. To test this hypothesis would require two bits of information, data from a public opinion survey and estimations by members of an SMO as to how the public would respond to the items. Thus, this hypothesis can be tested with data from one SMO, although several tests would be required before the hypothesis could be regarded as having been strongly confirmed. If there were doubts as to the preferences of the members of the SMO, they should also be measured.

Hypothesis 2: Attributions of public opinion vary significantly in comparisons of members of opposing SMOs, such that members of each SMO attribute relatively more support within the public for their respective preferred position. Testing this hypothesis does not require a measure of how the public really feels, but rather evidence of estimates made by members of two opposing SMOs.

The compositional survey of NARAL and the NRLC in 1980 ($N = 896$) provides a direct test of these two hypotheses. Table 5-4 gives the *attitudinal responses* of NARAL and NRLC members to 12 items dealing with whether abortion should be legally available (columns 1 and 3). Not surprisingly, the two groups differed significantly on each item with r being larger than .90 for eight of the items (column 4). The best estimate available as to how adults in the United States really would have responded to these items at the time is derived from the 1980 General Social Survey conducted by the National Opinion Research Center (NORC) of the University of Chicago. Column 2 of Table 5-4 gives the results of that survey. Columns 5 and 6 of that table show the average *attribution* or estimate made by NARAL and NRLC members as to how they thought a representative sample of adults in the United States would respond to the attitude items.

In the case of NRLC members, Hypothesis 1 was clearly supported. On each of seven items, NRLC members, who themselves oppose abortion, underestimated the amount of public support for legalized abortion. The average level of approval was really 64% compared to 47% as the level of approval estimated by NRLC members. However, the evidence from NARAL members does not support Hypothesis 1. On four of the items, NARAL members, who themselves support legalized abortion, overestimated support for legalized abortion among the public, but they also underestimated support on three items. It was on the "hard" items (mother's health, rape, serious defect) that they underestimated support, while they tended to overestimate support on the "soft" items (cannot afford, do not want more children, does not want to marry the man). NARAL members may have underestimated the

Table 5-4. Percentage of NARAL, Adults in the United States, and NRLC Approving of Legalized Abortion Being Available Under 12 Circumstances and Average Estimates by NARAL and NRLC Members as to How Adults in the United States Would Respond

Do you think it should be possible for a pregnant woman to obtain an abortion...	Percentage yes				Average level of approval of U.S. adults as estimated by		
	NARAL	U.S. Adults	NRLC	NARAL vs. NRLC (*r*)	NARAL	NRLC	NARAL vs. NRLC (*r*)
	1	2	3	4	5	6	7
If it is necessary to save the woman's life	99.8	NA	73.2	.40	84.6	84.6	.00
If the woman's own health is seriously endangered by the pregnancy	99.8	90.1	14.9	.86	77.4	62.8	.37
If she became pregnant as a result of rape	99.8	83.4	7.2	.93	81.3	65.3	.42
If she became pregnant as a result of incest	99.4	NA	7.7	.92	81.5	66.5	.38
If there is a strong chance of a serious defect in the baby	99.8	83.1	3.6	.96	74.1	54.4	.52
If the family has a low income and cannot afford more children	98.1	51.7	1.7	.96	59.0	43.3	.39
If she is not married and does not want to marry the man	97.6	48.4	1.6	.96	54.8	38.3	.40
If she is a teenager and her parents would not consent to her having an abortion	97.6	NA	1.6	.96	52.6	37.3	.37

Do you think it should be possible for a pregnant woman to obtain an abortion. . .	Percentage yes				Average level of approval of U.S. adults as estimated by		
	NARAL	U.S. Adults	NRLC	NARAL vs. NRLC (*r*)	NARAL	NRLC	NARAL vs. NRLC (*r*)
	1	2	3	4	5	6	7
If she is married and does not want any more children	97.4	47.1	1.4	.96	52.1	32.3	.49
If the woman wants to have an abortion but her husband would not consent to her having an abortion	96.1	NA	1.7	.94	50.1	36.6	.36
If tests determine that the baby would not be the sex desired by the parents	58.2	NA	1.4	.62	26.7	17.0	.28
If she wants to have an abortion for whatever reason	84.8	41.1	1.4	.84	46.0	31.0	.35
Average for 12 items	94.0	—	9.8	.86	61.7	47.4	.36
Average for 7 NORC items	96.8	63.6	4.5	.92	63.5	46.8	.42

Note. NA means the question was not asked in the 1980 NORC General Social Survey. All of the correlations in columns 4 and 7 are significantly different from zero ($p < .001$), except, of course, the correlation of .00 in column 7. The wording of the question for columns 5 and 6 was, "How do you think a current representative sample of the U.S. adult population would respond to these items concerning whether a pregnant woman should be able to obtain a legal abortion. For each circumstance, give your estimate as to the percentage of people in a representative sample of the U.S. adult population who would respond yes and no. Please give an estimate or guess for each item." This table reports only the average estimate of approval or yes answers, but the average estimate of disapproval would simply be 100 minus the number in column 5 or 6. Similarly, in columns 1-3, the people who said "don't know," left the item blank, or who gave some other uncodeable response were excluded from the analyses, and thus, the percentage who said no would be 100 minus the number given in column 1, 2, or 3.

extent to which members of the public would differentiate among the various circumstances. But, overall, NARAL members gave attributions that were uncanny in accuracy, the average estimated level of approval being 63.5% compared to the actual average level of approval of 63.6%. Given these mixed results, Hypothesis 1 was not strongly supported.

Hypothesis 2 stated that in a comparison of competing SMOs, members of each SMO would attribute *relatively* more support within the public for their respective preferred position. Table 5-4 shows that in 11 of 12 comparisons, the results are in this direction. NARAL members attributed significantly more support for legalized abortion to the public than did members of the NRLC. The 12th item is an unusual case because a sizable majority of both groups approved of legalized abortion being available if it is necessary to save the woman's life. Column 7 in Table 5-4 gives the point biserial correlation between group membership and attribution to the public, the average across 12 items being .42. Thus, Hypothesis 2 was strongly supported.

In this study, respondents were not asked to estimate the distribution of attitudes within their own group or within the opposing group. Had this been done, it is the author's expectation that they would have shown assimilation when estimating attitudes of in-group members, provided there was adequate variation in attitudes. It is less clear what would have happened had they been asked to estimate the attitudes of members of the opposing group. Casual observation suggests that when members of one of these SMOs selects, quotes, or cites a member of the out-group, they tend to choose one who has taken an extremely opposed view. The strategy, it seems, is not to influence the members of the out-group *but rather* to try to influence the public and policymakers. One way is to show how extreme or radical one's opponents are, thus establishing distance between the out-group and the group that one is trying to influence. But when asked to attribute views to the public, it is clear than an assimilation tendency does occur among members of competing SMOs on the issue that is of greatest concern to them. The evidence indicates that more confidence should be placed in Hypothesis 2 than in Hypothesis 1. We now turn to a consideration of whether Hypotheses 1 and 2 can be incorporated into a more comprehensive theory.

An Attributional Theory of Experiences and Resource Allocation in Social Movement Organizations

Given that the attributional tendency observed thus far is quite pervasive and extends to members of SMOs, is this merely an intriguing cognitive bias or might it have some practical consequences in the lives of people? Let us examine the possibility that it could have a significant influence on what people experience and how they behave. What follows is an attempt to weave a theory based on the assumption that the assimilative tendency in the attribution process is both *pervasive and consequential* in determining lines of action. The theory involves the following categories of people: (a) members of an SMO; (b) leaders of an SMO; (c) the public or electorate, including members of the SMO, nonmembers, and members of an opposing SMO; and (d) members of the elite, that is, people at the upper echelons who formulate and administer policy in society.

Attributions made to the public reveal part of a person's definition of the situation. Another important aspect in one's definition of the situation is an assessment of the extent to which current policymakers are acting in line with the preferences of the SMO. Given the ambiguity of social and political reality in modern society, both of these factors are dimensions on which there would be variance among members of an SMO. Although the two dimensions of attributions to the public and assessment of elite performance are continua in reality, they can be dichotomized for heuristic purposes. When intersected, they form the typology in Table 5-5.

Type A (upper left-hand cell of Table 5-5) would be a person who attributes favorable sentiment to the public and makes a favorable assessment of the current elite group. Such a person is likely to experience *satisfaction* that the goals of the SMO are being achieved. The only thing remaining is to maintain surveillance over elites if doubt remains as to whether the victory is final. Some goals may be achieved once and for all (e.g., conquering a particular disease) whereas other goals may have to be realized each year (e.g., controlling inflation). In the case of the former, the SMO might end or look for some "new frontier." For the latter, it may be more of a holding action. For instance, if the Zero Population Growth organization saw the society

Table 5-5. Theoretical Typology of the Attitude Attribution Process and its Relation to Experience and Strategic Decisions Regarding Resource Allocations.

	Elites acting in accordance with the preferences of our organization	Elites *not* acting in accordance with the preferences of our organization
Nonelites supportive or in agreement with preferences of our organization	Experience: Satisfaction Strategy: Maintain vigilance or surveillance over elites and nonelites if doubt remains as to whether victory is permanent; holding action. May look for "new frontiers."	Experience: Frustration Strategy: Focus on pressure and electoral politics; in this situation, people may experience anger and may often show an unwillingness to compromise. Willing to have issue put to popular vote as in a referendum.
Nonelites *not* supportive or in agreement with the preferences of our organization	Experience: Uneasiness Strategy: Focus on efforts to inform and educate the masses in an effort to influence public opinion; reluctance to have conflict settled by popular vote, initiative or referendum; the feeling of uneasiness is mingled with doubts about the future	Experience: Isolation Strategy: Depends upon the person's conception of how change is brought about in matters like this, (by changing the elites *or* by initiating change at the nonelite level): people in this situation may be prone to expressive or apparently meaningless violence.

achieve what it regarded as the preferred birth rate in a given year, this would offer no guarantee that 1 year or 5 years hence some more unfavorable situation might not reemerge. The establishment in the United States of a Department of Education, a goal of the teachers' union, did not assure its continued existence.

Type B (upper right-hand cell in Table 5-5) would be a person who attributes agreement between the public and the SMO but feels the elites have not been acting in line with what the SMO would prefer. It is expected that a person in such a situation would be especially likely to experience *frustration* since the elite may be seen as *arbitrarily* thwarting the achievement of the goals of the SMO (Berkowitz, 1969). Since the public is already seen as being in line with the preferences of the SMO, the public is not seen as in great need of further information or education. Therefore, the strategy for Type B would focus on mobilizing latent support among the nonelite in order to change the elites, either by lobbying the present ones or by trying to replace them. In a democracy, the latter would normally be accomplished through electoral processes. Type B people, sensing that their preferences have broad popular support without a corresponding responsiveness by the elites, might be most likely to experience indignation and anger. If they have confidence in the long-term possibility of translating public opinion into public policy in their society, they may show an unwillingness to compromise, sensing that time is on their side. Type B people would be quite willing to have the controversy decided by popular vote as in a referendum.

Type C (lower left-hand cell of Table 5-5) senses that the public is not supportive of the goals of the SMO while, at the same time, believing that the elites are acting to establish or maintain public policy that is consistent with the goals of the SMO. In recent years, the percentage of adults in the United States who favored legalizing marijuana was never especially large, averaging about 25% in five surveys between 1973 and 1980. Suppose that sometime during this time period, the Supreme Court had struck down the marijuana laws, ruling them an unconstitutional infringement of personal liberty and the right to privacy. Then, a person who was a member of an SMO with the goal of decriminalizing the use of marijuana, and who had an accurate sense of public opinion, would be a Type C person.

A Type C person is expected to experience *uneasiness* over the possibility that while public policy is currently consistent with the SMO's goals, this may change in the future, especially given the public sentiment that is seen as not consistent with the preferences of the SMO. In a complex modern society like the United States, social change can be initiated in various ways, for example, by executive order, as in the desegregation of the armed forces under President Truman; by Supreme Court decision, as in the desegregation of public schools under *Brown v. Board of Education*; or by an act of Congress, as in the desegregation of hotels and restaurants under the Public Accommodations Civil Rights Law. Even in case of congressional action, Senators may vote in a way that they know is inconsistent with the popular will, as in the Panama Canal Treaty and gun control laws (Schuman & Presser, 1978).

A Type C person is expected to be apprehensive about the future and to direct attention to the cause of the uneasiness, namely the unsympathetic public. The public is to be informed and educated in order to bring public opinion more in line with the goals of the SMO. For the present, however, such a person would be reluctant to have the conflict settled by popular vote in the form of a referendum. The feeling of pleasure or satisfaction in seeing the SMO's goals enacted as policy is tempered by doubts about what the future may hold.

Type D (lower right-hand cell of Table 5-5) would be a person who senses that the public is *not* in agreement with the SMO and that the elites are *not* acting in line with the preferences of the SMO. Such a person might be expected to experience *isolation* and alienation from the rest of society, particularly if the conditions are viewed as chronic and not readily amenable to change.

The strategy favored by Type D people might depend further on their conception of how social change can be most effectively brought about, for example, by trying to change the masses at the grass-roots level, by trying to change the people in elite positions, or by setting up an enclave that could serve as an example for the rest of society or humanity ("a city on a hill"). If Type D people see no effective way of initiating and bringing about desired changes, they may be prone toward acts of expressive or apparently meaningless violence, for example, the rampage of the "Weathermen" in Chicago in 1969. The typology in Table 5-5 leads to four hypotheses:

Hypothesis 3: The probability of SMO members experiencing satisfaction, frustration, uneasiness, isolation, and other emotions varies as a joint function of attitudinal attributions to the public and an assessment of whether policymakers are acting in line with the preference of the SMO.

Hypothesis 4: In an SMO, preferences for allocating resources vary as a joint function of attitudinal attributions to the public, an assessment of whether elites are acting in a way consistent with the preferences of the SMO, and feelings they experience in relation to this situation.

Hypothesis 5: Within an SMO, preferences for allocating resources for pressure and electoral politics vary as a direct function of the assimilation tendency, and are especially strong among members who attribute views to the public that agree with the SMO but who disapprove of current elite performance.

Hypothesis 6: Within an SMO, preference for allocating resources for informing and influencing the public through educational campaigns varies as an inverse function of the assimilation tendency, and is especially strong among members who attribute views to the public that disagree with the SMO but who approve of current elite performance.

Thus far, the focus has been on members of an SMO. Although there is some evidence that leaders might be more sensitive than nonleaders to the attitudes of group members, there is no reason to believe that leaders of an SMO would be immune from a tendency to assimilate. Leaders are faced with the dual problem of figuring out the status of the SMO in relation to the public and trying to determine how the members of the SMO would like to see the resources of the SMO expended.

Hypothesis 7: In their attributions to the public, leaders of an SMO overestimate the amount of support for their preferred position among the public.

Hypothesis 8: When members and leaders of an SMO tend to overestimate the amount of support for the preferences of the SMO among the public, the extent to which this assimilative tendency occurs varies as a direct function of the amount of confidence they have in the public, and the degree to which they have a positive attitude toward the public.

Hypothesis 9: In attributing preferences to the members of an SMO as to how resources should be allocated, leaders of an SMO attribute preferences that are more similar to their own preferences than is actually the case.

Hypothesis 10: When leaders of an SMO make decisions regarding the allocation of resources, they are influenced by their attributions to the public, by their assessment of current elite performance, and by their attributions to members as to what they think the members would have them do.

Hypothesis 11: When leaders sense a difference between how they think the resources of the SMO should be allocated and the preferences of the members regarding resource allocation, the result will frequently be a compromise accompanied by an explanation to the members and an effort to persuade them to the leadership's point of view.

There is also no reason to think the assimilation tendency would not occur among people in policymaking positions. Here it may be difficult to separate what elites really think the masses prefer from impression management (Hall, 1972). For example, consider Nixon's clever reference to support by a "silent majority" for his Vietnam policy (Rosenberg, Converse, & Verba, 1970). Also, the tendency to assimilate in attributions made by elites to nonelites might be diminished somewhat by the extensive use of polls by elites. However, evidence from polls on controversial issues is usually at least mildly ambiguous. Overall, it is probable that elites genuinely overestimate mass support for their decisions.

Hypothesis 12: Elites overestimate the support by nonelites for policy alternatives preferred by the elites.

It should be emphasized that these hypotheses must be regarded as speculative. The theory is grounded in a rather extensive set of observations of two SMOs, but beyond the evidence already presented pertaining to Hypotheses 1 and 2, no systematic evidence is offered here in support of the theory.

Conclusion

One of the difficult lessons of growing up is learning that the world looks different to other people from the way it looks to us. Recent evidence indicates that this lesson is imperfectly learned so that the egocentric bias or assimilative tendency is a characteristic pattern of adults as well as children (Ross, 1977). It is apparently difficult to resist attributing an attitude to others when it seems so eminently reasonable to us.

Just how far this assimilative bias extends is difficult to say. We know that it occurs when attributing views to the in-group and to the public or electorate within one's own society. It also appears that whites assimilate when attributing preferences to blacks. Since the corresponding tendency for blacks to assimilate when attributing preferences to whites, on the matter of desegregation, did not occur, one is tempted to point to status differences and the effect of these differences on interaction patterns. That is, since in the United States, whites dominate society, it is likely that a lot of the unequal status contact between blacks and whites involves inauthentic interaction. Blacks may have been constrained by power and status differentials, but whites may not have taken this adequately into account when attributing attitudes to blacks (Jones & Harris, 1967; Jones et al., 1971). Even constrained behavior can engulf the field. However, on other social issues, blacks tend to assimilate when attributing attitudes to whites at least as much as when whites attribute attitudes to blacks (Granberg et al., 1981). This suggests that there may, indeed, be something special, unique, or fundamental about the matter of associating with members of the out-group, that is, segregation-desegregation.

Future research should more adequately distinguish among nonmembership groups. There are groups whose goals are irrelevant to the goals of one's in-group. Clearly, this is different from a group whose goals are seen as antithetical to the goals of one's in-group. Granberg et al. (1981) operationalized reference group by whether the person felt close or closest to that social category of people. Although limited in their use of secondary analysis, logically one could ask what groups one feels distant from, as well as those groups to which one feels close. The idea of negative unit and sentiment relationship in Heider's theory (1958) has a clear parallel to the concept of a negative reference group (Newcomb, 1948). But when a group is not a positive reference group for the person, one should not necessarily infer from this that it is a negative reference group. It may be largely irrelevant in the individual's frame of reference.

When we deal with the opposing SMOs concerned with abortion, then it is likely that people active in one group have it as a positive reference group and the opposing group as a negative reference group. One testable hypothesis is that when attributing characteristics to groups, people overestimate the amount of homogeneity within the out-group and overestimate the amount of heterogeneity within the in-group (Stephan, 1977). To test this, people would have to estimate the amount of intratrait variance within groups rather than asking them to estimate the modal view.

In the broadest sense, what emerges as a theme in this analysis of the attribution of attitudes is a rather bizarre image of human interaction. Carried to the extreme, it involves everyone assimilating in their estimates of everyone else, a kind of fool's paradise. But it should be remembered that what has been hypothesized here are human tendencies that are by no means expected to be invariant. For instance, when it was hypothesized that elites would assimilate in their estimates of the views of nonelites, it was offered as a stimulus to future analyses, which should delineate the circumstances that determine when, and to what degree, this assimilative tendency occurs.

Some time ago, it was suggested that prior to negotiation in intergroup relations, each side should engage in role-playing and state the other side's position to the other side's satisfaction (Rapoport, 1962). This proposal was obviously based on the assumption that the negotiation process would otherwise be hampered by misconceptions and inaccuracies in the attribution process. And there may be times when the intergroup differences may be overestimated and the common interest underestimated. But there may also be other instances in which perfectly accurate attributions only serve to lay bare the conflict. In any event, it is clear that attributions are often involved in an integral way in influencing the course of intergroup relations, and the probability of successfully managing these relations will increase when we understand this attribution process more fully.

Acknowledgements. Data in this chapter on race relations were made available through the Inter-University Consortium for Political and Social Research. The collection of data on abortion activists was funded by the Research Council of the University of Missouri—Columbia. Analysis of that data was funded by NICHD Grant No. 1-HD-82834. The assistance and advice of Beth Wellman Granberg, David Leuthold, Richard Hardy, Terry Brown, Donald Denny, Mary Harbourt, Sherry Kilgore, April Nelson, Karen Mulhauser, Kay Harrold, and Ann O'Donnell are gratefully acknowledged. The typology in Table 5-5 developed out of discussion with Lynn Taylor. The chapter was written while the author was on sabbatical leave from the University of Missouri-Columbia and a guest scholar at the Sociologiska Institutionen, Göteborgs Universitet, Göteborg, Sweden. The author is solely responsible for the analyses and interpretation.

References

Berkowitz, L. (1969). The frustration-aggression hypothesis revisited. In L. Berkowitz (Ed.), *Roots of aggression.* New York: Atherton.

Brent, E., & Granberg, D. (1982). Subjective agreement with the presidential candidates of 1976 and 1980. *Journal of Personality and Social Psychology, 42,* 393-403.

Edwards, H. (1969). *The revolt of the Black athlete.* New York: Free Press.

Eiser, J. (1971). Enhancement of contrast in the absolute judgment of attitude statements. *Journal of Personality and Social Psychology, 17,* 1-10.

Fields, J., & Schuman, H. (1977). Public beliefs about the beliefs of the public. *Public Opinion Quarterly, 40,* 427-448.

Granberg, D. (1972). Authoritarianism and the assumption of similarity to self. *Journal of Experimental Research in Personality, 6,* 1-4.

Granberg, D. (1981). The abortion activists. *Family Planning Perspectives, 13,* 157-163.

Granberg, D., & Brent, E. (1974). Dove—Hawk placements in the 1968 election: Application of social judgment and balance theories. *Journal of Personality and Social Psychology, 29,* 687-695.

Granberg, D., & Brent, E. (1980). Perceptions of issue positions of presidential candidates. *American Scientist, 68,* 617-625.

Granberg, D., & Brent, E. (1983). When prophecy bends: The preference-expectation link in U.S. presidential elections, 1952-1980. *Journal of Personality and Social Psychology, 45,* 477-491.

Granberg, D., & Denney, D. (1982). The coathanger and the rose. *Transaction/SOCIETY, 19,* 39-46.

Granberg, D., & Jefferson, N., Brent, E., & King, M. (1981). Membership group, reference group, and the attribution of attitudes to groups. *Journal of Personality and Social Psychology, 40,* 833-842.

Granberg, D., & Jenks, R. (1977). Assimilation and contrast effects in the 1972 election. *Human Relations, 30,* 623-640.

Granberg, D., & Robertson, C. (1982). Contrast effects in estimating the policies of the federal government. *Public Opinion Quarterly, 46,* 43-53.

Granberg, D., & Seidel, J. (1976). Social judgments of the urban and Vietnam issues in 1968 and 1972. *Social Forces, 55,* 1-15.

Hall, P. (1972). A symbolic interactionist analysis of politics. *Sociological Inquiry, 42,* 35-75.

Heider, F. (1958). *The psychology of interpersonal relations.* New York: Wiley, 1958.

Hovland, C., & Sherif, M. (1952). Judgmental phenomena and scales of attitude measurement: Item displacement in Thurstone scales. *Journal of Abnormal and Social Psychology, 47,* 822-832.

Insko, C., Songer, E., & McGarvey, W. (1974). Balance, positivity, and agreement in the Jordan paradigm: A defense of balance theory. *Journal of Experimental Social Psychology, 10,* 53-83.

Jones, E., & Harris, V. (1967). The attribution of attitudes. *Journal of Experimental Social Psychology, 3,* 1-24.

Jones, E., Worchel, S., Goethals, G., & Grumet, J. (1971). Prior expectancy and behavior extremity as determinants of attitude attribution. *Journal of Experimental Social Psychology, 7,* 59-80.

Judd, C., Kenny, D., & Krosnick, J. (1983). Judging the positions of political candidates: Models of assimilation and contrast. *Journal of Personality and Social Psychology, 44,* 952-963.

Katz, D. (1960). The functional approach to the study of attitudes. *Public Opinion Quarterly, 24,* 163-204.

Kinder, D. (1978). Political person perception: The asymmetrical influence of sentiment and choice on perceptions of presidential candidates. *Journal of Personality and Social Psychology, 36,* 859-871.

King, M. (1978). Assimilation and contrast of presidential candidates' issue positions, 1972. *Public Opinion Quarterly, 41,* 515-522.

Korte, C. (1972). Pluralistic ignorance about student radicalism. *Sociometry, 35,* 576-587.

Markus, G. (1982). Political attitudes during an election year: A report on the 1980 NES panel study. *American Political Science Review, 76,* 538-560.

McGuire, W. (1980). In R. Evans (Ed.), *The making of social psychology: Discussions with creative contributors.* New York: Gardner.

McGuire, W. (1981). The probabilogical model of cognitive structure and attitude change. In R. Petty, T. Ostrom, & T. Brock (Eds.), *Cognitive responses in persuasion.* Hillsdale, NJ: Lawrence Erlbaum.

Newcomb, T. (1948). Attitude development as a function of reference groups. In M. Sherif (Ed.), *An outline of social psychology.* New York: Harper.

O'Gorman, H. (1975). Pluralistic ignorance and White estimates of White support for racial segregation. *Public Opinion Quarterly, 39,* 313-330.

O'Gorman, H., (1979) White and Black perceptions of racial values. *Public Opinion Quarterly, 43,* 48-59.

O'Gorman, H., & Garry, S. (1977). Pluralistic ignorance: A replication and extension. *Public Opinion Quarterly, 40,* 449-458.

Price, K., Harburg, K., & Newcomb, T. (1966). Psychological balance in situations of negative interpersonal attitudes. *Journal of Personality and Social Psychology, 3,* 265-270.

Rapoport, A. (1962). Rules for debate. In Q. Wright, W. Evan, & M. Deutsch (Eds.), *Preventing World War III: Some proposals.* New York: Simon & Schuster.

Romer, D. (1983). Effects of own attitude on polarization of judgment. *Journal of Personality and Social Psychology, 44,* 273-284.

Rosenberg, M., Converse, P., & Verba, S. (1970). *Vietnam and the silent majority: The dove's guide.* New York: Harper & Row.

Ross, L. (1977). The intuitive psychologist and his shortcomings: Distortions in the attribution process. In L. Berkowitz (Ed.), *Advances in experimental social psychology* (Vol. 5). New York: Academic Press.

Ross, L., Greene, D., & House, P. (1977). The "false consensus effect": An egocentric bias in social perception and attribution process. *Journal of Experimental Social Psychology, 13,* 279-301.

Schuman, H., & Presser, S. (1978). Attitude measurement and the gun control paradox. *Public Opinion Quarterly, 41,* 427-438.

Shaffer, S. (1981). Balance theory and political cognitions. *American Politics Quarterly, 9,* 291-320.

Sherif, C., Sherif, M., & Nebergall, R. (1965). *Attitude and attitude change: The social judgment-involvement approach.* Philadelphia: Saunders.

Sherif, M., & Hovland, C. (1961). *Social judgment: Assimilation and contrast effects in communication and attitude change.* New Haven, Yale University Press.

Smith, I. (1976). For Rhodesian government: No quick Black majority rule. *Columbia Daily Tribune,* August 26, p. 7.

Stephan, W. (1977). Cognitive differentiation in intergroup perception. *Sociometry, 40,* 50-58.

Travers, R. (1941). A study in judging the opinions of groups. *Archives of Psychology, 266,* 1-73.

Upshaw, H. (1962). Own attitude as an anchor in equal-appearing intervals. *Journal of Abnormal and Social Psychology, 64,* 85-96.

Wallen, R. (1943). Individual estimates of group attitudes. *Journal of Social Psychology, 17,* 269-274.

White, R. (1970). *Nobody wanted war: Misperception in Vietnam and other wars.* Garden City, NY: Doubleday.

Chapter 6

Stereotyping and Sampling Biases in Intergroup Perception

Myron Rothbart, Robyn Dawes, and Bernadette Park

In order for language to achieve its communicative function, it is essential that a given symbol be able to evoke a similar psychological representation across diverse individuals. Although many symbols or words succeed in eliciting highly similar meanings among different people, there is an important domain in which the discrepancies in meanings are at least as important as the similarities, and that is in the perception of the characteristics of human groups.

Many of the important classifications we use to describe people divide individuals into mutually exclusive social categories such as male-female, young-old, white-nonwhite, and so on. Since these categories are frequently exhaustive as well as mutually exclusive, an interesting implication arises. Whereas we can readily describe the properties of "chair" or "tree" without reference to one's self, any description of say, "men" or "women" will have reference to ourselves as members of one of those categories. The fact that one category includes one's self (in-group) and the other category does not (out-group) has, we shall argue, enormous implications for intergroup perception. One of these implications is that a group will be perceived differently by its own members than by outsiders, and it is this discrepancy in intergroup perception that constitutes the subject matter of this chapter.

The chapter is organized into two major sections. The first section deals with the internal, psychological mechanisms that lead to differing perceptions of a given social stimulus. In this section we will discuss evidence, and possible psychological mechanisms, for four important phenomena: (a) the perception of in-group superiority (ethnocentrism), (b) the tendency for a group to be perceived as more variegated and complex by in-group than out-group members (the perception of out-group homogeneity), (c) the tendency to exaggerate differences between own and other group (contrast and accentuation effects), and (d) the tendency for different groups to differentially encode the same event in accord with existing expectancies and goals (assimilation).

The second section focuses not on the internal psychological mechanisms that affect the interpretation of an event, but on the external, *inter*personal or social factors that constrain the sampling of events, and provide a different set of data available to in-group and out-group members. Following the second section we briefly discuss some of the general and applied issues that emerge from our analysis.

Internal Mechanisms that Constrain the Perception of Social Groups

Ethnocentrism

Urie Bronfenbrenner (1963) showed photographs taken in Russia to a class of fifth- and sixth-grade American school children. In response to photographs depicting a road lined with young trees, one child asked, "Why do they have trees along the road?" Bronfenbrenner was surprised at this question and turned it back to the class: "Why do *you* suppose they have trees?" Among the answers were, "So that people won't be able to see what's going on beyond the road," and, "To make work for the prisoners." Bronfenbrenner then asked why American roads have trees planted along the side, and received much less dramatic responses: "For shade," and, "To keep the dust down." Bronfenbrenner then asks the reader, "Where did the children get the idea that the Russians have different reasons than we have for planting trees?"

One answer to Bronfenbrenner's question had been suggested a half-century earlier by Sumner who coined the term "ethnocentrism" to describe the widespread perception of in-group superiority (Sumner, 1906). Sumner defined ethnocentrism as:

> the view of things in which one's own group is the center of everything and all others are scaled and rated with reference to it . . . Each group nourishes its own pride and vanity, boasts itself superior, exalts its own divinities, and looks with contempt at outsiders . . . Each state . . . regards itself as the leader of civilization, the best, the freest, and the wisest, and all others as inferior. (1906, pp. 13-14)

The ubiquity of ethnocentrism has been well-documented (cf. Brewer & Campbell, 1976), and its prevalence among historically stable naturally existing groups probably is not surprising, since we would expect people to favor the attitudes, values, and habits with which they are most familiar. More surprising is the work by Tajfel, Rabbie, and others (cf. review by Brewer, 1979) on the artificially created "minimal" group situation. Rabbie and Horwitz (1969) attempted to determine the minimal conditions necessary for establishing bias against an out-group. Although a purely randomly generated label alone (e.g., labeling group members as "blue" or "green") was not sufficient to generate a more favorable evaluation of the in-group, the pairing of those arbitrarily generated labels with a minimal "common-fate" (e.g., own-group winning or losing a raffle by the toss of a coin) was sufficient to generate in-group favoritism (ethnocentrism).

Tajfel (Billig & Tajfel, 1973; Tajfel, 1970) created arbitrary, mutually exclusive social categories (e.g., under- or overestimators of dots) and found that subjects would use these categories in selectively favoring in-group over out-group members when distributing rewards. Billig and Tajfel argued that simply labeling a person as a member of a group (e.g., a group M or group W member) was sufficient to establish in-group favoritism—contrary to the findings of Rabbie and Horwitz—but there seems to be some ambiguity in this research as to whether the subjects perceived the "M" or "W" label as random or as "meaningful." In the Rabbie and Horwitz research it is likely that subjects perceived the "blue" or "green" labels as truly random, but subjects in the Tajfel research may see the categories as potentially meaningful even though they are arbitrary from the experimenter's perspective. In summary, although there is still some argument as to how arbitrary the basis for social categorization can be and still elicit ethnocentrism, it is clear that the sufficient conditions are minimal indeed.

There is perhaps more disagreement about the possible causes of ethnocentrism. It is possible that subjects, for a variety of reasons, assume themselves to be worthwhile, and assume that others who are different from self are therefore less worthwhile. This interpretation is more of a cognitive than motivational one and could handle most of the Tajfel research, but not the findings of Rabbie and Horwitz. A more motivational explanation suggests that we wish to enhance our own esteem by exalting the groups that are similar to us and disparaging those that are different. Research by Cialdini, Borden, Thorne, Walker, Freeman, and Sloan (1976) on student identification with winning or losing college football teams, is consistent with this esteem hypothesis. Cialdini et al. found that when subjects were led to experience a loss in self-esteem, they were more likely to refer to a winning home team as "we" and a losing home team as "they" than subjects who experienced a boost in self-esteem.

In a series of experiments, Howard and Rothbart (1980) attempted to extend the implications of the earlier Tajfel work on social categorization. Since the Tajfel research was restricted to measures of reward allocation, it was not clear whether subjects were blindly following an implicit norm (cf. Tajfel, 1970), or whether they regarded the out-group as truly different from the in-group. In their first experiment, Howard and Rothbart categorized college students as under- or overestimators of dots and presented them with 48 behaviors, half of which were favorable and half unfavorable. Subjects were asked to sort them into two piles according to which behaviors they associate with under- and which with overestimators of dots. The results were quite clear: Subjects associated more favorable behaviors and fewer unfavorable behaviors with their own group. It seemed, then, that by activating a "we-they" distinction, they were also activating the implicit expectation that "we are better than they."

Since there was evidence that subjects tend to remember selectively instances consistent with prior expectancies (Rothbart, Evans, & Fulero, 1979), it was argued that the activation of in-group/out-group dichotomies should bias subjects' memory toward remembering more favorable in-group and/or more unfavorable out-group behaviors. In two other experiments Howard and Rothbart confirmed this prediction, and argued that these findings signaled the presence of an important self-confirming "loop." The simultaneous operation of two biases, ethnocentrism and selective memory for confirming events, transformed an implicit expectation into a "psychological data base" that was overrepresented with undesirable out-group behaviors. Thus, while the research by Tajfel and others points to the minimal conditions required to generate ethnocentric attitudes, the Howard and Rothbart data suggest further that such implicit expectancies are quickly transformed into concrete instances of out-group inscrutability. What originally began as an implicit expectancy, ends up as demonstrable examples of out-group inferiority, which in turn can be used to justify the original sense of in-group superiority.

It is clear that ethnocentrism is an enormously powerful source of discrepancy in the mutual perceptions of in-group and out-group members, and may well account for the profound hostility of ideologically diverse groups, as well as provide an answer to Bronfenbrenner's more mundane question about why the Russians' motives for planting trees differ from those of Americans. Moreover, we suspect it is extremely difficult to innoculate against ethnocentric bias, as the daily newspapers provide abundant evidence of formerly victimized groups who, upon achieving victory and/or nationhood, proceed to dehumanize their "enemies" in the same way that they, themselves, had been treated.

The perception of out-group homogeneity

Several years ago, the first author taught a seminar on race relations in which there were approximately equal numbers of black and white students. Often a white student would begin a question or statement with the preface, "Don't black people feel . . ." or, "If blacks would only . . . ." The white instructor would hear these comments and say to himself, "That is an interesting observation . . ." or "Good question . . . ." Then a black student would say, "Don't white people feel . . ." or "If whites would only . . ." Now the instructor would become much more discerning and say to himself,

> What do they mean, 'white people'? There are all kinds of white people, some conservative, some liberal, some Jewish, some gentile, some sensitive to the problems of minorities and some not. 'White people' is too broad and meaningless a category to use, and there is no way I can respond to the black's question or statement in its existing form.

Of course, the same response was likely going through the black student's mind when white students offered generalizations about blacks.

Much of the course was spent discussing the attitudes of "whites" and "blacks," yet the meaning that was evoked by these two of the most frequently used words in the class may have been vastly different for observer and object. Each group referred to the other as if it were homogeneous and monolithic, and each group viewed itself as if it were variegated and complex. This discrepancy in the perception of intragroup variability in in-group and out-group members can be thought of as the perception of out-group homogeneity.

Park and Rothbart (1982), in a series of experiments on the perception of out-group homogeneity, argued that it may be most useful to think of out-group homogeneity as closely related to the process of stereotyping, rather than as an isolated phenomenon. If we were to ask subjects, for example, "How variable are men on the dimension of interpersonal competitiveness?," women would probably be more likely to respond in terms of the stereotype, whereas men would be more likely to respond in addition to specific instances relevant to the dimension. Since we are therefore predicting greater use of the stereotype in judging the out-group than in judging the in-group, a measure of the *strength* of the stereotype could be a useful index of intragroup homogeneity. More specifically, we would expect that the most homogeneous perception of a group would occur when all members of a group are seen as possessing stereotypic traits and none are seen as possessing counterstereotypic traits. To the degree that a group is perceived as having more equal mixtures of stereotypic and counterstereotypic traits, we could say that the image of the group is more heterogenous and complex. Thus, we are predicting that *fewer stereotypic* and *more* counterstereotypic characteristics would be attributed to a group by in-group than by out-group members.

If it is true, however, that the out-group responds more in terms of the stereotype than the in-group, we immediately confront the problem of ethnocentrism described earlier. Since stereotypes of the out-group are frequently pejorative, does a greater reliance on the stereotype by the out-group merely reflect a greater attribution of undesirable characteristics to the out-group? Or is out-group homogeneity manifest on favorable as well as unfavorable attributes? It is necessary to answer this question if we are to learn whether ethnocentrism and out-group homogeneity are independent or related processes.

In the first of four experiments, subjects were presented with a series of attitude or belief statements that had been pretested and classified as either typically feminine or typically masculine in nature, and as socially desirable or undesirable. Male and female subjects were asked to estimate the proportion of either males or females who would agree with or endorse each of these attitude statements. It was predicted and found that each group would estimate that a smaller proportion of own-group members would endorse stereotypic items, and a larger proportion would endorse counterstereotypic items than would be estimated by the out-group. For example, consider the target group "females." The prediction is that female subjects would estimate fewer females as endorsing stereotypic items (e.g., those that indicate passive or nurturant behavior) than would be estimated by male subjects, while female subjects would estimate a larger proportion of females as endorsing counterstereotypic items (e.g., those that implied dominance or independence) than would be estimated by male subjects. The results from this experiment are presented in Figure 6-1. To eliminate individual (and group) differences in scale usage, each subject's data were standardized by setting the subject's mean equal to 0 and standard deviation to 1.

It is important to note that this effect held for both groups being judged, that is, for both males as the target group, and females as the target group. In addition, there is *no* interaction between this effect and the social desirability of the items. That is, subjects were just as likely to make estimates that followed the predicted pattern for favorable and unfavorable items, suggesting that the perception of out-group homogeneity is independent of more well-established ethnocentrism effects.

One of the striking aspects of this experiment is the nature of the two groups that were used. While it would be less surprising to find that two groups who have little or no contact with one another view each other as relatively homogeneous and undifferentiated (e.g., Americans and Turks), it is impressive to have demonstrated this phenomena with two groups who have almost continual contact, and a wealth of information about one another.

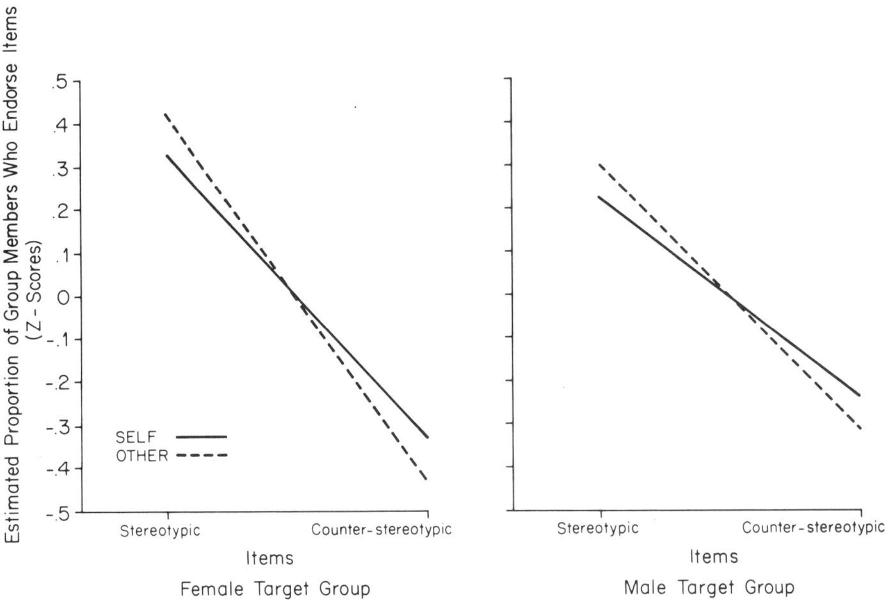

Fig. 6-1. Estimated proportion of group members who endorse stereotypic and counterstereotypic items as a function of in-group/out-group status (self/other) and sex of target group.

In the second experiment, Park and Rothbart (1982) were interested in the extent to which the perception of out-group homogeneity would be perceived among subgroups that varied along a dimension of typicality. For example, would we find evidence of greater homogeneity by out-group than in-group members when judging female physics majors (as contrasted with female English literature majors) and male dance majors (as contrasted with male economics majors)? In order to test this, male and female subjects again were asked to rate either male or female target groups. But now these target groups were actually subgroups of the larger category, such that subjects were asked to rate either female physics, economics, dance, or English literature majors, or male physics, economics, dance, or English literature majors. The data from this experiment are presented in Figure 6-2. Again, to eliminate individual (and group) differences in scale usage, each subject's data were standardized by setting the subject's mean equal to 0 and standard deviation to 1.

There are two points worth noting. The first is that in all eight of these subgroup conditions the out-group homogeneity effect is replicated such that the in-group (self) always estimates a smaller proportion of members as endorsing stereotypic and larger proportion as endorsing counterstereotypic items, relative to the estimates of the out-group (other). The perfect pattern of replication in all eight cells is a fairly convincing demonstration of the out-group homogeneity phenomenon. As in Experiment 1, there was again no interaction with the social desirability of the items, which again supports out-group homogeneity as a process independent of ethnocentrism.

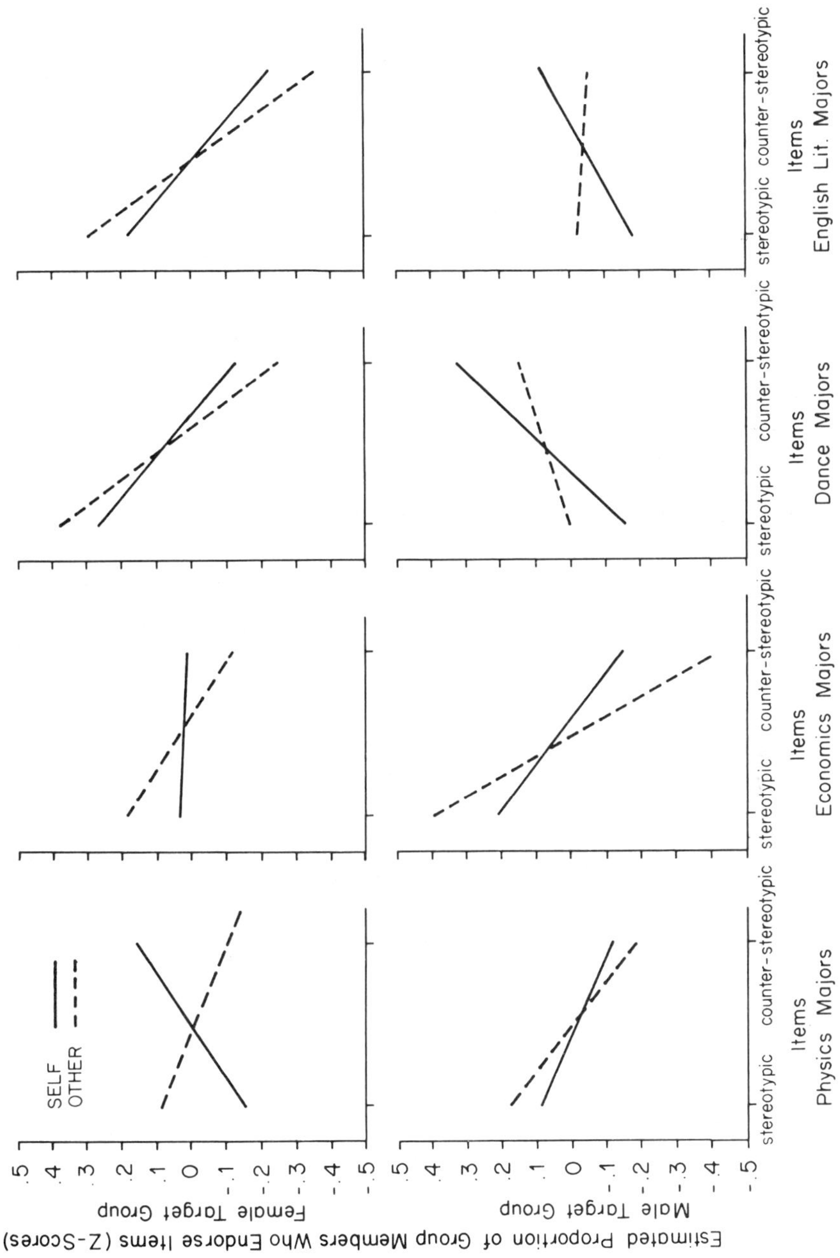

Fig. 6-2. Estimated proportion of group members who endorse stereotypic and counterstereotypic items as a function of sex of major in-group/out-group status (self/other) and sex of target group.

The second major point is best illustrated by the following examination of Figure 6-2. The top panel of graphs represents the judgments about women (as the target group). The solid line in the top panel represents the judgments about women, provided *by* women, and it is clear that the slope of this solid line varies dramatically as we move from "atypical" women on the left (physics and economics majors) to "typical" women on the right. Compare this with the slope of the dashed line (men judging women), which shows much less variability than for the solid lines. For the bottom panels (male target groups) again the solid line (now men judging men) shows more variability than the dashed line (women judging men).

A simple summary of this mass of findings is that each group sees much more variability among its subgroups (e.g., physics vs. dance majors) than does the out-group. It is as if the out-group member says, "Physics or dance, economics or English literature, the group's characteristics are still primarily male/female." The results of this experiment strengthen the findings of Experiment 1 by demonstrating the crossed interaction for a wider variety of stimulus groups, demonstrating greater differentiation of subgroups by in-group than out-group members, and confirming the independence of the out-group homogeneity and ethnocentrism effects.

In these first two studies men and women were used as the in-group and out-group. In a third experiment, an attempt was made to demonstrate the out-group homogeneity effect in a different group context, using a different set of measures. Whereas the stimulus groups previously judged may have represented rather large, abstract, and in some cases unfamiliar groups, the third experiment asked subjects to judge groups that were small, salient, and familiar. Women who belonged to three different sororities were asked to estimate the degree of similarity among the members of their own sorority and among the members of the two other sororities. All three sororities knew one another fairly well, lived in close physical proximity, and interacted with each other at a variety of functions. The data from this experiment is presented in Table 6-1, and again each subject's data are standardized.

When we consider each sorority as a target (i.e., within each column), the members of that sorority are judged to be least similar by in-group members and more similar by out-group members. This is true when sororities A, B, and C are judged.

Table 6-1. Judged Intragroup Similarity Within Three Sororities as Judged by the Three Sororities (*Z* Scores).

	Sorority being judged		
Sorority doing the judging	A	B	C
A	.08	.02	−.09
B	.33	−.33	.00
C	.84	.14	−.98

Note. The higher the number, the more similar the members of a given sorority are seen as being to one another. From Park, B., & Rothbart, M. (1982). Perception of out-group homogenity and levels of social categorization: Memory for the subordinate attributes of in-group and out-group members. *Journal of Personality and Social Psychology, 42*, 1051-1068. Copyright 1982 by the American Psychological Association.

This particular measure did not allow the investigators to separate out subject's ethnocentric judgments from their homogeneity judgments and all that can be concluded is that out-group members perceive greater similarity than do in-group members. (On a set of separate measures in this experiment, strong evidence for an ethnocentric bias among the three sororities was also found.)

At this point, the reader may rebel, arguing that we have demonstrated evidence for out-group homogeneity, but we have placed these experiments in the wrong section of the chapter. Since this section deals with differential encoding of a *constant* stimulus, can we rule out the possibility that people have more and/or different kinds of information about in-group than out-group members? Obviously, a central aspect of in-group/out-group relations is that of *differential contact* with own versus other group members, suggesting that the same information is not available to in-group and out-group members. In fact, this is quite a legitimate objection, but it is one we wish to address now, first with a theoretical analysis and then with an additional experiment.

Level of categorization in the encoding of in-group and out-group attributes. In the aforementioned course on the psychology of prejudice, each student described anonymously and in writing the nature of his or her negative attitudes and beliefs toward a particular group. In addition, each person was asked to try to explain the origins of their negative feelings about the group. Some of these accounts were discussed in class, and an attempt was made to identify the psychological processes underlying these causal explanations. In one particularly interesting case, a white male class member indicated that he disliked Chinese merchants, considering them untrustworthy and greedy. His attitudes, ostensibly, were based on one experience he had while in Singapore, when he patronized a shop owned by a Chinese proprietor. Our student purchased an item and insisted to the proprietor, who spoke very little English, that he was not given enough change. An argument ensued, and the proprietor finally gave our student the money he demanded. The student ascribed this incident of being short changed (if it was that) to a general characteristic of Chinese merchants.

When we discussed this case in class, the first question asked by the instructor was: "If the identical behavior had been associated with a white merchant, would he have inferred that white merchants are untrustworthy and greedy?" In other words, would he have attributed the behavior to the race of the proprietor if the proprietor were white? The fact is, as whites, it is almost inconceivable that we would conclude from an adverse interaction with another white person that it was their "whiteness" that was diagnostic of the adverse behavior, but this white student was willing to ascribe such adversity to Chinese merchants.

We wish to use this anecdote to develop our theoretical argument. Our student was encoding a very complex social event into memory, and it was necessary to store information both about the subject (the proprietor) and the predicate (the "undesirable" behavior). For the moment, we would like to defer a discussion of how the behavior (predicate) was encoded, and focus instead on the question of how the *subject* is encoded in memory. Although our student encoded the subject as "Chinese person," we must avoid the "stimulus error," and recognize that there are a plethora of social categories that could have been used to describe the proprietor: "male," "middle-aged," "bald-headed," "businessman," "thin person," "urbanite," and "jeweler," as well as "Chinese." Some of these attributes, such as "Chinese" or "male" are very general or global, and some are very specific, such as "bald-headed" or "jeweler." Our student clearly chose to encode this individual using a very general, undifferentiating attribute. We now wish to make two arguments: (a) We will tend to encode the characteristics of an out-group member using global, undifferentiating attributes, whereas we will tend to encode in-group members using more specific, differentiating categories (as well as using more global categories); and (b) the tendency to attach behavioral events to global rather than differentiating attributes will perpetuate the perception of a group as homogeneous, since differentiating subgroup categories are not available to attach to behavioral events.

To test this first assertion, a fourth experiment was conducted in which male or female subjects were presented with *identical* information about male or female characters in a news story. Each story described the behavior of either a male or female protagonist, along with his or her occupation, and other less important demographic information (e.g., age, residence). Each subject was asked to read one news story, with either male or female protagonist, and then completed several ratings concerning the quality of the written news account. Three days later, subjects were asked in an unexpected free and cued recall task to remember the character's sex, occupation, age, and residence. The investigators were interested in the extent to which in-group and out-group members would learn the most general information about the main character (the person's sex), as well as the extent to which they would learn subordinate information (the person's occupation). The relevant data are presented in Table 6-2, which contains the percentage of male and female subjects

Table 6-2. Accuracy of Recall for Sex and Occupation of Male and Female Stimulus Persons as a Function of In-Group/Out-Group Status.

Recall	As judged by	Male stimulus persons	Female stimulus persons	Male and female stimulus persons	$p<$
	Proportion of subjects accurately recalling sex of stimulus person				
Free	Self	.84	.91	.88	*ns*
	Other	.84	.76	.80	
Cued	Self	.98	.99	.98	*ns*
	Other	.98	.94	.97	
	Proportion of subjects accurately recalling occupation of stimulus person				
Free	Self	.29	.29	.29	.05
	Other	.21	.15	.18	
Cued	Self	.33	.46	.40	.01
	Other	.22	.22	.22	

Note. Number of males = 109. Number of females = 131. Total N = 240. From Park, B., & Rothbart, M. (1982). Perception of out-group homogeneity and levels of social categorization: Memory for the subordinate attributes of in-group and out-group members. *Journal of Personality and Social Psychology, 42*, 1051-1068. Copyright 1982 by the American Psychological Association.

Table 6-3. Accuracy of Recall for Occupation of Main Character as a Function of Favorability of Behavior and In-Group/Out-Group Status.

Recall	As judged by	Favorable character	Unfavorable character
Free	Self	.32	.26
	Other	.20	.16
	Difference	.12	.10
Cued	Self	.43	.36
	Other	.26	.19
	Difference	.17	.17

Note. From Park, B., & Rothbart, M. (1982). Perception of out-group homogeneity and levels of social categorization: Memory for the subordinate attributes of in-group and out-group members. *Journal of Personality and Social Psychology*, *42*, 1051-1068. Copyright 1982 by the American Psychological Association.

who were able to recall the sex and occupation of male and female protagonists during free and cued recall. While subjects were no more likely to recall the sex of in-group or out-group members, they were significantly more likely to recall the occupation of the main character if the main character was an in-group rather than an out-group member, and this was true for both free and cued recall. In half the stories subjects received, the main character behaved in a socially desirable manner, and in half they behaved in a socially undesirable manner. From Table 6-3 it is apparent that recall differences in memory for self and other are almost identical for favorable and unfavorable characters, again suggesting independence between out-group homogeneity and ethnocentrism.

The results of this experiment (Park & Rothbart, 1982, Experiment 4) suggests that even when identical information is available about the attributes of in-group and out-group members, subjects do not learn the same things about the two groups. Both groups remember well the global, undifferentiating information about the protagonist (their "maleness" or "femaleness") but the more differentiating information is remembered far better for the in-group member than the out-group member.

The importance of this "level of categorization" phenomenon in understanding discrepancies in social perception should not be underemphasized. We are, in effect, taking the ultimate phenomenological position and asserting that the stimulus person, as encoded by the in-group member, is not the same as the one encoded by out-group member. The consequences of this for the social inference process seem quite important to us. Consider, for example, the characteristics of a group such as feminists, a very large social category, which includes a variety of subgroups that vary dramatically in the nature and extremity of their political views. There is one subgroup that is essentially separatist and favor, literally, a world without males. There is a subgroup that is strongly pro-women's rights, nonseparatist, and strives to achieve equality with males within the existing political and economic structure. There is another group that wishes to achieve a nonsexist society, not through the business or professional world, but by concentrating on the artificiality and counterproductiveness of sex-typed roles for both males and females. There are also males who identify themselves as feminists. Many other points on a political continuum of beliefs are represented within the group "feminists," and there is overlap among the groups outlined previously.

How would such a complex group be psychologically represented by feminists (in-group members) and by nonfeminists (out-group members)? Reasoning from the results of the previous experiment, we would expect in-group members (feminists) to have learned a highly differentiated structure of the concept "feminists," recognizing that certain views, such as separatism, are associated with one subgroup of feminists, but not with others. To out-group members, who have failed to learn the differentiating categories, all the beliefs would presumably be attached to one (or few) undifferentiated categories, and it would be difficult, if not impossible, to discriminate among views that were characteristic of feminists, in general, from those that may characterize only a small subgroup.

The nonfeminists may characterize "feminism" by just one of these views (usually the most extreme, and in this case often the separatists) and the beliefs and actions of this subgroup (separatists) are attributed to the general category "feminists" (see Rothbart, Fulero, Jensen, Howard, & Birrell, 1978, for evidence indicating an over-representation of extreme individuals in group impressions). Many people outside the women's movement view feminists as anti-male and interpret many of the group's efforts for equality accordingly. This attribution would seem ridiculous to feminists (in-group members) who perceive their group as including women *and* men, Republicans and Democrats, separatists and nonseparatists, business executives and "head shop" owners.

This analysis is, of course, consistent with findings of Experiment 2 in Park and Rothbart (1982), where women, for example, saw enormous differences between women physics majors and women dance majors, whereas males saw those two groups of women as quite similar to one another (similarly, men saw large differences among diverse subgroups of men, but women did not).

Contrast and polarization effects

Dawes, Singer, and Lemons (1972) sought evidence for a contrast effect in intergroup attitudes. Specifically, they wanted to see whether Doves and Hawks during the Vietnam War would exaggerate the discrepancy between their own views and those of the opposing side. Moreover, Dawes et al. wanted to determine whether this effect was purely semantic (i.e., restricted to settings in which subjects were asked to scale or categorize items), or whether the effect was genuinely perceptual, and had implications beyond the use of psychologists' rating scales.

In Experiment 1, the researchers generated three mild, moderate, and extreme Dove statements and three mild, moderate, and extreme Hawk items, for a total of eighteen attitude statements. Self-defined Doves and Hawks were recruited as subjects, and each subject was presented with (almost) all possible pairs of the eighteen statements and asked to judge which of the two statements was more extreme. The results were quite clear: When a Dove item was paired with a Hawk item, Doves typically regarded the Hawk item as more extreme, while Hawks regarded the Dove item as more extreme. Consider, for example, the pairings of any of the three moderate Dove items with any of the three moderate Hawk items. Averaged over the nine possible pairings, 78% of the Doves regarded the Hawk items as more extreme and 68% of the Hawks regarded the Dove items as more extreme.

Because the measure of extremity was comparative rather than categorical, Dawes et al. (1972) concluded that this evidence for the contrast effect was not an artifact of implicit differences in subjects' definition of category boundaries. To assess Doves' and Hawks' images of one another more directly, a second experiment was run.

In Experiment 2, a new group of Hawks and Doves were recruited and asked, under an accuracy set, to write statements that would be endorsed by the typical Dove (Hawk) on campus. A still different group of Hawks and Doves were given these items and asked if they agreed or disagreed with the item; further, if they disagreed, they were asked to indicate whether they did so because the item was worded "too strongly" or "too mildly." Table 6-4 presents the mean number of Dove-written and Hawk-written statements rejected by Doves and Hawks, together with the reason for rejection. It is clear that Doves reject more Hawk-written (than Dove-written) statements, and the Hawks reject more Dove-written (than Hawk-written) statements; further, the reason for the vast majority of rejections is that the statements are too strong.

The findings from Experiment 2, then, suggest that subjects' images or stereotypes of the typical person holding opposing views is too extreme. Although subjects' task was to write items that the opposition would endorse, they consistently overestimated the extremity of the views held by the opposing side. To the degree that subjects overestimate, and therefore inaccurately describe opponents' views, we can be more confident that the contrast effect is not restricted to rating scale judgments, but has real implications for our impressions of others with all the attendant consequences for ameliorating or exacerbating intergroup conflict.

A number of different interpretations have been offered for the Dawes et al. (1972) findings, some of them only subtly different from others. As we see it, there are three

Table 6-4. Dove and Hawk Rejection of Hawk-Written and Dove Written Statements and Reason for Rejection.

	Reason	
Statement	Too strong	Too mild
Dove Rejection		
Dove-written	7.84	3.00
Hawk-written	9.32	3.36
Hawk rejection		
Dove-written	15.68	1.44
Hawk-written	11.40	2.00

Note. From Dawes, R. M., Singer, D., & Lemons, F. (1972). An experimental analysis of the contrast effect and its implications for intergroup communication and the indirect assessment of attitude. *Journal of Personality and Social Psychology*, *21*, 281-295. Copyright 1972 by the American Psychological Association.

central interpretations of the effects previously described: (a) a perceptual-cognitive interpretation, which asserts that the discrepancies in judgment are attributable to "real" differences in our assumptions about what other groups are like (clearly, this is the interpretation preferred by Dawes et al.); (b) a bias, presumably motivational in character, to disparage others' views by characterizing them as extreme, that is, "my views are moderate, your views are intemperate." This interpretation assumes that judgments of extremity are synonymous with judgments of opprobrium, and the judgment of extremity is basically an evaluative reaction. Although this interpretation is not necessarily at variance with the first interpretation, it nonetheless seems to us that there is a significant difference between the two, a difference that is akin to the difference between the affective and cognitive components of an attitude. The second interpretation assumes that the judgment is primarily affective and makes no assumptions about the perceived attributes or characteristics of the stimulus object. The first interpretation assumes the judgment is based on the perceived characteristics of the stimulus object and although an affective reaction may be an expected concomitant of the perceived attributes, the assumption is that the affective reaction is not the central component of the contrast effect. (c) The third interpretation is an "accentuation" interpretation, which again bears a number of similarities to the previous interpretations. The accentuation interpretation, as described by Eiser and Osmon (1978) and Judd and Harackiewicz (1980), seems to assume that the contrast effect is primarily perceptual in character, but comes about because judgments of stimuli along one dimension are polarized (accentuated) by the presence of another, correlated dimension. In the case of the Dawes et al. (1972) research, the judgment of extremity may be accentuated by the subject's degree of disagreement with the opposing viewpoint. One peripheral dimension (liking-disliking) may accentuate the focal dimension (degree of extremity). Since the accentuation principle is elaborated elsewhere in this book (cf. Chapter 3), we will not discuss it further here.

There is yet another possible interpretation of the Dawes et al. (1972) findings that differs from the preceding alternatives. It is probably clear to the reader that the subjects' task in the second experiment in Dawes et al. is remarkably similar to the first two experiments reported in Park and Rothbart (1982). In both instances, subjects are asked, in effect, for their stereotype of the out-group. Dawes et al. accomplished this by asking subjects to generate statements that they thought the "typical" out-group members would endorse. Park and Rothbart provided subjects with statements (both stereotypic and counterstereotypic) and asked what proportion of the out-group would endorse the item. In both instances, in-group members judged themselves *as less stereotypic* than did out-group members. Put another way, in both sets of experiments, (a) in-group and out-group members showed a significant *discrepancy* in their estimates of the characteristics of a group, and in both instances, (b) the discrepancy was in the direction of out-group members being more likely than in-group members to perceive the group as conforming to the stereotype.

We are, of course, making a major assumption that in the Dawes et al. (1972) research the items constructed by the out-group were, to some degree, stereotypic of the target group, in the same way that stereotypic items in the Park and Rothbart (1982) research were characteristic of a majority of the target group. If the items written by the out-group were ones that in-group and out-group members did not both regard as stereotypic, then the Park and Rothbart analysis does not apply.[1]

If the Dawes et al. (1972) and the Park and Rothbart (1982) experiments are tapping the same stereotyping processes, then the latter experiments could clarify the interpretation of the former. First, it would suggest that subjects are not simply disparaging the out-group by labeling them as "extreme." Recall that in the Park and Rothbart Experiments 1 and 2, out-group members were equally likely to assign both more bad and *good* stereotypic qualities than were in-group members, as well as less good and bad counterstereotypic qualities. As we stated earlier, this result suggested that out-group homogeneity was independent of ethnocentrism.

Are the data presented in this chapter amenable to an "accentuation" interpretation? There is clearly abundant experimental evidence in favor of an accentuation effect (Eiser & Osmon, 1978; Judd & Harackiewicz, 1980; Tajfel & Wilkes, 1963), but it is not clear that this is the best interpretation of the Park and Rothbart (1982) and Dawes et al. (1972) data. Clearly, when mutually exclusive groups judge one another, they will differ on peripheral (like-dislike, similar-dissimilar, agree-disagree) dimensions as well as on focal ones, and it would be impossible to ensure that no dimensions other than the focal one comes into use. As we understand the accentuation principle, however, it is not clear to us that it would make any predictions regarding subjects' memory for the superordinate or subordinate attributes of in-group and out-group members. We have proposed that subjects' judgments of out-group extremity and/or homogeneity may be mediated by the failure to learn the differentiating or subordinate attributes of out-group members, and we have provided tentative evidence for this prediction in Park and Rothbart's Experiment 4. Hopefully, further research and thought will clarify whether our interpretation based on "levels of categorization" is or is not congruent with an accentuation interpretation.

Differential encoding of behavior as a function of expectations and goals

In the previous section it was suggested that when we observe social events we are, in effect, encoding in memory information about a behavior (the predicate) with a causal agent (the subject). We have already discussed the way in which information about the subject is differentially encoded by in-group and out-group members, and we wish to turn now to the interpetation of behavioral events.

Actual differences between groups (cultural, experiential, or goal-orientation) may lead to different interpretations of what objectively is the same behavior. There is a fairly healthy literature documenting cultural, racial, and sex differences in behavioral interaction such as physical distance in conversation, eye contact, posi-

---

[1]The fact that the in-group rejected the items as applying to *one's self* does not mean that the in-group judges did not regard the items as stereotypic of their group. We may personally reject the item "wants at least two color TV sets," even though we are Americans and feel the item is stereotypically endorsed by a majority of Americans. In short, judges may or may not regard themselves as typical of their group.

tioning of the body, and voice rate and tone (LaFrance & Mayo, 1976; Sussman & Rosenfeld, 1982). There is also some work that looks at differential perception of the same objective stimulus as a function of such group differences. Abbey (1982) investigated male and female subjects' interpretations of behavioral interactions of male-female dyads. After listening to a conversation between a male-female pair, the male subjects judged the female participant as more seductive and promiscuous than did female subjects. The male subjects were also more attracted to the opposite-sex member of the target dyad than were female subjects. Finally, the male subjects also rated the male stimulus person as more flirtatious, seductive, and promiscuous than did the female subjects. It appears that the dimension of "sex" was used more by the male subjects in interpreting the entire interaction. To the extent that groups differ in the dimensions along which they interpret behavior, this could potentially lead to very different sets of information being stored for the same behavioral episode.

In a similar study, Sagar and Schofield (1980) investigated black and white children's perceptions of aggressive behavior. School-age children in an integrated school were shown cartoon drawings depicting black and white actors engaging in a variety of aggressive acts toward black and white targets, and were asked to rate the stimulus persons on a variety of dimensions. Race of the stimulus person was manipulated by shading the cartoon figures. Both black and white children rated the actor as more rude, mean, thoughtless, playful, threatening, unfriendly, and less likeable than the target. In addition, although the information presented was identical, the behaviors were rated as more mean and threatening when paired with a black than a white stimulus person. Of the four behaviors used by Sagar and Schofield, two were obviously aggressive and involved physical contact (bumping in the hallway, poking a student in the classroom), and two were more ambiguously aggressive and did not involve physical contact (requesting food from another student, using another's pencil without asking). Subjects were asked to indicate how threatening each of the behaviors was, and while there was agreement among the black and white children as to the aggressiveness in the two obvious behaviors, for the two that were more ambiguous, white children said they were more threatening than did the black children. This suggests an interesting possible interaction in the perceptual processes related to the stimulus materials.

We know there is a main effect such that both black and white children rate the behaviors as more mean and threatening when paired with a black than a white actor. We also know that white children are more likely than black children to see the ambiguous behaviors as threatening. It would also have been interesting to test for an interaction predicting that while black and white children agree on how threatening the white actor is (and it is less than for the black actor), the white children judge the black actor to be more threatening than do the black children. (This comparison is not directly available from Sagar and Schofield's presentation of the data because they are not broken down for judgments of the ambiguous vs. obviously aggressive acts.) Such an interaction would be supported by the following line of argument. Upon perceiving the black actor, the stereotype "aggressive" is activated, and hence ambiguously aggressive behaviors are more likely to be encoded as aggressive than when the perpetrator is white, since the category "aggressive" would not have been activated. In addition, according to the out-group homogeneity principle, white children should use the stereotype of blacks to a greater degree than black children, thus resulting in an interaction. In terms of category accessibility then (Bruner, 1957), black stimulus persons would be more likely to be described as aggressive, and in addition, out-group homogeneity would predict this affect to be stronger for white than black observers.

Social Forces that Constrain the Sampling of Events for In-Group and Out-Group Members

In this section, we will attempt to survey a number of important external, interpersonal factors that may result in differential perception of a target group by own versus other members. Whereas the first section of the chapter dealt with psychological factors that lead to differential encoding of the in-group and out-group behaviors, we now turn to social-psychological variables that lead to differential sampling of events for in-group and out-group members, which provide a different set of data available to in-group and out-group members.

Public and private behavior

Since the ultimate in-group/out-group dichotomy reduces to self-other differences, it is instructive to look at the well-established self-other differences in attribution of traits (Goldberg, 1978, 1981; Nisbett, Caputo, Legant, & Maracek, 1973). It has been demonstrated that when people are asked to describe both themselves and others in terms of trait adjectives, *and* can mark an alternative, "depends on situation," they are far more likely to use the "depends on situation" option for self than other. There has been a great deal of research and thought on this problem (cf. recent review by Watson, 1982), but variables relating to the *number* and *kind* of events sampled by self and others must be important. We sample our own behavior over the full range of our activities, whereas others sample over a much smaller range. Even others who know us quite well do not sample our dreams, fantasies, impulses, and bathroom habits. Consider facing the word *kind* and having to decide whether or not that applies to self. Others look at us and, perhaps, see the trait as applicable. But we look at ourselves and, while we have available the same public behaviors that lead others to attribute kindness to us, we are also aware of our petty and selfish impulses and fantasies, which are far less likely to be expressed to others. This observation is hardly original with us, as the public-private distinction serves as a focal point for the theories of Freud, Jung, Goffman, and others. The point is, there are public and private behaviors and, by definition, others only have access to the former and not the latter. The same reasoning applies to groups greater than one, as it is clear that there are some things that blacks will say to blacks and not to whites, some things that women will say to one another but not to men, and so on. Such restricted sampling may well account for some of the differences in perceived variability and extremity by in-group and out-group members.

Aside from the public versus private distinction, there are a number of other "external" forces that affect sampling that can be lumped under the general rubric of situational constraints. Since the term "situational" can refer to virtually anything, it may be more useful to decompose this general class into more specific ones. More precisely, we want to argue that at least three types of situational constraints can be distinguished: (a) the effects of social or occupational roles on the range and values of behaviors that are sampled; (b) the effects of intergroup, as opposed to interpersonal, interactions on behavior sampling; and (c) the effects of the presence of out-group members on the range of in-group behaviors.

Social and occupational roles

In a study by Ross, Amabile, and Steinmetz (1977), pairs of students were asked to take part in a "quiz game," with one member of the pair randomly designated as "questioner" and the other "contestant." The questioner was asked publicly to generate questions that would be "challenging but not impossible" for the contestant. Questioners were effective at this task, and after the question-answer session the players were asked to rate the general knowledge of self and other. Although the "questioners" did not rate themselves significantly more knowledgeable than the contestants, the contestants did perceive themselves as far less knowledgable than the questioner. Clearly, the "contestants" were unable to correct adequately for the fact that questioners were *instructed* to ask questions to which the answerer would be unlikely to respond. The immediacy of the questioner's astuteness and the answerer's dullness were stronger than any higher-order tendency to adjust or compensate for the unrepresentativeness of the questions. Interestingly, the questioners did not show this bias, presumably because they could not avoid sampling their own areas of ignorance, as well as their specialized knowledge (contestants only sampled the latter).

We professors benefit from this phenomena. Most of our students see us in only one context—the lecture hall. In that context, they only hear us lecture about things we know and understand and, not surprisingly, we do not lecture on topics that we find puzzling and difficult. Our students do not see us botching some home repair job or interpersonal encounter, nor do they hear us fumbling over an explanation of Avogadro's number to our children. We do see ourselves, however, in these settings, and this selective exposure may explain why many professors have a less exalted view of one another than do students.

A less benign example of the effects of social and occupational roles on the perception of groups concerns the prevalence of racist attitudes among white police who work in black slum communities. White police who patrol black areas sample almost exclusively negative behaviors from blacks, as the job of the police, at least as defined in this country, is to deal with criminal behavior. Since the police's sample of white behavior is predominantly favorable (whites' behaviors are sampled from within their own comparatively safe neighborhoods), police are sampling almost entirely from the cells containing unfavorable black and favorable white behaviors (see Fig. 6-3). Given the disproportionate sampling of cells b and c in Figure 6-3, it would be extremely difficult for even the most fair-minded individual not to come away from this sample space without believing in group differences between whites and blacks (cf. Lyons, 1970). Moreover, the problem is unlikely to be corrected unless data are

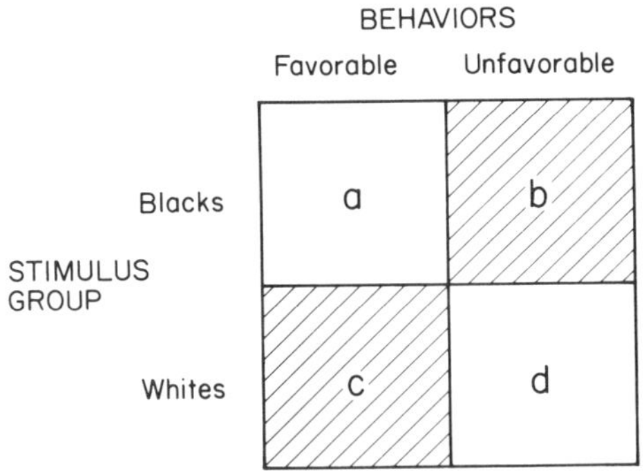

Fig. 6-3. A white policeman samples white and black behaviors. Cross-hatched cells are most heavily sampled.

sampled from the underrepresented cells, either by changing the definition of the job or by choosing police who are more likely to sample unrepresented behaviors (e.g., black police officers or white police officers who patrol white slum communities as well).

Intergroup versus interpersonal interaction

In a recent book on intergroup processes, Turner and Giles (1981) emphasize the difference between interpersonal and intergroup interaction. When a striking worker and a policeman interact with one another on a picket line, the behavior will be greatly constrained by the social categories that are important to the situation; that is, the police respond to the potential disruptiveness of the worker and the worker responds to the police as a symbol of established and oppressive authority. They are very unlikely to respond to one another as individuals with, say, common interests in fishing, baseball, sex, and family.

To the degree that the roles of the two parties are constrained, for example, by virtue of conflict or historical precedent, each will perceive the behaviors of the out-group along only highly restricted aspects, usually related to the dimensions along which the groups differ. Imagine, for example, a conflict between two adjacent neighborhood groups over the issue of blocking off a street. Assume our own group wishes to block the street and the other group wishes to keep it open. We know that our own group is heterogeneous, with some people in it who are wise and some who are foolish, some happy and some sad, but all of whom have one, and only one, common bond: the desire to close the street. But the only thing we know about the out-group is what they do have in common: their desire to keep the street open. Knowledge of our own group is not restricted solely to the issue dividing the in-group and out-group, but knowledge of the out-group *is* restricted in that way.

The effects of the presence of out-group members. A third potentially important constraint is that the presence of out-group members may serve to define the in-group's behaviors in a way that is consistent with the stereotype of the group. The extent to which women behave in a "feminine" way may be magnified by the presence of men, and the extent of men's "masculine" behavior may be magnified by the presence of women. This phenomenon may also apply to other dimensions along which populations can be divided (e.g., race, national origin). Americans in Europe often seem more American than they do in the United States, and one of us knows a colleague, born in Brooklyn, who teaches on the West Coast and develops a Western drawl whenever he returns to the East. A black student, known to the first author, has suggested that black students expressed more militant views in the presence of whites than in the presence of other blacks. This possibility could never have occurred to any of us, being white, since by definition we would never have been able to sample the behavior of "blacks only." It is as if group-related behavior is defined in part by the presence of others who are different. There are probably a number of different reasons for this phenomenon, but its implications are enormous for intergroup perception. It implies, in a sense, that the out-group *is* more extreme than the in-group or, more precisely, it suggests that a group behaves in a more extremely stereotypic fashion when out-group members are present, in comparison to "in-group members only." Given that we sample our own group under two conditions, with and without the presence of out-group members, whereas we only sample other groups under one condition (when we out-group members are present), it is not surprising that we perceive ourselves as more heterogeneous and less extreme than others see us.

A handful of studies exists in this area and the evidence for different behavior in the presence of out-group members is mixed. In a naturalistic study using coding of videotaped discussions among all male, all female, or mixed groups, Piliavin and Martin (1978) report little evidence to suggest that subjects altered their behavior in the presence of out-group members. What few interactions they did find between subjects' behavior and the sex composition of the group suggest there was less sex-typed behavior in the mixed than unmixed groups. In an earlier study using participant observers and a somewhat less rigorous coding procedure, Aries (1976) did find that the sex composition of a group resulted in differences in subject's behavior such that a greater amount of sex-typed behavior was observed in the mixed groups and a lesser amount in the unmixed groups. It is certainly plausible that under particular circumstances the presence of out-group members has not effect on the behavior of in-group members. What is needed is a more rigorous and extensive investigation of the conditions under which in-group members behave differently in the presence of out-group members, and the conditions under which they do not.

A recent study by Skrypnek and Snyder (1982) suggests that one's behavior toward a target is influenced by whether the target is believed to be an in-group or out-group member. In the study, male-female pairs of unacquainted individuals interacted to divide up a series of job-like tasks that varied in their sex-typedness. The male subject was always designated the perceiver and was led to believe that the female target subject was a female or a male, or was given no information concerning the sex of the target. Throughout the experiment, subjects had no visual or verbal contact with one another. The male perceiver chose to divide tasks in a manner consistent with the perceived sex of the target. Moreover, following several such interactions, the female target also chose to divide the tasks in a manner consistent with the sex she was perceived to be. This may, however, have been due to inferences the female targets made concerning the sex of the male perceiver, rather than any adjustment in their perceptions of themselves. Nevertheless, the idea is intriguing that knowledge of a target's group membership results in differential behavior toward the target and may, under certain circumstances, elicit behavior that conforms with the perceiver's beliefs. Previous work by Zanna and Pack (1975) found that a target will alter her behavior in accordance with the perceived preferences of a desirable other. Whether or not this alteration of behavior occurs in interactions other than those with desirable others is left for future research. It seems likely that the perceived expectations of others, whether desirable or not, do influence the behavior of the individuals.

There are several studies suggesting that the imagined presence of the out-group tends to produce more stereotypic behavior from in-group members. Deconchy (cited in Doise, 1978) asked Catholic students to free associate to the word "God" and provide their responses on a questionnaire. Half of the students were told the questionnaire came from a religious body and half were told it came from an anti-religious group. In response to the "religious" questionnaire, the associations were quite diverse, but in response to the "anti-religious" questionnaire, associations were drawn more uniformly from the catechism. That is, the associations were more stereotypically "religious" in the imagined presence of an anti-religious group.

Doise (1969) asked students of a particular architecture school, Y, to fill out a questionnaire consisting of statements about the characteristics of Y as an architecture school. Subjects were asked to indicate how much they agree with these items, which were actually either stereotypic or counterstereotypic beliefs about Y. In one condition they simply filled out the questionnaire, but in another condition they first imagined how a rival school, Z, would fill out the questionnaire and then they filled it out themselves. Under the "imagined rival" conditions, Y's judgments were more extremely stereotypic than they were under the control conditions.

Both of these studies provide at least presumptive evidence that the imagined presence of an opposing group produces more extremely stereotypic responses than would otherwise occur. Clearly, more research is needed on this interesting problem, particularly since these results, if taken at face value, suggest some very limiting conditions on intergroup contact as a means for ameliorating conflict.

Overview

We have examined a body of evidence indicating important discrepancies in the way in-group and out-group members perceive the characteristics of a group. These discrepancies include the ways in which a group's behaviors are interpreted, evaluated, and remembered. Moreover, these discrepancies are not restricted to the perceptions of unfamiliar groups, or to groups locked in ideological conflict, but extend to groups that are highly familiar (e.g., men and women) and hold similar values (e.g., members of different sororities).

We have argued that the source of these discrepancies can be localized both in the internal psychological mechanisms that lead to the encoding of a given stimulus, and in external social-psychological forces that lead to the availability of different samples of behavior to in-group and out-group members. The evidence considered thus far strongly indicates that a group is judged in more stereotypic terms by out-group than in-group members. We have argued that this discrepancy is associated with the perception of greater homogeneity and possibly greater extremity in the characteristics of out-group members.

We now wish to extend this argument and assert more generally that our mental representations of groups include both stereotypic and individual components, and that the relative mix of these two components is an important determinant of how we perceive both out-groups and in-groups. We view the stereotypic component as embodying generic, culturally shared features, generated in large part by "secondary" sources such as media, schools, and parents, whereas the individual component incorporates concrete, episodic experiences generated by "primary" interaction with specific individuals or specific groups of individuals. We have already argued that out-group members' representations of a group embody a larger share of stereotypic than individuating information. It is important to stress that the mix of stereotypic to individuating information varies not only with in-group or out-group status, but differentiates *among* in-groups and among out-groups as well. This analysis implies, of course, that we can have stereotypes of the in-group as well as the out-group, although the former is more likely to be attenuated by our own presence. There is some evidence consistent with this possibility in data presented earlier. Consider once again the Dawes et al. (1972) data in which Doves and Hawks evaluated attitude statements written by Doves and Hawks and decided whether they were (a) accurate, (b) too strong, or (c) too mild (Table 6-4). As already indicated, subjects were more likely to reject as extreme statements written by the out-group than statements written by the in-group. But it is also true that even for statements written by the in-group, a statement was far more likely to be rejected as too strong than as too mild. In other words, even in trying to write "endorsable" statements for their own group, subjects exaggerated the extremity of the group opinion.

In summary, we think it is useful to think of group impressions as varying in the degree to which they embody stereotypic images. As we move from few to many individuals, and from familiar to unfamiliar groups, we are far more likely to employ uniform stereotypes in our impressions of groups. This phenomenon is clearly present in the differential perceptions of in-groups and out-groups, but this analysis also implies that we may also hold stereotypic conceptions of the in-group, and some out-groups are more likely to be stereotyped than others. The main point of this line of argument is that group impressions are complex amalgamations of generalized features and specific instances, and the relative mix of these two components may be important determinants of how extreme and how monolithic we perceive a group to be.

Problems for further research

We are currently investigating a number of problems we hope will tell us more about the use of social categories in the social inference process and, most importantly, are trying to understand something about the ways in which people alter their category use as a consequence of facing disconfirming information. This is a complex question because the outcome depends upon the relative power of a number of opposing forces. For example, we have argued that the perception of out-group homogeneity is self-perpetuating, because we fail to learn the differentiating characteristics of the out-group. On the other hand, there is evidence from the judgment literature indicating that people will use the most differentiating information available on which to base their inferences. To the degree that there is *utility* in perceiving the differentiating features of the out-group, out-group members should eventually learn those features.

A second problem of considerable importance, in our view, concerns the relationship between the properties of the class and the properties of the members of the class. Certainly there should be *some* relationship between the observed characteristics of specific feminists we encounter and our views of feminists in general. We suspect, however, that while there is *some* relationship between the class and the members of the class, the relationship is a loose one that allows for some massive discrepancies. In our future work, we hope to examine this relationship more closely since it is a central problem for the general field of cognition, as well as for the area of intergroup perception.

Implications for social conflict

We have examined various sources of discrepancy in the mutual perceptions of groups, and it should be noted that these discrepancies are not restricted to groups physically isolated from one another, or to groups locked in conflict. Since discrepancies in the perception of group characteristics are a major concomitant, if not cause, of intergroup conflict, it is worth considering the implications of this paper for understanding social conflict. One implication is that the line between "realistic" and "nonrealistic" sources of conflict becomes thin indeed when we consider the *differential sampling* of behaviors for in-group and out-group members. Is the "reality" of a group its behavior among its in-group members, or its behavior in the presence of out-group members? Although it may be possible to label as "unrealistic" the various sources of bias in the *interpretation* of social events, this task becomes more difficult when we recognize the array of psychological and social forces that provide different samples of behavior to in-group and out-group members. A more constructive implication of our analysis is that by restructuring the social setting in a way that elicits underrepresented behaviors, as in the example of white police who patrol black slums, it may be possible to ameliorate some forms of intergroup conflict.

A troubling issue for students of social conflict concerns the mixed effects of intergroup contact (Amir, 1976). It now seems clear that even equal status contact does not ensure a reduction in denigrating stereotypes, a result that is not surprising in light of research discussed earlier on the polarizing presence of out-group members. On the one hand, if our images of out-group members are to become more complex, contact is necessary in order to learn about dimensions along which out-group members differ. On the other hand, it seems clear that contact can strengthen stereotypes by polarizing out-group behavior. One potential remedy is to structure *extended* contact that encourages out-of-role behavior. Arranging extended contact between opponent groups in a way that does not elicit conflict related behavior is no mean task, but one such episode is reported by Tom Wicker (1975) in a recounting of a 10-day journey on a troop train from Seattle to Norfolk spent with 2 other whites and 27 blacks:

> That 10 days had been the time of [Wicker's] discovery that black people were just that—people, individuals, human as he was, hurting, laughing, loving, worrying in much the same fashion about much the same things, whatever the inexcusable and ineradicable differences in their experience.
>
> The blacks still were preoccupied, as he was, with families, jobs, schooling, girls. No two of them were much alike in temperament or personality. Some he liked, some he did not. One was better read than he; another was mentally deficient, or so it seemed; another had a flashing wit; still another organized a profitable black market for food and tobacco, out of whatever obscure sources of supply. Some [created] disciplinary problems, as both the white boys did. Others shared plans and memories as equals with young Tom Wicker. Since in 10 days all the men on the car got only one shower—at the St. Louis YMCA, to which they were marched from the city's magnificent old railroad station one blessed evening—it turned out that whites when dirty smelled as bad as blacks when dirty. In such close quarters, it became apparent that black penises were no bigger than white and no more thought about by their possessors, which was constantly. The only major difference, other than skin color, was that, with one or two exceptions, the blacks were not as well educated as the whites, although all had gone to school. (Wicker, 1975, pp. 162-163, reprinted by permission of the Bodley Head, Ltd. from *A Time to Die* by Tom Wicker)

To the degree that contact can occur under conditions that deemphasize in-group/out-group boundaries, and permit intragroup variability to emerge, contact may be beneficial. As with most remedies for intergroup conflict, however, nature seems to have provided far more opportunities to fail than to succeed.

Discrepancies in intergroup perception are socially important and theoretically interesting. Since a nuclear, and probably final, war may be launched because either the United States or Union of Soviet Socialist Republics perceives the other's intentions as unalterably malignant, it is hoped that future work will clarify the way in which we alter the basis of our categorization of out-group members and suggest ways in which discrepancies in the perception of group characteristics can be minimized.

Acknowledgments. Preparation of this chapter was supported in part by National Science Foundation Grant BNS-8203731 to the first author. We are grateful to Mary Rothbart for her comments on an earlier draft.

References

Abbey, A. (1982). Sex differences in attributions for friendly behavior: Do males misperceive females' friendliness? *Journal of Personality and Social Psychology, 42,* 830-838.

Amir, Y. (1976). The role of intergroup contact in change of prejudice and ethnic relations. In P. Katz (Ed.), *Towards the elimination of racism.* New York: Pergamon Press.

Aries, E. (1976). Interaction patterns and themes of male, female and mixed groups. *Small Group Behavior, 7,* 7-18.

Billig, M., & Tajfel, H. (1973). Social categorization and similarity in intergroup behavior. *European Journal of Social Psychology, 3,* 27-52.

Brewer, M. B. (1979). In-group bias in the minimal intergroup situation: A cognitive motivational analysis. *Psychological Bulletin, 86,* 307-324.

Brewer, M. B., & Campbell, D. T. (1976). *Ethnocentrism and intergroup attitudes: East African evidence*. New York: Halstead Press (Sage Publications).

Bronfenbrenner, U. (1963). "Why do the Russians plant trees along the road?" *Saturday Review, 46*(95), 96.

Bruner, J. S. (1957). On perceptual readiness. *Psychological Review, 64,* 123-152.

Cialdini, R. B., Borden, R. J., Thorne, A., Walker, M. R., Freeman, S., & Sloan, L. R. (1976). Basking in reflected glory: Three (football) field studies. *Journal of Personality and Social Psychology, 34,* 366-375.

Dawes, R. M., Singer, D., & Lemons, F. (1972). An experimental analysis of the contrast effect and its implications for intergroup communication and the indirect assessment of attitude. *Journal of Personality and Social Psychology, 21,* 281-295.

Doise, W. (1969). Intergroup relations and polarization of individual and collective judgments. *Journal of Personality and Social Psychology, 12,* 136-143.

Doise, W. (1978). Groups and individuals: Explanations in social psychology. New York: Cambridge University Press.

Eiser, J. R., & Osmon, B. E. (1978). Judgmental perspective and value connotations of response scale labels. *Journal of Personality and Social Psychology, 36,* 491-497.

Goldberg, L. R. (1978). Differential attribution of trait-descriptive terms to one's self as compared to well-liked, neutral and disliked others: A psychometric analysis. *Journal of Personality and Social Psychology, 36,* 1012-1028.

Goldberg, L. R. (1981). Unconfounding situational attributions from uncertain, neutral and ambiguous ones: A psychometric analysis of descriptions of one's self and various types of others. *Journal of Personality and Social Psychology, 41,* 517-552.

Howard, J., & Rothbart, M. (1980). Social categorization and memory for ingroup and outgroup behavior. *Journal of Personality and Social Psychology, 38,* 301-310.

Judd, C. M., & Harackiewicz, J. M. (1980). Contrast effects in attitude judgment: An examination of the accentuation hypothesis. *Journal of Personality and Social Psychology, 38,* 390-398.

LaFrance, M., & Mayo, C. (1976). Racial differences in gaze behavior during conversations: Two systematic observational studies. *Journal of Personality and Social Psychology, 33,* 547-552.

Lyons, R. D. (November 29, 1970). Miami police study hints bigotry arises early from slum duty. *The New York Times*, p. 32.

Nisbett, R. E., Caputo, C., Legant, P., & Maracek, J. (1973). Behavior as seen by the actor and the observer. *Journal of Personality and Social Psychology, 27,* 154-165.

Park, B. M., & Rothbart, M. (1982). Perception of outgroup homogeneity and levels of social categorization: Memory for the subordinate attributions of ingroup and outgroup members. *Journal of Personality and Social Psychology, 42,* 1051-1068.

Piliavin, J. A., & Martin, R. R. (1978). The effects of sex composition of groups on style of social interaction. *Sex Roles, 4,* 281-296.

Rabbie, J. M., & Horwitz, M. (1969). Arousal of ingroup-outgroup bias by a chance win or loss. *Journal of Personality and Social Psychology, 13,* 269-277.

Ross, L. D., Amabile, T. M., & Steinmetz, J. L. (1977). Social roles, social control and biases in social perception processes. *Journal of Personality and Social Psychology, 35,* 485-494.

Rothbart, M., Evans, M., & Fulero, S. (1979). Recall for confirming events: Memory processes and the maintenance of social stereotypes. *Journal of Experimental Social Psychology, 15,* 343-355.

Rothbart, M., Fulero, S., Jensen, C., Howard, J., & Birrell, P. (1978). From individual to group impressions: Availability heuristics in stereotype formation. *Journal of Experimental Psychology, 14,* 237-255.

Sagar, H. A., & Schofield, J. W. (1980). Racial and behavioral cues in black and white children's perceptions of ambiguously aggressive acts. *Journal of Personality and Social Psychology, 39,* 590-598.

Skrypnek, B. J., & Snyder, M. (1982). On the self-perpetuating nature of stereotypes about men and women. *Journal of Experimental Social Psychology, 18,* 277-291.

Sumner, W. G. (1906). *Folkways*. Boston: Ginn and Co.

Sussman, N. M., & Rosenfeld, H. M. (1982). Influence of culture, language and sex on conversational distance. *Journal of Personality and Social Psychology, 42,* 66-74.

Tajfel, H. (1970). Experiments in intergroup discrimination. *Scientific American, 223,* 96-102.

Tajfel, H., & Wilkes, A. L. (1963). Classifications and quantitative judgment. *British Journal of Psychology, 54,* 101-114.

Turner, J. C., & Giles, H. (Ed.). (1981). *Intergroup behavior*. Chicago: University of Chicago Press.

Watson, D. (1982). The actor and the observer: How are their perceptions of causality divergent? *Psychological Bulletin, 92,* 682-700.

Wicker, T. (1975). *A time to die*. New York: Quadrangle/The New York Times Book Company.

Zanna, M. P., & Pack, S. J. (1975). On the self-fulfilling nature of apparent sex differences in behavior. *Journal of Experimental Social Psychology, 11,* 583-591.

Chapter 7

Language and Intergroup Attitudes

Ellen Bouchard Ryan, Miles Hewstone, and Howard Giles

Introduction

Somewhat surprisingly, social psychologists have traditionally been rather reluctant to consider speech in their formulations of social behavior (notable exceptions are Brown, 1965; Lambert, 1967; Robinson, 1972). However, this oversight has recently and gradually been corrected with a series of studies on language from a social-psychological perspective (e.g., Fraser & Scherer, 1982; Giles & St. Clair, 1979). It is clear that the way we speak and how listeners interpret our speech has important consequences for our interactions with others. Furthermore, the social-psychological approach to the study of such influences makes unique theoretical and methodological contributions to the wider discipline of language science.

We propose that this nascent discipline of the "social psychology of language" can play an especially influential role in the study of intergroup relations. In the present chapter we focus specifically upon language in interethnic behavior (see Giles, 1977; Giles & St. Jacques, 1979). A certain language, or speech style, can often be a necessary attribute for membership in a particular ethnic group, a salient cue for interethnic categorization, an important dimension of ethnic identity, and an ideal medium for facilitating intragroup cohesion (see Fishman, 1977). Our approach to the study of language and intergroup attitudes seeks to integrate the psychological processes underlying various social judgments with the sociostructural influences on ethnic groups as perceived by their members.

Many of the original and current studies in the social psychology of language have been concerned with attitudes toward different varieties of language and speech and the traits attributed to speakers of these varieties (Ryan & Giles, 1982; Scherer & Giles, 1979). Thus the present chapter, while contributing some insights and new perspectives to the general study of attitudes, also reveals the breadth and depth of associated research in the study of language. It is not possible here to discuss in detail the contributions of other disciplines to the investigation of language attitudes (e.g., sociological—Fishman, 1971; sociolinguistic—Labov, 1966) or to assess the strengths and weaknesses of complementary approaches to language and ethnicity (see Giles & Johnson, 1981). Suffice it to say that there is a long historical tradition to the imposition of a hierarchy on dialects and speech styles and that this aspect of prescriptivism has led to a variety of empirical and nonempirical analyses. The general result of such a hierarchy is that some forms of accented speech are rated lower on linguistic ability by "the system" (see Shuy & Fasold, 1973); and it is this essential fact that underlies all approaches. The present social psychological approach places an emphasis on individuals and their display of attitudes toward in-group and out-group members, as elicited by language and as reflected in its use.

In this chapter, we shall review the assessment procedures utilized, the findings from speaker evaluation research, the determinants and mechanisms posited to account for these, and finally extend the analysis by introducing a speculative model of language and intergroup attitudes.

Assessment Procedures

Taking a variety of definitions of attitude as their basis (see Eiser, 1980), studies of language attitudes have adopted a diverse set of perspectives and methods, as presented at length in Agheyisi and Fishman's (1970) catalogue of surveys, interviews, case studies, autobiographies, commitment measures, and speaker evaluations. However, three primary types of methodology are considered within the framework put forward by Ryan, Giles, and Sebastian (1982); this distinguishes among analysis of societal treatment of language varieties, direct assessment, and indirect assessment. The latter approach is of primary importance for the readership of this volume, because it is here that social psychology has made its primary contribution.

The first methodological approach refers to content analyses of the treatment accorded to language varieties within the society. Although rarely afforded any attention, the primary source of information concerning views about language varieties lies in their public treatment (e.g., official language policies, use by various subgroups, and use in different institutional settings). This approach does encompass a variety of techniques (see Fishman, 1966), but has thus far remained distinct from social-psychological inquiry. However, given the growing interest in richer, more social, and less experimental studies of social cognition, as exemplified in recent work on social representations (e.g., Moscovici, 1976), the way lies open for a rapprochement. Indeed, it can be argued that the social-psychological study of social representations may provide a useful theoretical background and some innovative tools to guide this work.

Language attitudes have, of course, also been measured directly with questionnaires bearing explicitly on language evaluation (how favorably a variety is viewed); language preference (e.g., which of two languages or varieties is preferred for certain purposes in certain situations); desirability and reasons for learning a particular language; evaluation of social groups that use a particular variety; self-reports concerning language use, desirability of bilingualism, and bilingual education; and opinions concerning language policies. Important contributions in this vein have been made by Fishman, Cooper, and Ma (1971) and Gardner and Lambert (1972). The primary limitation of this approach is that demand characteristics may call forth certain socially desirable responses and repress others. Both Labov (1966) and Giles (1970) have also indicated inaccuracies in respondents' perceptions of their own speech styles while, of course, the linguistic and nonlinguistic behavior of the interviewer may be crucial (see Olmedo, 1981).

The third method of measurement, indirect assessment of attitudes by means of speaker evaluation, forms the foundation of the social-psychological perspective on language attitudes (Giles & Powesland, 1975). The matched-guise technique (Lambert, 1967) has been used to elicit people's evaluative reactions to various speech styles, accents, dialects, and languages. Judges are told that they are to hear the voices of different speakers, usually reading the same passage of "neutral" verbal material, and are asked to evaluate the speakers on a series of rating scales. The speech is, in fact, produced by one set of speakers using realistic guises of different languages or speech characteristics. When believable matched-guises are unavailable, the contrasted speech styles may be represented by distinct speakers. The matched-guise technique has the advantage of eliminating the effects of the more idiosyncratic variations in speech, but in so doing it may rule out some of the other characteristics that normally covary with different speech varieties. Lambert (1967, p. 94) argues that the indirect speaker-evaluation paradigm is "particularly valuable as a measure of group biases in evaluative reactions"; and perhaps its major strength lies in its ability to reveal spontaneous attitudes, while direct attitude questionnaires may reflect mainly socially desirable responses.

The classic study using this indirect method was that of Lambert, Hodgson, Gardner, and Fillenbaum (1960). English-Canadian and French-Canadian subjects rated in-group and out-group speakers (i.e., English-Canadian and French-Canadian speakers). English-Canadians were found to view the in-group as superior to the out-group, while the French-Canadian subjects seemed to have adopted the inferior position assigned to them by the majority culture around them—a kind of self-denigration. It should also be mentioned that Tajfel's (1959) explanation of these data was slightly different. He pointed out that the French-Canadians accentuated the difference between the groups more than the English-Canadian subjects did on certain dimensions relating to socioeconomic success. He therefore interpreted these responses as a form of categorical differentiation (see Doise, 1978).

This first study precipitated an outpouring of further studies on language evaluation, the results of which are reported in the following. However, before moving to these findings it should be acknowledged that the speaker evaluation technique has had its critics (e.g., Lee, 1971; Robinson, 1972). The essence of these critiques was that providing subjects with vocal stimulus cues alone might be too limiting and artificial a procedure to be meaningful as an evaluative task. Replies followed from Giles and Bourhis (e.g., 1976) and will not be repeated here; suffice it to say that we see no basic methodological objections to research of this type. However, a number of limitations to speaker-evaluation research need to be addressed in future elaborations of the paradigm. For instance, in the typical study, other individuating cues (linguistic and nonlinguistic) are absent; message content is personally uninvolving and innocuous; target speakers are unfamiliar, anonymous others; the evaluative task is highly abstract, formal, and asocial; the experimenter is high status and often speaks the standard language variety; and the dependent measures are lacking in complexity (see Giles & Ryan, 1982, for a constructive critique). Nevertheless, despite the inevitable restriction of these findings to specific situations, this body of research does point to language as an important cue across a range of social judgments.

Findings from Speaker Evaluation Research

Basic in-group/out-group comparison

Empirical research in various parts of the world (see Giles & Powesland, 1975; Ryan, 1979) has yielded a generally consistent pattern of results: speakers of "high" or powerful speech styles are rated highly on competence and traits related to socioeconomic status, while speakers of "low" or powerless speech styles are evaluated less favorably along these dimensions, even by judges who themselves have "subordinate" ethnic speech markers (Labov, 1966; Lambert, 1967). In other social contexts, however, the language varieties of many of the latter groups may be imbued with pride by their own speakers (and sometimes conceded by the "superior" group) on the human traits of solidarity, integrity, social attractiveness, and persuasive quality. This subsection presents a selective review of some of the earlier research, classified according to its cultural context.

Studies in Britain (beginning with Cheyne, 1970, and Strongman & Woolsey, 1967) have established the overriding prestige attributed to received pronunciation (RP) over regional and foreign accents as well as lower class accents (e.g., Giles, 1970, 1971). British studies have also revealed that nonstandard speech is evaluated along several dimensions. Thus, although downgrading their own speech on scales concerned mainly with social status or competence, nonstandard speakers in Britain have shown accent loyalty on personality rating scales related to social attractiveness and integrity.

Research in Canada, where use of the matched-guise technique originated, has yielded an abundance of interesting results. French-Canadian listeners were shown to view speakers of European French as more intelligent, likeable, and ambitious than speakers of their own Canadian French (d'Anglejan & Tucker, 1973; Lambert et al., 1960) and upper class French-Canadian speakers were rated more favorably than lower class French-Canadians (Brown, 1969). Interestingly, 'toughness' emerged as a positive characteristic of lower class French-Canadian speech in d'Anglejan and Tucker's study (see also Labov's 1966 study of working class speech in New York City).

Research carried out in the United States added further weight and crosscultural validity to the emerging perspective on language attitudes. Thus speakers with ethnic dialect variations from standard American English (e.g., black English and Spanish-influenced speech styles) have consensually received low ratings on socioeconomically related evaluations such as intelligence, industriousness, and confidence (e.g., Ryan & Carranza, 1975; Williams, Hewet, Miller, Naremore, & Whitehead, 1976). Much of the work of Williams et al. was in educational settings and involved teachers' evaluations of pupils. Children speaking nonstandard or ethnic speech styles (blacks and Mexican Americans) were generally downgraded on a number of dimensions, such as projected scholastic success. Ratings of perceived and actual status were shown to be predictable from linguistic analyses of the voice samples. For example, those rated lower in status were found to have a greater incidence of silent pausing and more grammatical and phonological deviations from standard English than their higher-status counterparts. Although the early studies provided a valuable data base for further theorizing, it may be argued that much was overlooked or ignored in the haste for experimental data. A brief overview of recent elaborations gives a more accurate picture of contemporary research activity.

One extension of earlier work has been to investigate the accentedness with which various speech styles have been represented, rather than to present them as if no such variation existed in reality. Thus Ryan, Carranza, and Moffie (1977) investigated reactions to Spanish accentedness. They demonstrated that college student listeners can make rather fine discriminations among varying degrees of accentedness in rating a speaker's personality attributes and speech. Small increments in accent were associated with gradually less favorable ratings of status, solidarity, and speech characteristics (see also Brennan & Brennan, 1981; Giles, 1972). Accent broadness has also been investigated in naturalistic contexts (Bourhis & Giles, 1976), where it has been found that the use of an out-group language, but with a distinctive ethnic accent, does not detract from the speaker's perceived ethnicity in the eyes of other in-group members (see Giles, 1979). The degree of accent can also form the basis of inferences concerning the speaker's attitudes and motives (Segalowitz & Gatbonton, 1977).

Another direction in which researchers have expanded upon the type of stimulus language used is by investigating speech shifts enacted by speakers in interpersonal interaction. Thus listeners' attitudes have been assessed in relation to speakers who converge towards, or diverge away from, their interlocutor on various linguistic dimensions (e.g., Bourhis, Giles, & Lambert, 1975). As Genesee and Bourhis (1982) have shown in their recent examination of language choices in a store clerk-client setting, the evaluative consequences of particular choice patterns can be examined dynamically after each conversational turn.

Once differences in status perceptions for contrasting language varieties had been established, researchers moved toward understanding the mechanisms underlying these evaluations. The factor originally singled out by Lambert (1967) was differential ethnic-group stereotypes. A key extension of this notion has involved the interaction between social class and speech evaluations (see class-related standard, Giles & Powesland, 1975). Various speech styles (both regional and ethnic) appear to be strongly associated with particular social class levels by both in-group and out-group members. Research confirming or disconfirming such expectations through background information about the speakers has shown the power of these class associations (Ryan & Sebastian, 1980; Thakerar & Giles, 1981). For ethnic speakers with a mildly nonstandard accent, listeners who accurately identify their ethnicity evaluate their speech differently from listeners who incorrectly identify them as members of the standard speech group (Fraser, 1973; Sebastian, Ryan, & Corso, in press). Another factor involved in devaluation of out-group speech is the discomfort aroused by hearing speech different from one's own and the expectation that one will be unable to comprehend the message fully (Sebastian, Ryan, Keogh, & Schmidt, 1980).

Listeners have often been asked to evaluate speakers along several dimensions. Particular language varieties are likely to be more highly evaluated along some dimensions than along others. For example, Adorno (1973) found that Mexican-American parents considered English to be important for practical reasons, but Spanish was valued for idealistic and personal reasons. As Ryan and Carranza (1977) have argued, these attitudes appear to reflect the functional separation of Spanish and English for many Mexican-Americans. This is consistent with Fishman's (1971) discussion of diglossia and, as Giles (1979) points out, in most bicultural societies there are quite explicit norms for the appropriate language to be used in formal and informal contexts. Given this last fact, Ryan and Carranza (1977) emphatically propose the need to examine reactions toward speech varieties across different contexts.

An illustration of how the context of language can be built into research is provided by Carranza and Ryan (1975). English and Spanish speakers in the United States were heard reading two types of texts, one in a home context and the other in a more formal school context. In addition, adjective rating scales representing two dimensions were used. Status-stressing scales were expected to reflect the actual societal status differences between speakers of English and Spanish, while solidarity-stressing scales were expected to be more related to affective group identification values. High school students (bilingual Anglo-American and Mexican-American) all preferred English in the school context, but they showed no strong preference in the home context. Similar differentiation of evaluations according to school and home contexts was observed for standard and Spanish-accented English by Ryan and Carranza (1975). In both studies, the difference between ratings for the contrasting varieties was greater for status scales than for solidarity scales.

Beyond evaluative reactions

The studies reviewed thus far have concentrated primarily on evaluations of the speaker evoked by various ethnic speech styles. While these judgments in themselves are important, it is also of interest to study their influence on further ratings and upon behaviors toward the speaker.

Judgments concerning the quality of the content of the speaker's message have followed the same pattern found in the more affective judgments. For example, the same composition or question-answer is evaluated as substantially better if the speaker uses a high-status speech style (Seligman, Tucker, & Lambert, 1972). Likewise, listeners rate messages given them in a relatively difficult communication task more favorably when they are provided in a prestige pronunciation (Sebastian et al., 1980; Taylor & Gardner, 1970).

Another important domain where speech style influences message reception is that of persuasion or attitude change. In a study examining attitudes of regional listeners to capital punishment, Giles (1973) presented the same argument in several different speech styles. Although the argument given in RP was rated as the best, the most persuasive communications were the regionally accented ones. It appeared that the RP speakers, although perceived as high on expertness, were perceived as low on trustworthiness. A further study (Powesland & Giles, 1975) established the importance of listeners' identification with the speaker for successful persuasion. RP listeners were most influenced by an argument in RP style while regionally accented listeners were again more influenced by a regionally accented message. Cacioppo and Petty (1982) argue that certain speech characteristics affect persuasion only at a peripheral level in inducing a resistance or willingness to go along with the speaker's message while other speech traits affect persuasion in a more cognitive, durable manner by inducing more actual thinking about issue-relevant information. The circumstances under which ethnic speech styles would affect either of these two routes to persuasion remain to be investigated.

An additional dependent measure that has been employed is evidence of cooperative behavior. Giles, Baker, and Fielding (1975) used the matched-guise technique in a face-to-face, real-life context (i.e., a speaker addressing a high school audience) to test whether subjects would provide more written information to and about an RP speaker than they would when the same speaker presented the message with a regional (Birmingham) accent. The findings indicated that the listeners did indeed write much more for the RP speaker than the Birmingham speaker. Thus accent was shown to influence the audience's quantity of information output in a direction entirely consistent with predictions from traditional matched-guise research. In a similar vein Bourhis and Giles (1976) examined the role of accent on compliance with a request carried over the public address system to a theatre audience. Members of the audience were asked to help with a short audience survey. Again, many more people completed the survey questionnaire when the announcer's speech style was RP.

Two further studies reveal one of the junctures at which language research can feed back into mainstream social-psychological research on attitudes by offering innovative methodological possibilities. Dealing with language offers the opportunity to examine the translation of language attitudes into particular speech styles or linguistic behavior when the listener is called upon to respond to the speaker. At the same time, this allows us to underline the view that the speakers' language attitudes mediate their strategies of self-presentation and impression management. Indeed, such a perspective is a core feature of speech accommodation theory that provides a set of propositions outlining the psychological conditions necessary for speakers to converge toward, maintain, or diverge away from the linguistic attributes believed to be characteristic of their interlocutors (e.g., Thakerar, Giles, & Cheshire, 1982). Thus Bourhis and Giles (1976) showed that when in-group members (in this case learners of the Welsh language) were ethnically threatened by an out-group (English) speaker, they conveyed their attitudes toward this speaker and his language via their own speech. All respondents broadened their Welsh accents in their replies, and some even introduced Welsh words and phrases in their answers. A further study along these lines was carried out in the ethnolinguistically potent context of Belgium (Bourhis, Giles, Leyens, & Tajfel, 1979). Here it was found that Flemish-speaking subjects conveyed their attitudes linguistically toward a Francophone speaking English, whom they perceived as ethnically threatening. Depending on the strength of the perceived threat, and hence how extreme the attitudes evoked, they adopted different strategies of differentiating their speech from that of the Francophone (including switching from English to Flemish).

Language attitudes in applied contexts

Language attitudes play a role in numerous applied contexts, such as personnel interviews, educational settings, medical consultations, and legal situations. In addition, language attitudes underpin language planning strategies and influence the outcome of educational programs for minority ethnolinguistic groups. These various applications have been studied in a variety of projects, only some of which can be mentioned here (see Kalin, 1982). Nonetheless, this brief summary should underline the fundamental social significance of this research area.

In the occupational field, language may be particularly important in the personnel interview, where first impressions are so telling. A number of studies have investigated whether a job applicant's ethnic accent has an effect on employers' decisions about job suitability (e.g., de la Zerda & Hopper, 1979; Giles & Johnson, 1981). Hopper and Williams (1973) showed that speech characteristics (for standard American, black, Mexican-American, and Southern white speakers) were relevant to employment decisions but they decreased in importance as the social status of the job decreased. Similarly, Kalin, Rayko, and Love (1980) revealed discrimination against foreign-accented applicants for higher-status positions; at the same time, these speakers were judged more suitable for lower-status jobs. The effect of such double discrimination would seem to be the inhibiting of upward social mobility for ethnic speakers.

In the educational field, the work of Williams et al. (1976) revealed various biases shown by teachers in their assessments and evaluations of non-standard-accented children. The work of Edwards (e.g., 1979) has also brought attention to important issues, although not bearing directly on ethnicity issues. He demonstrated that the perception of poor speech characteristics of children led their teachers to make negative inferences about their social background and unfavorable evaluations of their personalities. These studies alert us to the possibility of self-fulfilling prophecies, whereby the speech of the child or the language attitudes of the teacher can have potentially devastating effects (see also Seligman et al., 1972). Also relevant to this context is research on the importance of attitudes in second-language learning. Studies in Canada have shown that attitude is more consistently correlated with achievement in the second language than is aptitude and that the manner in which attitudes predict language learning differs for majority and minority group students (see Gardner, 1982).

In the medical field, research has focused primarily on social class variables. It has revealed effects of social class on the frequency of communication difficulties and the amount of information provision (Pendleton & Bochner, 1980), while there may also be some relation to diagnoses offered (Fielding & Evered, 1980). In each case, working-class patients appear disadvantaged relative to middle-class patients.

Almost certainly, attitudes to nonstandard usage can also affect forensic situations, such as police and courtroom decision-making; and research has begun to examine the influence of speech style in such contexts (Lind & O'Barr, 1979). For instance, in an Australian study, Seggie (1983) adopted the matched-guise technique using RP, broad Australian, and Asian accents. Subjects listened to a message in which an "accused" protested his innocence to one of three crimes. The results showed an interesting interaction between speech style and crime. RP speakers were seen as more guilty when the crime was theft, but the broad Australian accented speaker was more severely judged when the crime was violent. Further research might investigate such questions as whether evidence by standard speakers is seen as more reliable and substantial than evidence given by non-standard-speaking witnesses and whether juries are prejudiced by the speech style of accused persons in their verdicts.

A final important area is that of language planning; this refers to the conscious, predictive approach to changes in language form, use, and status (Rubin & Jernudd, 1971). Here language attitudes are very influential as planners need to determine how speakers in the community feel about the varieties superseded and those to assume prominence. Ryan (1981) has recently outlined a framework for using particular language attitude patterns to predict which language planning strategies and goals would be workable. In particular, whether various forms of bilingual education can be effective for minority children in a given society is considered in relation to the language attitudes of both the majority and minority groups.

Mechanisms and Determinants

Lambert (1967) and Robinson (1972) proposed early in the development of this field of study that speech samples evoke group stereotypes in a two-stage cognitive process: accent/language → social categorization → personality judgments. This conclusion, in light of our review encompassing another decade of research, is stated rather too starkly. In response to data concerning the monotonic relationship between degree of accentedness and speaker evaluation (e.g., Ryan et al., 1977), Robinson (1979) suggested that group identification may be more tentative and complex and that categories need not have rigid borders (see Giles, Scherer, & Taylor, 1979; Mervis & Rosch, 1981). Secondly, we may point to the slight relationship between direct measures of attitudes toward ethnic groups and indirect measures of language attitudes (e.g., Kalin et al., 1980; Lambert et al., 1960). Similarly, the null or positive effects of identifying ethnic group membership for nonstandard speakers (Arthur, Bradford, & Farrar, 1974; Bourhis & Giles, 1976) argue against the proposition of any simple isomorphism between attitude toward ethnic groups and toward the languages of those groups. Thirdly, the fact that listeners take into account the appropriateness of speech for particular contexts argues for a more complex model of evaluation.

Moving beyond Robinson's simplified model, Ryan et al. (1982) presented an organizational framework which not only drew explicit attention to important sociostructural determinants but also attempted to provide a typology of the various language attitude profiles apparent in different speech communities. In their scheme, contrasting language varieties can be characterized in terms of two interrelated sociostructural dimensions: standardization and vitality.

Standardization is the more static dimension, referring to the extent to which norms for correct usage (Fishman, 1971) have been codified, adopted, and promoted for a particular variety. This might be accomplished through the compilation of dictionaries and grammars while the acceptance of a variety may be advanced by elites and government. Therefore, white middle-class English might be placed toward the standard pole while Mexican-American- or West-Indian-accented English might be placed more toward the nonstandard pole in the United States and United Kingdom, respectively. Vitality is the more dynamic dimension, reflecting the range and importance of functions served by language varieties (Fishman, 1971) and the social pressures towards shifts in language use. Giles, Bourhis, and Taylor (1977) have provided a simplified taxonomy of relevant nonpsychological factors affecting ethnolinguistic vitality: status—the economic, social, political, and historical power wielded by its speakers; demographic strength—the number and distribution of its speakers; and institutional support—the contribution made to the maintenance of the variety by national, governmental, and community bodies. The more ethnolinguistic vitality factors an ethnic group has in its favor, the more likely that its members would act collectively in pursuing goals of group survival. Notwithstanding the separation here, Ryan et al. emphasize that standardization and vitality are mutually influential. They are also inherently similar in that their influence upon language attitudes is seen to be mediated by respondents' subjective or cognitive perceptions of their value (Bourhis, Giles, & Rosenthal, 1981).

In this vein, Ryan et al. (1982) propose a two-dimensional framework wherein the language varieties of particular ethnic groups may be placed at any given time according to their levels of standardization and vitality. Perhaps not surprisingly, the languages of dominant ethnic collectivities are more often than not clustered in the high standardization and vitality quadrant, whereas the languages of subordinate collectivities are found usually in the low standardization and vitality counterpart. Changes in language attitude patterns are seen to follow mainly from increasing or decreasing vitality of contrasting varieties. As a social-psychological consequence of a substantial increase in vitality, speakers of a nonstandard variety (and sometimes speakers of the standard as well) come to consider cognitive alternatives to the society's power structure.

In Figure 7-1, we have outlined the basic factors determining speaker evaluations by in-group and out-group members. Although the dimensions underlying evaluations undoubtedly vary somewhat across intergroup contexts, Ryan et al. (1982) argue for social status and group solidarity as the primary universal dimensions. Of critical importance to the ultimate evaluations of two language varieties (LV1 and LV2) along these two evaluative dimensions are their relative standardization and vitality. As illustrated in detail in the previous section, however, the specific reactions elicited in any given assessment depend as well on characteristics of the immediate situation, speakers, and judges selected. The importance of socially motivated cognitive processes will be developed in the next section.

While openly admitting the possibility of many other patterns and complexities, Ryan et al. (1982) identified four distinct language-preference profiles. They are based on evaluations of two contrasting language varieties: LV1 refers to the variety of the dominant ethnolinguistic group and LV2 to that of the subordinate group. These patterns contrast in terms of whether judgments by the in-group and out-group

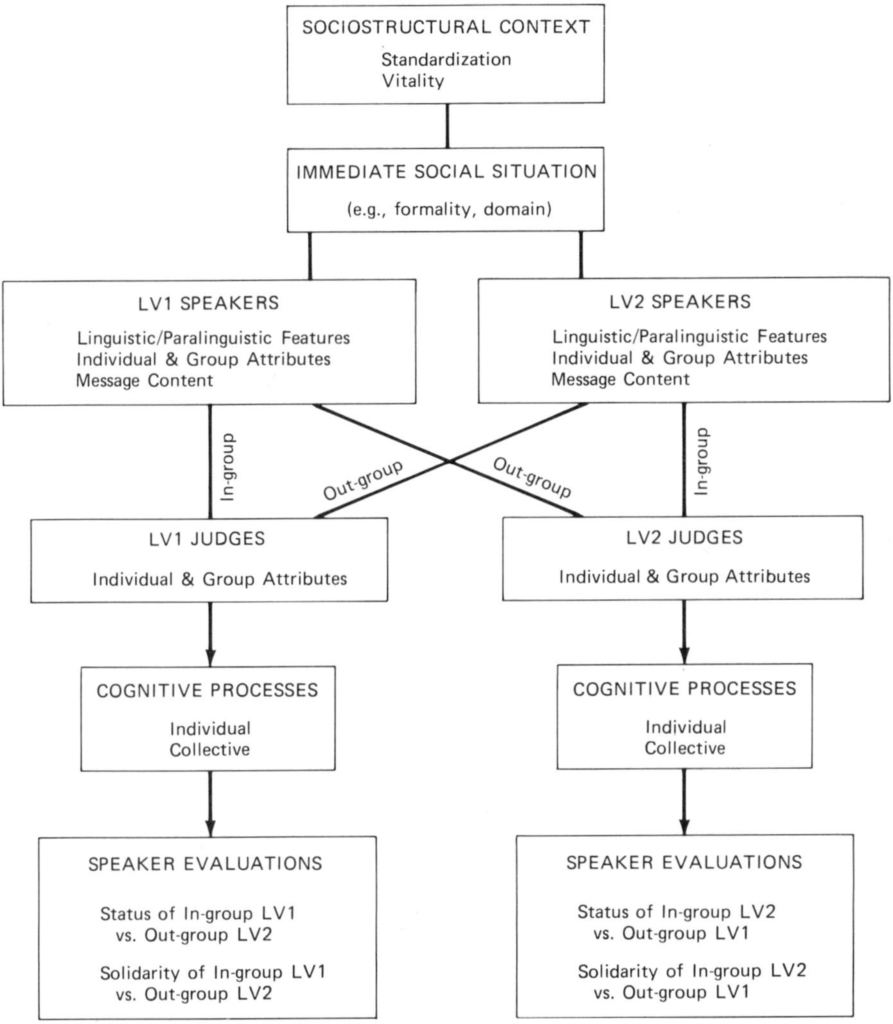

Fig. 7-1. Determinants of speaker evaluations by in-group and out-group members.

are similar or different and whether judgments along the status dimension coincide with those along the solidarity dimension. The language attitude patterns are presented in Table 7-1, in which the status and solidarity columns indicate in-group and out-group preferences as outlined in our earlier work. The other columns reflect our intergroup elaboration of these distinctive profiles as presented in the section on the intergroup model of language attitudes. Patterns A (preference by both groups for the dominant group), B (status preference for the dominant group, solidarity preference for in-group), and D (status preference for the dominant group, solidarity preference for the subordinate group) represent paradigms of increasing perceived vitality for LV2. Pattern C (in-group preference) reflects the sense of equal status, as for example when French and British listeners rate representatives of each others'

Table 7-1. Intergroup Model of Language Attitude Patterns for Two Contrasting Language Varieties.

	Judges							
	LV1 speakers			LV2 speakers			Relative vitality of LV2	Relative standardness of LV1
Type of preference	Status	Solidarity	Cognitive processes	Status	Solidarity	Cognitive processes		
A. Preferance for dominant group	LV1	LV1		LV1	LV1			
A1			Individual			Self-hate	Low	Low
A2			Collective (explanation)			Social Mobility	Very Low	Low
B. Status preference for dominant group/Solidarity preference for in-group	LV1	LV1	Justification	LV1	LV2	Social Creativity	Low-Medium	Low
D. Status preference for dominant group/Solidarity preference for subordinate group	LV1	LV2	Token appeasement	LV1	LV2	Social Creativity	Low-Medium	Low-Medium
C. Preference for in-group	LV1	LV1	Competitive differen-tiation	LV2	LV2	Social Competition	Medium-High	Medium

language varieties. Alternatively, it could exist when LV2 is experiencing a revival in in-group loyalty and pride. Identifying these four profiles is particularly useful in allowing for crosscultural comparisons in terms of the basic underlying dimensions and in providing for a relatively straightforward integration of past and future work.

Framework for Extending Research on Language Attitudes

Extending language attitude research in fruitful directions depends upon a clear understanding of the factors affecting their assessment in the speaker-evaluation paradigm. This section is a speculative attempt to extend the Ryan et al. framework and take into account more explicitly the social-psychological processes underlying intergroup relations. To this end, we shall introduce three areas: (a) Tajfel and Turner's social identity theory; (b) Tajfel's functional model of social stereotyping; and (c) a hierarchical, differentiating approach to evaluative judgments.

Tajfel and Turner's (1979) social-psychological theory of intergroup relations and social change can be summarized as follows. We categorize the social world and, hence, perceive ourselves as members of various social groups. Such knowledge of ourselves as group members is defined as our social identity, and it may be positive or negative according to how our in-groups fare in social comparison with relevant out-groups. It is argued that we strive to achieve a positive identity by seeking dimensions that afford favorable comparison with out-groups; in other words, we aim to achieve positive "psychological distinctiveness." Language comes into the picture when a group regards its own language or speech variety as a dimension of comparison (Giles et al., 1977). Naturally, there are also instances of language being salient but affording unfavorable intergroup comparisons.

What happens when an individual experiences negative social identity? First, he or she may pursue a strategy of individual mobility, trying to pass into the dominant group by acquiring its characteristics, leaving the in-group to attain a new positive identity. This is likely if intergroup boundaries are perceived as "soft" and permeable. Linguistically, the individual will converge on what are believed to be the out-group's linguistic habits and discard in-group speech markers. If individual mobility through language is widespread, the in-group will not be maintained and "language death" will result.

A second type of strategy applicable if individual mobility fails or is thwarted by the existence of impermeable intergroup boundaries is social creativity. This is redefining the in-group/out-group comparison in various ways, including the following: taking other, low-status groups or fellow members of the in-group for social comparisons; reevaluating as positive in-group characteristics previously seen as negative (e.g., "black is beautiful"); or inventing new more favorable dimensions of intergroup comparison. The last two forms of social creativity occur when groups divergently flaunt their supposedly debased or substandard speech forms, exhume dead languages and dialects, and indigenize technological vocabulary or create new orthographies and forms of slang.

The third strategy type, outright social competition, is likely to be adopted when the previous strategies have failed. Though members still identify with their subordinate in-group and make unfavorable intergroup comparisons, they perceive alternatives to the status quo in the sense of acknowledging that the social hierarchy of groups is changeable. Numerous situations where language has been the focus of civil unrest can be regarded as intense linguistic illustrations of this strategy.

What does the dominant group do in response? Assimilation of a large enough number of the subordinate group by individual mobility would threaten the dominant group's psychological distinctiveness so that the latter is likely to reassert this by diverging away from the "social climbers." Subordinate group creativity or competition, if threatening enough, would be likely to elicit reciprocal competition in the form of verbal derogation or overtly oppressive political acts.

Complementing social identity theory, Tajfel (1981) also attempted to specify the individual and collective functions served by stereotyping in intergroup relations. Two individual cognitive functions were proposed with reference to principles of categorization and physical judgments. The first of these is to make a complex social world orderly and predictable by, for example, accentuating intracategory similarities and intercategory differences. The second function is to preserve and defend the individual's value system—a function that arises from judgments of categories associated with socially valued rather than neutral differentials. Stereotypes serve two major social collective functions for group members as a whole in intergroup contexts. The first may be titled a "social explanatory" function and refers to the creation and maintenance of group ideologies that justify and explain intergroup relations, particularly reactions to and treatment of out-group members. The second collective function concerns the role of stereotyping in preserving, creating, or enhancing positively valued differentiations between the in-groups and relevant out-groups. It is argued that the contents of stereotypes (the particular traits attributed to groups), which vary from one intergroup relationship to another, will depend on which group function(s) they serve in the social context under consideration.

The social explanatory function is exemplified in recent work on social dimensions of attribution (e.g., Hewstone & Jaspars, 1982; Hewstone, Bond, & Wan, in press; Hewstone, Jaspars, & Lalljee, 1982) that illustrates the role of causal attributions in intergroup relations and particularly how the explanation of social behavior and outcomes varies as a function of group memberships of actors and perceivers. We suggest that a fruitful avenue for the elaboration of this social explanatory function is in terms of the naive or commonsense "theories" shared by laypeople (see Ajzen, 1977; Eiser, 1982). The study of such beliefs can be seen, in very different ways, in Schank and Abelson's (1977) work on "scripts" and in the European work on social representations. Recently, Moscovici and Hewstone (1983) have explicitly integrated social representations and social explanations, showing how representations form a frame of reference or implicit explanatory framework.

Taking an alternative perspective, Applegate and Delia (1980) argue for a constructivist approach to social perception. They propose that people develop a construct system to aid in their analysis and understanding of other people and their behaviors. Within constructivism, children are said to develop constructs that are progressively more differentiated than global, integrated rather than diffuse, abstract rather than concrete, and in perspective rather than egocentric in order to cope with increasing social complexity. They state further that any group of adults will contain some individuals with highly differentiated constructs and others with primitive constructs, due to different ranges of social experience.

It is our belief that the social experience of the changing relationships between in- and out-group will also have an influence on the organization and complexity of constructs brought to bear in the evaluation of contrasting language varieties. In other words, and in line with the two previous approaches outlined, we reason that the developing intergroup belief structures and strategies attending group memberships will inspire progressively more differentiated and hierarchically organized evaluative dimensions in order to function so as to preserve or enhance positive social identities. However, as we shall see shortly, the precise relationship perceived as existing between the contrasting groups may crucially determine the evaluative pattern and its associated social attributions.

What then could such a hierarchical network of evaluative constructs look like if we concede that two general factors, status and solidarity, are insufficient for our purposes? We would suggest the following increasingly differentiated levels: (a) global evaluation; (b) status versus solidarity; (c) within both status and solidarity, group-oriented versus person-oriented; and (d) within each of the above, middle-class-oriented versus working-class-oriented. The importance of differentiating between group- and person-centered aspects of evaluation has been discussed by Tajfel and Turner (1979), and this distinction elaborated within the context of status-solidarity by Giles and Ryan (1982). For example, within the status dimension traits can emphasize the group (e.g., superior and advantaged) or the individual (e.g., ambitious and assertive). Similarly, within solidarity traits can emphasize the group (e.g., in-group pride and loyalty) or the individual (e.g., sincere and forgiving). The class-orientedness of both positive and negative traits was highlighted most clearly by Giles, Smith, Ford, Condor, and Thakerar (1980), who showed that sex-trait stereotypes overlapped with social class stereotypes. Whereas previous research had been interpreted as showing that masculine and feminine characteristics were attributed to speakers of different dialects, listeners were more likely in part to have been attributing class stereotypes instead. Of particular relevance to us, some person-oriented status and solidarity traits were found to be more associated with the middle class (e.g., ambitious, opportunistic, poised, and snobbish) whereas other person-oriented traits were found to be more associated with the working class (e.g., robust, impulsive, sincere, and coarse). The same lesson can be applied to ethnic speaker-evaluation research to the extent that certain status and solidarity traits have inherent class connotations as well (not to mention, of course, sex, age, and other social category overlaps).

An Intergroup Model of Language Attitudes

While the identification of sociostructural determinants, evaluative dimensions, and types of language attitude profile presented by Ryan et al. (1982) is more advanced in terms of intergroup dynamics than the simple categorization model, owing to its consideration of group cognitive alternatives and the cognitive representation of societal forces, it does not go far enough. We also suggest that it is not always the case that perceptions of vitality and standardization determine the structure of language attitudes through the awareness of cognitive alternatives; the reverse sequence is theoretically possible. In this vein, we offer an extended model that accounts for more of the complex cognitive processes underlying language attitudes.

Our intergroup model is summarized in abbreviated form in Table 7-1 and is an extension of the Ryan et al. classification on a number of levels. The four language attitude profiles A-D are now organized into a distinct temporal pattern conceived to be some of the important phases of an intergroup cycle (see Taylor & Giles, 1979). Pattern A is divided into two subcategories, the first of which (Al) is characterized by a belief structure of "self-hate" (see Milner, 1981) among LV2 judges who accept a global downgrading of representatives of their own group. The evaluative preference for in-group speakers by LV1 judges which only needs to be global in character, functions for individual categorization and value preservation purposes. In this situation, responsibility for the inferiority of its members is attributed to the subordinate group. The A2 subcategory arises when certain individuals from the LV2 community come to attribute their own personal circumstances as being due to the negatively valued group of which they are members. They begin to see that the power position of LV1 speakers is reflected in their positive status traits (e.g., educated, intelligent) which allows them the privilege of greater solidarity attributes (e.g., benevolence, sociability). An acceptance of this ideology and a movement psychologically toward members of the dominant group is reflected in their differentiation of status from solidarity judgments in favor of LV1 (see Tajfel, 1959). The dominant group has little need to change the nature of its stereotype although it might function for them now quite satisfactorily as an explanation for the socioeconomic disparity between the two groups. Especially in pattern A2, the standardization and vitality of LV2 is perceived to be very low.

Pattern B emerges for LV2 when passing is either not possible or is undesirable according to in-group dictates or sanctions. In search of a positive identity, subordinate group members not only differentiate between the status and solidarity dimensions as in pattern A2 but also now attempt to search out qualities within these factors that may be conceived in their own favor. Because of objective criteria against LV2 in terms of status attributes, it would be easier for them to search out evaluative superiorities along the subjective and more malleable solidarity factor. An appreciation—or even creative redefinition—of the group-oriented versus person-oriented characteristics of solidarity may then come about wherein their language patterns can be seen to be valued for group survival and distinctiveness along the former dimension (Fishman, 1977). This may lead to a further differentiation within the person-oriented traits culminating in an upgrading of positive in-group traits (e.g., working-class traits such as robust and sincere) with a simultaneous downgrading of negative out-group traits (e.g., middle-class traits such as opportunistic and snobbish). It is possible that this evaluative creativity would then spread to neutral attributes (i.e., not related to either social class), shifting these also in the favor of LV2. In response to early signals of such sociolinguistic redefinition, the dominant group may begin to differentiate between status and solidarity aspects of their own global evaluations in favor of their own in-group, accentuating the former factor's favorability now more as a justification for their apparent superiority. Indeed, it is possible that the discriminatory practices levied against LV2 speakers in the applied contexts referred to earlier are a concomitant feature of pattern B which began perhaps its initial momentum alongside pattern A2. Thus, pattern B (see Table 7-1) can be viewed as an end product of this temporal sequence of evaluative events. Under these conditions of social creativity, although the standardization of LV2 has received perhaps only a little impetus, the vitality of the group begins to be strengthened with in-group identification and pride thereby being fostered.

Next, pattern D is characterized by the subordinate group's realizations that group- versus person-oriented differentiation could occur within the status factor as well and that it may have social attributional significance for them (Hewstone & Jaspars, 1982). However, the main distinguishing feature of this pattern is the evaluative differentiation that occurs within the dominant group community (LV1 judges) especially with regard to the group- versus person-oriented attributes of status and solidarity. The latter trend could come about when LV1 judges perceive that their positive group-oriented status traits may be linked to historically unfair advantages. Perhaps reluctantly, although less so among those members of the dominant group who possess a liberal ideology (Tajfel, 1981), they come to accept that LV2 has positive out-group solidarity traits of its own and they themselves negative in-group counterparts. In other words, they concede pattern B as represented by LV2 speakers. The function of the dominant group's evaluative orientation here might be termed "token appeasement" to convey its pseudoegalitarian motive, which aims to inhibit a more general awareness of cognitive alternatives and a further strengthening of perceived vitality among LV2 speakers. Moreover, the strategy of token appeasement might also be manifest in the increased adoption of LV2 speech in some informal media situations (e.g., TV sports, entertainment).

However, if the ethnolinguistic vitality and in-group identification of the subordinate group are bolstered, the contrary might happen, resulting in pattern C. This could happen, for instance, if LV2 speakers attributed LV1's remaining positive status characteristics to oppressive measures on the part of that group. Social competition would ensue evaluatively and behaviorally, and LV2 judges would downplay the group-oriented status advantages of LV1 and/or perhaps evaluatively redefine them more negatively (Eiser, 1975). In addition, subordinate group members would now come to differentiate in favor of the in-group, person-oriented status qualities (e.g., robust and assertive) while denigrating some person-oriented out-group ones (e.g., opportunistic). This would induce a swift counterreaction from the dominant group whereby they would articulate a highly differentiated judgmental and attributional pattern of their own in favor of their own person-oriented status and solidarity traits. This counterreaction would function stereotypically for dominant group members so as to differentiate themselves from LV2 speakers, thereby aiding restoration of their positive in-group distinctiveness. Moreover, it is conceivable that they would create new judgmental dimensions of comparison besides those of status and solidarity in their favor (as perhaps would LV2 speakers for their part). Ultimately, and perhaps in direct opposition to the constructivist approach according to which increasing social experience leads to greater evaluative differentiation, both dominant and subordinate groups might revert to a global evaluation factor of generalized in-group positivity and out-group negativity. In other words, superficially narrow and rigid stereotypes might be underlaid by complex intergroup belief structures and stereotype functions. Dominant group members might then attribute this judgmental state of affairs to the inherent, primitive aggressive stance of LV2 individuals. Correspondingly, these subordinate group members, observing the out-group's intransigence, might no longer attribute the cause of the situation to historical intergroup conditions but to the inherent power-seeking qualities of most LV1 individuals.

A number of possibilities might occur at this point, which are beyond the scope of Table 7-1. These depend not only on a transaction between the psychological resilience of the subordinate ethnolinguistic group, on the one hand, and the strength of the dominant group's reactions and sanctions on the other, but also on the ever-fluid sociostructural conditions prevailing. It is possible that LV2 might fall back to one of the previous pattern types and even ultimately to pattern A. However, the dominant group might have to concede—perhaps in part due to superordinate pressures from without—and grant complementary prestige to LV2 on dimensions valued to them that are in no sense psychologically or structurally inferior (see Taylor & Simard, 1979). Finally, it is possible that a reversal of pattern A might emerge whereby the dominant global evaluation is in favor of LV2 owing to a reversal of the power relations between the groups (see Bourhis, 1983).

A number of features of our intergroup model are worthy of further focus. First, we hypothesize that evaluative differentiation occurs (and particularly with respect to the subordinate variety) on solidarity traits prior to status ones. Second, and in accord with a number of researchers who have underlined the fact that social groups are not homogeneous entities, different individuals in a speech community can be found who represent several of the phases outlined in our analysis. In other words, the subordinate group may simultaneously include various individuals—or subgroups of them—who possess patterns A, B, D, or C. Third, the language preference of LV1 and LV2 speakers may involve different mechanisms. The profiles for the dominant group may be accounted for best by our extension of Tajfel's (1981) functional stereotyping approach, whereas those of the subordinate group may be more readily interpreted by the intergroup belief systems and strategies of Tajfel and Turner (1979). Fourth, the dichotomy we have used between dominant and subordinate language varieties is oversimplified since groups are often associated with more than one variety. For instance, Price, Fluck, and Giles (1983) have shown that West Welsh preadolescents appear evaluatively positive toward speakers of their own in-group language (Welsh) whereas they denigrate those who speak English with a typical West Welsh accent. Furthermore, as evaluative patterns change and are differentiated according to the prevailing belief structures of the contrasting communities, the language patterns are also likely to change over time (Aitchison, 1981). In other words, what were typical of LV1 and LV2 speech samples as related to pattern A may be quite different from those manifest in pattern C (Giles, 1979). This conceptual notion raises difficult issues with respect to stimulus control. Fifth, we see various relationships between the language attitudes model presented here and the more behaviorally oriented frameworks of ethnolinguistic identity theory (Giles & Johnson, 1981) and the intergroup model of second-language acquisition (Giles & Byrne, 1982), linkages that obviously await further theoretical elaborations. Suffice it to say, however, that patterns A, B, and D (and especially A2) might include some of the attitudinal prerequisites for LV2 speakers to be motivated toward proficiency in LV1 and to converge closely toward speakers of the latter variety. Pattern C, on the other hand, can reflect the conditions necessary for inhibiting native-like proficiency in LV1 among LV2 speakers and could moreover foster the accentuation of in-group speech markers among the latter in interethnic encounters.

Conclusions

Space has precluded a more detailed elaboration of our intergroup model. Moreover, it is difficult to illustrate the above sequential patterns among and within types with actual data as current language attitude studies are typically impoverished in terms of the complexities of their dependent measures (evaluatively and attributionally), independent data on the intergroup belief structures of their listeners, and historical perspectives of social change. We hope that whether our particular analysis holds up after empirical scrutiny or not, language attitude researchers will come to appreciate more the urgent need for a robust theoretical orientation. As illustrated in Figure 7-1, the determinants of speaker evaluations are much more diverse than originally outlined by Lambert (1967) and Robinson (1972). In particular, we have argued here for the importance of taking account of social attributional processes, intergroup dynamics, and cognitive representations of societal forces.

Finally, more studies across disciplines have been conducted via the speaker-evaluation paradigm using language as a social cue to impression-formation than any other single paradigm. Strangely, such studies are rarely reported in texts on person-perception, impression-formation, and impression-management. It is hoped that we have helped underscore their crucial importance in many social and applied contexts and that the analysis we have formulated will have ramifications in other judgmental arenas.

Acknowledgment. Miles Hewstone acknowledges with gratitude the financial support of the Leverhulme Trust during the time in which this chapter was written.

References

Adorno, W. (1973). *The attitudes of selected Mexican and Mexican American parents in regards to bilingual/bicultural attitudes*. Unpublished doctoral dissertation, U.S. International University.

Agheyisi, R., & Fishman, J. A. (1970). Language attitude studies: A brief survey of methodological approaches. *Anthropological Linguistics, 12,* 131-157.

Aitchison, J. (1981). *Language change: Progress or decay*? Bunpay, Suffolk: Fontana.

Ajzen, I. (1977). Intuitive theories of events and the effects of base-rate information on prediction. *Journal of Personality and Social Psychology, 35,* 303-314.

d'Anglejan, A., & Tucker, G. R. (1973). Sociolinguistic correlates of speech styles in Quebec. In R. W. Shuy & R. W. Fasold (Eds.), *Language attitudes: Current trends and prospects*. Washington, D.C.: Georgetown University Press.

Applegate, J. A., & Delia, J. G. (1980). Person-centered speech, psychological development, and the contexts of language usage. In R. N. St. Clair & H. Giles (Eds.), *The social and psychological contexts of language*. Hillsdale, NJ: Lawrence Erlbaum.

Arthur, B., Bradford, G., & Farrar, D. (1974). Evaluation reactions of college students to dialect differences in the English of Mexican-Americans. *Language and Speech, 17,* 255-270.

Bourhis, R. Y. (Ed.). (1983). *Conflict and language planning in Quebec.* Clevedon, Multilingual Matters.

Bourhis, R. Y., & Giles, H. (1976). The language of cooperation in Wales: A field study. *Language Sciences, 42,* 13-16.

Bourhis, R. Y., Giles, H., & Lambert, W. E. (1975). Social consequences of accommodating one's style of speech: A cross-national investigation. *International Journal of the Sociology of Language, 6,* 55-72.

Bourhis, R. Y., Giles, H., Leyens, J., & Tajfel, H. (1979). Psycholinguistic distinctiveness: Language divergence in Belgium. In H. Giles & R. N. St. Clair (Eds.), *Language and social psychology*. Oxford: Blackwell.

Bourhis, R. Y., Giles, H., & Rosenthal, D. (1981). Notes on the construction of a "subjective vitality questionnaire" for ethnolinguistic groups. *Journal of Multilingual and Multicultural Development, 2,* 145-155.

Brennan, E. M., & Brennan, J. S. (1981). Accent scaling and language attitudes: Reactions to Mexican-American English speech. *Language and Speech, 24,* 207-221.

Brown, B. (1964). *The social psychology of variations in French Canadian speech styles*. Unpublished doctoral dissertation, McGill University, Montreal.

Brown, R. (1965). *Social psychology*. New York: The Free Press.

Cacioppo, J. T., & Petty, R. E. (1982). Language variables, attitudes, and persuasion. In E. B. Ryan and H. Giles (Eds.), *Attitudes towards language variation: Social and applied contexts*. London: Edward Arnold.

Carranza, M. A., & Ryan, E. B. (1975). Evaluative reactions of bilingual Anglo and Mexican American adolescents toward speakers of English and Spanish. *International Journal of the Sociology of Language, 6,* 83-104.

Cheyne, W. (1970). Stereotyped reactions to speakers with Scottish and English regional accents. *British Journal of Social and Clinical Psychology, 9,* 77-79.

de la Zerda, N., & Hopper, R. (1979). Employment interviewers' reactions to Mexican American speech. *Communication Monographs, 46,* 126-134.

Doise, W. (1978). *Groups and individuals: Explanations in social psychology*. Cambridge: Cambridge University Press.

Edwards, J. (1979). *Language and disadvantage*. London: Edward Arnold.

Eiser, J. R. (1975). Attitudes and the use of evaluative language: A two-way process. *Journal for the Theory of Social Behaviour, 5,* 235-248.

Eiser, J. R. (1980). *Cognitive social psychology*. New York: McGraw-Hill.

Eiser, J. R. (1982). Attitudes and applied research. In P. Stringer (Ed.), *Confronting social issues: Some applications of social psychology* (Vol. 1). London: Academic Press.

Fielding, G., & Evered, C. (1980). The influence of patients' speech upon doctors: The diagnostic interview. In R. St. Clair & H. Giles (Eds.), *The social and psychological contexts of language*. Hillsdale, NJ: Lawrence Erlbaum.

Fishman, J. A. (1966). *Language loyalty in the United States*. The Hague: Mouton.

Fishman, J. A. (1971). *Sociolinguistics: A brief introduction*. Rowley, MA: Newbury House.

Fishman, J. A. (1977). Language and ethnicity. In H. Giles (Ed.), *Language, ethnicity, and intergroup relations*. London: Academic Press.

Fishman, J. A., Cooper, R., & Ma, R. (1971). *Bilingualism in the barrio*. Bloomington: Indiana University Press.

Fraser, B. (1973). Some "unexpected" reactions to various American-English dialects. In R. W. Shuy & R. W. Fasold (Eds.), *Language attitudes: Current trends and prospects*. Washington, D.C.: Georgetown University Press.

Fraser, C., & Scherer, K. R. (Eds.). (1982). *Advances in the social psychology of language*. Cambridge: Cambridge University Press.

Gardner, R. C. (1982). Language attitudes and language learning. In E. B. Ryan & H. Giles (Eds.), *Attitudes towards language variation: Social and applied contexts*. London: Edward Arnold.

Gardner, R. C., & Lambert, W. E. (1972). *Attitudes and motivation in second-language learning*. Rowley, MA: Newbury House.

Genesee, F., & Bourhis, R. Y. (1982). The social psychological significance of code switching in cross-cultural communication. *Journal of Language and Social Psychology, 1,* 1-28.

Giles, H. (1970). Evaluative reactions to accents. *Educational Review, 22,* 211-227.

Giles, H. (1971). Patterns of evaluation in reactions to RP, South Welsh and Somerset accented speech. *British Journal of Social and Clinical Psychology, 10,* 280-281.

Giles, H. (1972). Evaluation of personality content from accented speech as a function of listeners' social attitudes. *Perceptual & Motor Skills, 34,* 168-170.

Giles, H. (1973). Communicative effectiveness as a function of accented speech. *Speech Monographs, 40,* 330-331.

Giles, H. (Ed.). (1977). *Language, ethnicity and intergroup relations*. London: Academic Press.

Giles, H. (1979). Ethnicity markers in speech. In K. R. Scherer & H. Giles (Eds.), *Social markers in speech*. Cambridge: Cambridge University Press.

Giles, H., Baker, S., & Fielding, G. (1975). Communication length as a behavioral index of accent prejudice. *International Journal of the Sociology of Language, 6,* 73-81.

Giles, H., & Bourhis, R. Y. (1976). Methodological issues in dialect perception: Some social psychological perspectives. *Anthropological Linguistics, 18,* 294-304.

Giles, H., Bourhis, R. Y., & Taylor, D. M. (1977). Towards a theory of language in ethnic group relations. In H. Giles (Ed.), *Language, ethnicity and intergroup relations*. London: Academic Press.

Giles, H., & Byrne, J. (1982). An intergroup approach to second language acquisition. *Journal of Multilingual and Multicultural Development, 3,* 17-40.

Giles, H., & Johnson, P. (1981). The role of language in ethnic group relations. In J. Turner & H. Giles (Eds.), *Intergroup behavior*. Oxford: Blackwell.
Giles, H., & Powesland, P. F. (1975). *Speech style and social evaluation*. London: Academic Press.
Giles, H., & Ryan, E. B. (1982). Prolegomena for developing a social psychological theory of language attitudes. In E. B. Ryan & H. Giles (Eds.), *Attitudes towards language variation: Social and applied context*. London: Edward Arnold.
Giles, H., & St. Clair, R. N. (Eds.). (1979). *Language and social psychology*. Oxford: Blackwell.
Giles, H., & St. Jacques, B. (Eds.). (1979). *Language and ethnic relations*. Oxford: Pergamon Press.
Giles, H., Scherer, K., & Taylor, D. M. (1979). Speech markers in social interaction. In K. R. Scherer & H. Giles (Eds.), *Social markers in speech*. Cambridge: Cambridge University Press.
Giles, H., Smith, P., Ford, B., Condor, S., & Thakerar, J. (1980). Speech styles and the fluctuating salience of sex. *Language Sciences, 2,* 260-282.
Hewstone, M. (Ed.). (1983). *Attribution theory: Social and functional extensions*. Oxford: Blackwell.
Hewstone, M., Bond, M. H., & Wan, K.-C. (in press). Social facts and social attributions: The explanation of intergroup differences in Hong Kong. *Social Cognition*.
Hewstone, M., & Jaspars, J. (1982). Intergroup relations and attribution processes. In H. Tajfel (Ed.), *Social identity and intergroup relations*. Cambridge: Cambridge University Press.
Hewstone, M., Jaspars, J., & Lalljee, M. (1982). Social representations, social attribution and social identity: The intergroup images of 'public' and 'comprehensive' schoolboys. *European Journal of Social Psychology, 12,* 241-269.
Hopper, R., & Williams, F. (1973). Speech characteristics and employability. *Speech Monographs, 40,* 296-302.
Kalin, R. (1982). The social significance of speech in medical, legal and occupational settings. In E. B. Ryan & H. Giles (Eds.), *Attitude towards language variation: Social and applied contexts*. London: Edward Arnold.
Kalin, R., Rayko, D. S., & Love, N. (1980). The perception and evaluation of job candidates with four different ethnic accents. In H. Giles, W. P. Robinson, & P. M. Smith (Eds.), *Language: Social psychological perspectives*. Oxford: Pergamon Press.
Labov, W. (1966). *The social stratification of English in New York City*. Washington, D.C.: Center for Applied Linguistics.
Lambert, W. E. (1967). The social psychology of bilingualism. *Journal of Social Issues, 23,* 91-109.
Lambert, W. E., Hodgson, R., Gardner, R. C., & Fillenbaum, S. (1960). Evaluational reactions to spoken languages. *Journal of Abnormal and Social Psychology, 60,* 44-51.
Lee, R. (1971). Dialect perception: A critical review and reevaluation. *Quarterly Journal of Speech, 57,* 410-417.
Lind, E. A., & O'Barr, W. M. (1979). The social significance of speech in the courtroom. In H. Giles & R. N. St. Clair (Eds.), *Language and social psychology*. Oxford: Pergamon Press.

Mervis, C. B., & Rosch, E. (1981). Categorization of natural objects. In M. R. Rosenzweig & L. M. Porter (Eds.), *Annual Review of Psychology, 32,* 8- ? .

Milner, D. (1981). Racial prejudice. In J. Turner & H. Giles (Eds.), *Intergroup behavior*. Oxford: Blackwell.

Moscovici, S. (1976). *Social influence and social change*. London: Academic Press.

Moscovici, S., & Hewstone, M. (1983). Social representations and social explanations: From the "naive" to the "amateur" scientist. In M. Hewstone (Ed.), *Attribution theory: Social and functional extensions*. Oxford: Blackwell.

Olmedo, E. L. (1981). Testing linguistic minorities. *American Psychologist, 36,* 1078-1085.

Pendleton, D. A., & Bochner, S. (1980). The communication of medical information in general practice consultations as a function of patients' social class. *Social Science and Medicine, 14,* 669-673.

Powesland, P. F., & Giles, H. (1975). Persuasiveness and accent-message incompatibility. *Human Relations, 28,* 85-93.

Price, S., Fluck, M., & Giles, H. (1983). The effects of language of testing on bilingual pre-adolescents' attitudes toward Welsh and varieties of English. *Journal of Multilingual and Multicultural Development, 4,* in press.

Robinson, W. P. (1972). *Language and social behavior*. Harmondsworth: Penguin.

Robinson, W. P. (1979). Speech markers and social class. In K. R. Scherer & H. Giles (Eds.), *Social markers in speech*. Cambridge: Cambridge University Press.

Rubin, J., & Jernuud, B. (Eds.). (1971). *Can language be planned? Sociolinguistic theory and practice for developing nations*. Honolulu: East-West Center.

Ryan, E. B. (1979). Why do low-prestige language varieties persist? In H. Giles & R. N. St. Clair (Eds.), *Language and social psychology*. Oxford: Blackwell.

Ryan, E. B. (1981). *Language planning from an attitudinal perspective*. Paper presented to the International Conference on Language Planning and Public Policy, Cancun, Mexico.

Ryan, E. B., & Carranza, M. A. (1975). Evaluative reactions of adolescents toward speakers of standard English and Mexican American accented English. *Journal of Personality and Social Psychology, 31,* 855-863.

Ryan, E. B., & Carranza, M. A. (1977). Ingroup and outgroup reactions toward Mexican American language varieties. In H. Giles (Ed.), *Language, ethnicity and intergroup relations*. London: Academic Press.

Ryan, E. B., Carrranza, M. A., & Moffie, R. W. (1977). Reactions toward varying degrees of accentedness in the speech of Spanish-English bilinguals. *Language and Speech, 20,* 267-273.

Ryan, E. B., & Giles, H. (Eds.). (1982). *Attitudes towards language variation: Social and applied contexts*. London: Edward Arnold.

Ryan, E. B., Giles, H., & Sebastian, R. J. (1982). An integrative perspective for the study of attitudes toward language variation. In E. B. Ryan & H. Giles (Eds.), *Attitudes towards language variation: Social and applied contexts*. London: Edward Arnold.

Ryan, E. B., & Sebastian, R. J. (1980). The effects of speech style and social class background on social judgments of speakers. *British Journal of Social and Clinical Psychology, 19,* 229-233.

Schank, R., & Abelson, R. (1977). *Scripts, plans, goals, and understanding*. Hillsdale, NJ: Lawrence Erlbaum.

Scherer, K. R., & Giles, H. (Eds.). (1979). *Social markers in speech*. Cambridge: Cambridge University Press.

Sebastian, R. J., Ryan, E. B., & Corso, L. (in press). Social judgments of speakers with differing degrees of accent. *Social Behavior and Personality*.

Sebastian, R. J., Ryan, E. B., Keogh, T. F., & Schmidt, A. C. (1980). The effects of negative affect arousal on reactions to speakers. In H. Giles, W. P. Robinson, & P. M. Smith (Eds.), *Language: Social psychological perspectives*. Oxford: Pergamon Press.

Segalowitz, N., & Gatbonton, E. (1977). Studies of the non-fluent bilingual. In P. A. Hornby (Ed.), *Bilingualism: Psychological, social and educational implications*. New York: Academic Press.

Seggie, I. (in press). Attributions of guilt as a function of accent and crime. *Journal of Multilingual and Multicultural Development, 4*.

Seligman, C., Tucker, G. R., & Lambert, W. E. (1972). The effects of speech style and other attributes on teachers' attitudes toward pupils. *Language in Society, 1*, 131-142.

Shuy, R. W., & Fasold, R. W. (1973). *Language attitudes: Current trends and prospects*. Washington, D.C.: Georgetown University Press.

Strongman, K., & Woolsey, J. (1967). Stereotyped reactions to regional accents. *British Journal of Social and Clinical Psychology, 6*, 164-167.

Tajfel, H. (1959). A 1959 note on Lambert's 'Evalutional reactions to spoken language'. *Canadian Journal of Psychology, 13*, 86-92.

Tajfel, H. (1981). Social stereotypes and social groups. In J. C. Turner & H. Giles (Eds.), *Intergroup behavior*. Oxford: Blackwell.

Tajfel, H., & Turner, J. C. (1979). An integrative theory of intergroup conflict. In W. G. Austin & S. Worchel (Eds.), *The social psychology of intergroup relations*. Monterey, CA: Brooks/Cole.

Taylor, D. M., & Gardner, R. C. (1970). The role of stereotypes in communication between ethnic groups in the Philippines. *Social Forces, 49*, 271-283.

Taylor, D. M., & Giles, H. (1979). At the crossroads of research into language and ethnic relations. In H. Giles & B. St. Jacques (Eds.), *Language and ethnic relations*. Oxford: Pergamon Press.

Taylor, D. M., & Simard, L. (1979). Ethnic identity and intergroup relations. In D. J. Lee (Ed.), *Emerging ethnic boundaries*. Ottawa: University of Ottawa Press.

Thakerar, J. N., & Giles, H. (1981). They are—so they speak: Noncontent speech stereotypes. *Language and Communication, 1*, 251-256.

Thakerar, J. N., Giles, H., & Chesire, J. (1982). Psychological and linguistic parameters of speech accommodation theory. In C. Fraser & K. R. Scherer (Eds.), *Advances in the social psychology of language*. Cambridge: Cambridge University Press.

Williams, F., Hewett, N., Miller, L. M., Naremore, R. C., & Whitehead, J. L. (1976). *Explorations of the linguistic attitudes of teachers*. Rowley, MA: Newbury House.

Part III

Salience, Schematic Processing, and Attitude Change

Chapter 8

Dimensional Salience, Judgment, and Attitudes

Joop van der Pligt and J. Richard Eiser

The manner in which people form judgments and evaluations has been the subject of much research interest in recent years. This research has identified several judgmental heuristics that function as adaptive strategies of selective effort. One picture that emerges is that of the "cognitive miser" (Taylor, 1981) who selectively processes a subset of the information available in order to structure his or her social environment. If our perceptual and decision processes are not to be overwhelmed by the mass of information available to us, we need to be guided by considerations of cognitive economy.

This tendency of the perceiver to attend selectively has been studied in a wide variety of research areas under the heading of *salience*. Salient stimuli are assumed to have a disproportionate influence on people's judgments. The idea of differences in the salience of information has a long history. For instance, Asch's (1946) seminal work drew attention to the differences between *central* and *peripheral* traits in person perception. Research in the field of impression formation has focused on the relative salience of items within a particular context. Considerable evidence showed that negatively valenced information is more influential than positive information in the formation of an overall evaluation of a person (e.g., Anderson, 1974; Hodges, 1974; Fiske, 1980; van der Pligt & Eiser, 1980). Current work in attribution focuses on salience in context, and shows that people attribute causality to distinctive and hence salient stimuli (Taylor & Fiske, 1978). Another research area incorporating "salience" in its conceptual framework is that concerned with the relationship between attitudes and behavior. Fishbein and Ajzen's (1975) theory of reasoned action traces the causes of behavior through a series of intervening processes to the individual's salient beliefs.

The concept of salience in one form or another is implicit in many theories in social psychology. Most of the research just cited, however, defines salience in terms of stimulus properties (e.g., negative or distinctive stimuli are more salient). In the current analysis we will focus on salience in relation to a person's attitude toward particular issues. As a consequence, more attention will be paid to affect, evaluation, and cognitive balance. Although recent developments in social cognition tend to pay more attention to these factors (e.g., Zajonc, 1980; Fiske, 1981; Higgins, Herman, & Zanna, 1981; van der Pligt, 1981), much research on salience casts human beings as *mere* cognitive organisms, whose processing of information takes place in an evaluative vacuum.

In the first part of this chapter, we introduce the notion of *dimensional salience* and its role in attitudinal judgment. In the second part, we investigate salience effects in the context of expectancy-value formulations of decision-making and processes of attitude change.

Dimensional Salience

We assume that when subjects perform a typical judgment task in which they rate a series of attitude statements, they will discriminate more between different items in terms of attributes they consider salient than those considered nonsalient. A given dimension can be said to be particularly salient for individuals if they give particularly extreme or polarized judgments along it.

Tajfel and Wilkes (1964) provided an operational definition of salience based on the criterion of priority and frequency of mention. The point here is that one can decide which dimensions are to be treated as salient for a given individual *before* looking at his or her judgments. In an attempt to provide an answer to the question of *why* a particular dimension or stimulus attribute is more salient than another, Tajfel links salience with "value." According to Tajfel, the association of value with a particular attribute is a special case of superimposing a classification on a series of stimuli: It enhances the salience of the attribute with which it is associated, and leads to increased polarization of judgment along the focal dimension. The effects of the evaluative properties of the response language are discussed in more detail in Chapter 3. According to accentuation theory, the more the differences along a specific dimension are systematically related to differences in value, the more salient that dimension is. This implies that a salient dimension is a dimension that is relevant to an individual's evaluations of the stimuli he or she is required to judge.

The notion that individuals discriminate between objects of judgment in terms of those dimensions they see as salient is basically a statement about *how* people attempt to interpret their environment. One branch of social psychology that examines such processes directly is that of cognitive balance.

Cognitive balance

Balance theory, and related theories of cognitive consistency, attempt to describe how individuals try to explain their social environment. As a description of "objective" reality, such theories are obviously gross oversimplifications—but it is precisely because of this that they can contribute to our understanding of the selective nature of social cognition. One of the implications of research in this field is the importance of self-evaluation. The unqualified formulation of cognitive consistency assumes a positive self-concept (see, e.g., Osgood and Tannenbaum's 1955 congruity model).

This assumption has received considerable empirical support (e.g., Edwards, 1959; Goldberg, 1978) and plays an important role in many current research areas, such as the attribution of success and failure.

If we move on to consider work on cognitive balance, we have to include the central principle that the perceptual field is organized according to certain rules about how things are related. Wertheimer (1923) referred to this rule as *Prägnanz*, meaning that there is a human tendency to perceive things in such a way that they fit well together. This notion of Prägnanz has been taken up by Heider (1958), and applied to relations among human beings. His work on the unit relation is an attempt to explain what an individual does when confronted with a situation that does not fit together. Heider describes the individual's attempts to make sense of an incongruent stimulus situation.

One way of preventing or solving imbalance is by cognitive restructuring. In other words, the tendency to prefer balanced to imbalanced cognitive structures may manifest itself in a tendency to see as more salient those dimensions in terms of which a given structure appears to be balanced. Substantial support for this suggestion is provided by Cohen (1971). However, as we have seen, it is not just consistency that is important, but also consistency with a positive self-evaluation. It would then be predicted that individuals see as most salient those dimensions that result in a balanced set of judgments consistent with a positive evaluation of themselves.

These principles suggest a possible answer to the question of *why* one particular dimension or stimulus attribute is more salient than another. In the remainder of this chapter we will apply the notion of *dimensional salience* to a number of issues in social cognition. First, we will return briefly to the judgment of attitude statements and the link between extremity of judgment and preference. We will then focus on the relevance of dimensional salience in the context of expectancy-value models of human decision-making. Third, empirical evidence concerning dimensional salience and attitudes will be presented. Finally, we will give a few examples of the effects of *manipulated* dimensional salience on attitude.

Dimensional Salience, Preference, and Judgment

The increased accentuation of judged differences in social judgment and categorization has been discussed in detail in Chapter 3. The major conclusion of that research was that judges will give more polarized ratings of attitude statements on *salient* dimensions, that is, those dimensions that allow individuals to describe their position in evaluatively positive terms, and the positions they disagree with in negative terms.

It appears, therefore, that some judges *prefer* to use some scales, and others *prefer* to use other scales. In short, polarization (i.e., the extent to which an individual makes extreme discriminations along a given scale) may be a sign of *preference*. Van der Pligt and van Dijk (1979) provided direct evidence of this relationship between polarization and preference. When subjects were given a choice of labels with which to describe attitude statements, the labels they preferred were evaluatively congruent with their own position. Furthermore, when the same labels were combined in the form of rating scales, greater polarization was again shown by judges whose own positions were closer to the positively labeled extreme. Further evidence for the link between extremity of response and salience to the individual of a particular dimension is provided by Tajfel and Wilkes (1964).

Following work on the availability heuristic (Tversky & Kahneman, 1974) it has been argued that salient information is the most available for retrieval and the most likely to serve as a cue for judgment. Research on attribution has shown that more information is retained about a salient other (e.g., McArthur & Post, 1977; Taylor & Fiske, 1975). This evidence suggests that salience affects the way in which data are organized in memory. The attitudinal aspects of these interactions among judgment, salience, and memory have been studied by Eiser, van der Pligt, and Gossop (1979). Their results show that categorizing attitude statements along a salient dimension improves recall.

Thus, salient dimensions are dimensions along which the individual can present the relationships between relevant stimuli in a way that is both descriptively accurate and evaluatively congruent with a positive self-evaluation. Furthermore, categorizations along salient dimensions are more accessible to memory retrieval and more likely to serve as cues for judgments. Finally, salient dimensions constitute the frame of reference the individual *prefers* when judging different attitudinal positions on an issue.

The question of salience is just as important from the standpoint of phenomenal causality. Consider the following hypothetical experiment in which subjects would be asked to rate a series of statements about the Falklands War, on scales such as peace-loving/war-mongering and patriotic-unpatriotic. We would expect the latter scale to be more salient for the pro-war subjects, and the former dimension more salient for the anti-war subjects. The pro-war judges would then show more *polarization* in their judgments, *prefer* to see the war as an issue of patriotism, and be more prepared to use the word "patriotic" to describe their own position. Further evidence for this preference for evaluatively congruent attributes comes from studies on the issue of nuclear energy (Eiser & van der Pligt, 1979; van der Pligt, van der Linden, & Ester, 1982). These attributions can be assumed to function not only as descriptions but also as explanations. For instance, the anti-war judge might argue that if one values peace one should oppose the war, so that the reason why some people opposed the war and others supported it is at least partly *because* some people value peace more than others.

Expectancy-Value Models and Salience

Early attempts to describe how people make decisions were largely based on economic theory. For instance, Edwards' (1954) subjective expected utility model (SEU) describes the universe of decisions in terms of three basic variables: options, probabilities, and utilities. Similar models were proposed by Rosenberg (1956) and others (see Feather, 1959). More recently, Fishbein and Ajzen (1975) advanced a similar model. Their theory of reasoned action traces the causes of behavior through a series of intervening processes to the person's salient beliefs. Fishbein and Ajzen (1975) opt for an expectancy-value formulation of attitude, along the same lines as the previously mentioned models. People's attitudes toward an object or behavior are estimated by multiplying their evaluation of each outcome or attribute associated with the behavior or object with their subjective probability that the behavior or object has that outcome or attribute. These products are then summed for the total set of beliefs to obtain an estimate of the person's attitude. The model specifies that a person's intention to perform a given behavior can be expressed as a simple linear weighted sum of a person's attitude and subjective norms connected with the behavior.

Since the introduction of this model research has shown a renewed interest in attitudinal phenomena (for reviews see Eagly & Himmelfarb, 1978; Cialdini, Petty, & Cacioppo, 1981). The theory of reasoned action has been applied to a wide variety of behaviors and a considerable amount of supporting evidence has accumulated in both experimental and naturalistic settings (see Ajzen & Fishbein, 1977, 1980).

In the current analysis we will emphasize the importance of *salience of beliefs* in the context of expectancy-value research. The considerable appeal of the expectancy-value approach has made it the cornerstone of applied research on decision-making. Unfortunately most research in applied settings is mainly concerned with *prediction*. For researchers working in applied settings, such as consumer behavior, the predictive power of a model provides a highly useful tool. As a consequence, the *descriptive* validity of the model receives less attention and seems to be taken for granted. As long as one can predict, it seems irrelevant to understand *how* decisions are made. It is simply assumed that the individual decision-maker uses the rules incorporated in the model. The major argument to be put forward in the present section is that increasing the predictive validity of a model does not necessarily lead to improved understanding of the decision-making process. It will be argued that a more explicit incorporation of *belief salience* could improve our understanding of *how* people come to their decisions.

The role of thought

More than two decades of research in cognitive psychology have clear negative consequences for the descriptive validity of expectancy-value models. The major conclusion of this research, going back as far as the early work of Miller (1956) and Simon (1957), is that combining enormous quantities of information in one's head exceeds the computational capacity of anyone but an idiot savant (cf. Fischhoff, Goitein, & Shapira, 1982). Research by Slovic (1974) indicated that it is difficult to learn and use a weighted sum decision rule when there are many cues or unusual relationships between the cues and the predicted variable. These results suggest that people could not use the decision rule assumed by expectancy-value models even if they tried. Furthermore, evidence presented by Fischhoff et al. (1982) shows that many of the axioms upon which the model is based are contradicted by empirical evidence. For instance, perceptions of values and probabilities are not independent (see also Sundstrom, DeVault, & Peele, 1981), probability assessments tend to be poorly calibrated (Lichtenstein, Fischhoff, & Phillips, 1977) and the reliability of values of desired outcomes is fairly modest and not consistent across different situations. More generally, many decisions and behaviors may be enacted relatively "mindlessly" at a reduced level of cognitive activity (see Chapter 9).

All these analyses suggest that the conscious thought preceding a decision may be of a relatively simple nature, given the difficulty of processing complex information. People seem to rely on simple heuristics for making probability judgments and hardly seem to think about more complex combinations of values or utilities involved in a decision. In other words, people's decision processes seem relatively inarticulated and are hardly compatible with the sort of rigorous, systematic thinking required by expectancy-value formulations that involve a considerable number of beliefs. The model presents an overintellectualized view of the cognitive processes people go through when making decisions, forming attitudes, or choosing alternative actions.

Applications of expectancy-value models

Some expectancy-value approaches seem aware of the above problems. For instance, Fishbein & Ajzen (1975) acknowledge that a person is capable of attending to or processing only five to nine items of information at a time, and argue that a person's attitude toward an object is primarily determined by no more than five to nine beliefs about the object. These beliefs are termed *salient*. Since it is impossible to obtain a precise measure of the beliefs determining an individual's attitude, they suggest one should obtain the *modal salient beliefs* in a given population, by simply asking a representative sample of the population to elicit their beliefs about a specific object. The most frequently elicited beliefs are then considered the *modal* salient beliefs for the population. However, Fishbein and Ajzen go on to say that nonsalient beliefs too can be used to measure attitudes, and place little weight on the distinction between salient and nonsalient beliefs. According to Fishbein and Ajzen (1975, p. 222) their model "is applicable to any set of beliefs, whether they are salient or non-salient, new or old." Responses to nonsalient belief statements are regarded as inferences consistent with the salient beliefs held by the person, and are seen as predictive of his or her attitude. The most unfortunate consequence of this type of reasoning is that many applications of this expectancy-value model use a considerable number of beliefs concerning possible consequences of a specific behavioral action. Given a sufficiently large set of probabilities and values, one can, of course, always devise a rule "predicting" decisions or attitudes at a reasonable level of proficiency. In regression terms, the expansion of the set of independent variables makes it relatively easy to find a set of predictors with a reasonable correlation with the dependent variable.

The inclusion of considerable numbers of belief statements seems the rule rather than the exception in expectancy-value research. Most applications use 20 or more belief statements concerning possible consequences or attributes. These statements have to be rated in terms of likelihood *and* valence. For instance, Ajzen and Fishbein (1980) in their overview of steps in the construction of a standard questionnaire within the framework of their theory include 20 belief statements in their example. Other examples are Fishbein and Coombs (1974; 24 items), Jaccard and Davidson (1972; 15 items), Smetana and Adler (1981; 54 items) and Sundstrom et al. (1981; 27 items). All these examples show a reasonable predictive power, that is, the model "worked." Unfortunately, it is difficult to know what this proves. Does it prove that the individual used the model? Or have we finally stumbled upon a set of items that correlates well with the actual decision, without reflecting the actual decision process? As we have seen, research in cognitive psychology suggests that the latter interpretation is more likely to be correct than the former. The crucial question that remains, however, is *why* a person holds a particular attitude. We will argue that the inclusion of a measure of perceived importance or salience could provide more information concerning *why* a person holds a specific attitude. Furthermore, inclusion of this variable enables the researcher to reduce the analysis of the decision-making process to manageable and more realistic proportions.

Attitudes and Salience: Some Empirical Findings

Salience and nuclear energy

A number of studies on the issue of nuclear energy have shown that separate dimensions of the issue appear differentially salient for the different attitude groups. Otway, Maurer, and Thomas (1978) conducted a factor analysis on 39 belief statements about nuclear power. Their analysis yielded four factors designated as "psychological risk," "economic and technical benefits," "sociopolitical risk," and "environmental and physical risk." They further compared the 50 most pro- and 50 most anti-nuclear respondents so as to determine the contributions of beliefs and evaluations within each of these factors to respondents' overall attitudes. For the pro group, the economical and technical benefits factor made the most important contribution, whereas for the anti group, the risk factors were more important. Their results showed a clear relationship between attitudinal position and salience of the various aspects of nuclear energy (salience being inferred from regression weights).

Two other studies on the issue of nuclear energy resulted in similar findings to the Otway et al. study, without relying on factor analysis. Eiser and van der Pligt (1979) conducted a study on the development of a nuclear waste reprocessing plant at Windscale in Northwest England. Subjects rated a list of 11 possible consequences of the proposed development, and were also asked to rank the five possible consequences they personally thought were most important. The percentages of pro and anti subjects choosing each of the consequences among the most important five showed marked differences. The pro subjects most frequently chose the strength of the UK economy (75% vs. 17% for the anti group) and the UK's ability to meet future energy demands (92% vs. 22%). The anti subjects focused on the possible restrictions on civil liberties (83% vs. 17%) and the risk of nuclear terriorism (72% vs. 4%). The rank correlation between the two sets of percentages was −.50, indicating that the two attitude groups *saw the issue in very different terms*. The relationship between an overall measure of subjects' attitude and an index score based on their ratings of the 11 possible consequences was strongly affected by their perceived importance of the belief statements. The index score based on the five items perceived as most important correlated 0.86 with subjects' attitudes. A similar calculation on the six remaining less important items for each subject resulted in a correlation of only 0.44. Results of this study show that a simple measure of importance or salience does provide interesting information on the *structure* of people's attitudes toward an issue. Inclusion of this variable shows that different attitude groups will tend to disagree not only over the likelihood and evaluation of certain attributes or consequences but also over their importance.

In a more recent study (van der Pligt, van der Linden, & Ester, 1982) a sample of the general population (n = 638) was asked to select the three possible consequences of nuclear energy which they found most important. Eight possible consequences of nuclear energy were presented. Results showed that subjects' attitude was strongly related to the perceived importance of the various potential consequences. The two attitude groups (pro and con nuclear energy) showed marked differences in their selection of the three most important possible consequences. The pro group regarded the possible economic benefits of nuclear energy and the ability to meet future energy demands are most important. These two aspects were selected by 65% and 64%, respectively, of the pro-nuclear respondents, while only 9% and 8% of the anti subjects regarded these aspects as important. The anti group regarded the risk of nuclear accidents (68% vs. 7% for the pros) and the possible adverse consequence for the environment (74%vs. 12% for the pros) as most important. We further calculated an index score for each subject based on those consequences he or she selected among the three most important. The correlation between the scores based on the three most important consequences and a direct measure of subjects' attitude toward nuclear energy was .83. A similar calculation on the remaining (less important) consequences yielded a significantly lower correlation (.65).

In this study we also asked subjects to estimate the prevalence of both pro- and anti-nuclear attitudes in various segments of the population (van der Pligt, Ester, & van der Linden, 1983). Results supported the "false consensus" hypothesis, both pro- and anti-nuclear subjects perceived their "own" attitude to be more common among the various population groups. This bias was most clear-cut for the extreme attitude groups. Furthermore, the extreme attitude groups made more extreme trait evaluations about others with pro or anti attitudes toward nuclear energy. These findings are in accordance with those reported by Judd and Johnson (1981; see also Chapter 4) and suggest that the more extreme subjects find nuclear attitudes more "diagnostic" (i.e., more informative concerning a person's traits) than do the relatively moderate subjects. It is worth noting that affective intensity increases with attitude extremity (Suchman, 1950) and that subjects with extreme and involving attitudes find the attitude issue of central concern. Therefore, the issue of nuclear energy would probably be more salient for the extreme attitude groups, which would lead the extreme subjects to see someone's position on the issue as more informative concerning internal traits and dispositions.

Summarizing, results of these studies indicate that individuals with opposing attitudes see different aspects of the issue as salient, and hence, disagree not only over the likelihood of the various potential consequences but also over their importance. Attitude scores based on this subset of important aspects were generally more strongly related to subjects' standpoint on the issue than attitude scores based on less-salient beliefs. Furthermore, it seems fair to conclude that each attitude group has its own reasons for holding a particular attitude. The pro group saw the potential economic benefits of nuclear energy as most important, while the anti group attached greater value to environmental and public health aspects. This finding not only has important practical implications for communication and mutual understanding between the protagonists in the nuclear debate, but also demands a conception of attitudes that takes such differential salience into account.

Salience and health

Another example of the selectivity of people's conception of a particular issue can be seen by directly examining which aspects of the issue are seen as most salient by those with different attitudes on the issue. In a study by Eiser, van der Pligt, and Friend (1983) on the issue of cigarette smoking, 15-year-old students from two comprehensive schools participated in group discussions on this issue. Arguments generated spontaneously in the course of free discussions were considered as reflections of the attitude structures of the individuals concerned. It was hypothesized that individuals who adopt different positions on an issue, such as smoking, may see different aspects of that issue as "salient" or subjectively important. We assumed that when a person spontaneously introduces a theme into such a discussion, that theme is one that they regard as relatively "salient" or important. Attitudinal differences between smokers and nonsmokers may therefore be reflected in how they respectively attempt to structure discussions about smoking.

The results of the content analysis of the tape recordings of the discussions showed clear differences in the aspects of the issue which were most "salient" to the smokers and nonsmokers, respectively, in the sense of being most likely to be introduced by them into the discussion. Nonsmokers, as would be expected, were more likely to mention the dangers and costs of smoking, as well as parental attitudes. Smokers emphasized, relatively, the benefits and pleasure of smoking, and were more inclined to argue that smoking was no worse than a variety of other habits. Results indicated that most smokers are aware of the potential negative consequences but regard the risk as a vague increase in the probability of cancer 20 years from now. The health consequences clearly are less salient for the smokers than for the nonsmokers. Research by Smith (1982) confirms these findings. His subjects tended to suppress beliefs relating smoking to lung cancer. The smokers made hardly any mention of it and seemed to be paying no attention to it.

The major implication of this finding is that persuasive communications should take account of which aspects of an issue are most salient to different individuals. Research by McKennell and Thomas (1967) and van der Rijt (1979) on adults' and adolescents' smoking habits and attitudes indicated that anti-smoking campaigns, premised on the assumption that smokers need *only* be informed of the link between smoking and lung cancer, are unlikely to be very effective.

Summary

It has been argued that people rely on relatively simple heuristics, and that the analytic mode of thought that seems to be implied by the expectancy-value approach is based on a rather optimistic view of our capacity to process complex information. The risk of including large numbers of belief statements is that the researcher may be stuck with associative responses, evaluatively congruent with the person's attitude, but generated without serious contemplation.

Inclusion of the concept of *salience* and *importance* enables the researcher to describe the decision process in much simpler terms which are more or less in line with the computational ability of the human brain. Research presented in this chapter suggests that perceptions of importance or salience are relatively valid, that is, ranking procedures result in similar findings as post hoc calculated regression weights. Furthermore, salient beliefs tend to show higher correlations with overall attitude measures than nonsalient beliefs, and ability to predict overall attitude is not affected by the exclusion of nonsalient beliefs. Incorporation of *salience* also provides useful information concerning the structure of people's attitudes. People with different attitudes toward an issue not only tend to have different perceptions of the likelihood and valence of the various possible consequences and/or attributes, but also tend to disagree on which aspects are most important.

It is necessary to discuss two possible criticisms of the above line of reasoning: (a) that cognitive models do not have to mirror the thought processes they try to explain; and (b) that retrospective reports of conscious thought processes are suspect. The first point states that the theory or model should be regarded as an analysis in terms of intervening variables (i.e., beliefs), but only in descriptive terms. The model thus describes a decision process without making assumptions about the intervening thought processes. As long as the model provides reasonable predictions, we should not worry about what goes on inside the black box. However, there have been many applications of expectancy-value models that claim not only to predict, but also explain, decision processes. A notable example is the theory of reasoned action (Ajzen & Fishbein, 1980). The second argument is based on an increasing body of research suggesting a relatively poor insight into our own cognitive processes (e.g., Nisbett & Ross, 1980). One could argue, therefore, that asking people which aspects they think are most important does not provide relevant data. However, studies on the issue of nuclear energy resulted in highly reliable findings concerning perceived importance or salience. Eiser and van der Pligt (1979), van der Pligt et al. (1982), Woo and Castore (1980), and Otway et al. (1978) all showed that attitudinal differences were highly related to perceived differences in salience. Findings of these studies were very similar although widely different measures of salience were used, ranging from post hoc calculated weights to self-reports.

From a practical point of view, these considerations have a number of important consequences. It may not be necessary to convince smokers further of the link between smoking and lung cancer, but for some it may be worthwhile trying to make this link more personally relevant, while, at the same time, taking more account of those dimensions of smoking that are seen as most important by smokers. Similar remarks can be made in the context of the nuclear debate. Nuclear opponents not only question the economic benefits of nuclear energy, but also regard them as less important. Similarly, the nuclear proponents not only regard the risks as less probable but also regard environmental and political risks as less important.

The preceding discussion shows that people use relatively simple heuristics in coming to an overall evaluation *and* that different attitude groups see a particular issue in different terms, that is, use a different "frame of reference." In the next section, we will consider some of the effects of manipulations of people's frames of reference on their attitudes.

Salience and Attitude Change

The literature is full of examples of how experimental instructions can influence how subjects interpret situations and task requirements, and hence how subjects behave. For instance, the way in which risk decisions are "framed"—that is, the way in which choices are presented to subjects—can strongly influence subjects' preference. Similarly, levels of cooperation in mixed-motive games such as the Prisoner's Dilemma can be dramatically changed by alternative modes of presentation of equivalent sets of payoffs (Pruitt, 1967), as well as by other manipulations that influence how subjects interpret the purpose of the experiment (e.g., Eiser & Bhavnani, 1974). As we have argued in relation to Fishbein and Ajzen's (1975) theory of reasoned action, there is more to choice than expected value. One needs to know how the consequences of actions are judged and interpreted—and hence what aspects are salient for the individual.

Our purpose here is not, however, to document the range of manipulations that produce effects consistent with such an analysis. We shall not, for example, consider manipulations of salience in terms of distinctiveness, and their influence on causal attributions (Taylor & Fiske, 1975, 1978). Instead, we shall address ourselves here to a narrower question. If people with different attitudes toward an issue construe that issue in terms of different salient dimensions, can one influence people's attitudes by influencing the dimensions they see as salient? One study that suggests an affirmative answer is that by Eiser and Mower White (1974b) concerned with adolescent attitudes toward adult authority. On the basis of evidence (Eiser & Mower White, 1974a; see Chapter 3) that pro- and anti-authority adolescents showed greater degrees of polarization on different scales, 12- to 13-year-old subjects were required to indicate their own agreement or disagreement with a set of statements under one of three conditions. The *control* group was simply asked to rate their agreement. The *pro-bias* group was told that the questionnaire was "a survey designed to find out if you are the kind of person who is obedient, helpful, polite, and cooperative as opposed to the sort of person who is disobedient, unhelpful, rude and uncooperative." The *anti-bias* group was told that it was "designed to find out if you are the kind of person who is bold, adventurous, creative and with-it, as opposed to the sort of person who is timid, unadventurous, uncreative, and old-fashioned" (Eiser & Mower White, 1974b, p. 90). Thus, this study involved a deliberate and quite blatant manipulation of "demand characteristics" through the labeling of the attitude continuum. The results were as predicted. The pro-bias group produced the most pro-authority attitude responses and the anti-bias group the most anti-authority responses.

Less direct manipulations of salience were employed by Eiser and Ross (1977) and Eiser and Pancer (1979). Both these studies required subjects to write short essays incorporating words from lists provided by the experimenter with clearly biased value connotations, and demonstrated short-term attitude shifts toward positions more evaluatively congruent with the connotations of such words. In the Eiser and Ross (1977) study, subjects were Canadian university students who had to write an essay on the issue of capital punishment. The study was presented as concerned with problems in the field of psycholinguistics, but the words that subjects had to incorporate conveyed clear negative evaluations of either capital punishment (e.g., callous, sadistic) or, in the other condition, of the abolitionist position (e.g., oversentimental, starry-eyed). Eiser and Pancer (1979) applied a similar methodology in the context of teenagers' attitudes to authority, one difference being that the bias in favor of pro and anti positions was conveyed by evaluatively positive as well as evaluatively negative terms.

One area where attempts at persuasion may involve selective emphasis on particular aspects or attributes is commercial advertising. In an attempt to simulate some of the effects of such selective emphasis, Eiser, Eiser, Patterson, and Harding (1983) had teenagers evaluate a list of 21 common foods after being informed whether each of these was relatively "high," "medium," or "low" in terms of *one* specific class of nutrient (iron, protein, fat, carbohydrate, calorie). Broadly, subjects' judgments of which foods were most "good for you" (but not which were most "pleasant") corresponded more closely with the categorizations they had learned than in a control condition where no specific information was provided.

These findings, therefore, imply that some changes in attitude can be produced by manipulations that direct subjects' attention to certain features of an attitude object or issue and away from other features. It is a matter of conjecture how much continued exposure to biased language or selective information will tend to influence attitudes and behavior in the longer term. Nonetheless, we do have large numbers of evaluative words in our language and we do use them frequently. It does not seem unreasonable to suppose that a large part of the intended function of such words is to persuade others as well as to justify one's own selective interpretation of events.

Conclusions

In this chapter we have attempted to spell out briefly the implications of a simple argument: People's cognitive and evaluative processes are selective. We cannot attend equally to all the information to which we are exposed, hence we need to make choices concerning the amount of processing space or time we can allocate to any piece of information. However the *way* we allocate our processing capacity can have profound effects on our attitudes, our decisions, and our behavior (as the following two chapters also testify).

We have used the term salient to refer to stimuli or stimulus attributes that attract a relatively large amount of attention from a given individual, are described as relatively important, and/or have a relatively large influence on judgments and evaluations. This definition thus categorizes stimulus properties in terms of subjective reactions. Why do we need such a roundabout definition? Why can we not define the properties of salient stimuli more objectively?

There are two parts to the answer. The first part is that there *are* ways of predicting the salience of stimuli on the basis of "objective" stimulus features, but these features are not absolute but rather relative to other stimuli, which form the perceiver's frame of reference. More distinctive stimuli are more salient and attract disproportionate attention (Taylor & Fiske, 1978; Fiske, 1980; see also Chapter 10). Distinctiveness, however, though "objectively" definable (up to a point at least) is not a property of individual stimuli per se, but instead a property of the relationship of individual stimuli to their context.

The second part to the answer is that we fall back on a definition in subjective terms because of the extent to which different individuals will see different stimuli or attributes as salient. This is particularly noticeable in the field of attitudes where the stimuli are frequently highly complex and multidimensional issues that are open to many alternative interpretations. We have used the phrase "dimensional salience" to express the idea that different dimensions of an issue may be differentially salient for different individuals and we have discussed a number of ways in which such dimensional salience can influence judgments and preferences.

This chapter has been concerned principally with salience as a consequence of individual attitude-cognitive structures rather than with salience as a consequence of the distinctiveness of stimuli in context. The problem we have faced, therefore, is analogous to that faced by anyone who seeks to deal with individual differences. The argument that such individual differences have a major influence may be intuitively appealing, but if we cannot predict which individuals will do what, the presence of such differences may simply be a nuisance that we are forced to allow to inflate our error variance.

We have suggested a very simple but, we believe, important clue to a possible solution to this problem. We contend that individual differences in dimensional salience are, to a large extent, *nonrandom*. Instead, such differences tend to be systematically related to the valence or direction of an individual's attitude toward an issue (and to some extent also to the extremity of that attitude). People with different attitudes toward an issue tend to see different aspects of the issue as salient. What is more, the kinds of aspects they see as salient are also predictable on the basis of evaluative content. Attributes that are evaluatively consistent with a person's attitude are more likely to be seen as salient than evaluatively inconsistent attributes.

This association between attitudes and dimensional salience could imply influences in both directions. It could be that people's attitudes and values lead them to see as salient those aspects of an issue in terms of which their own opinions seem most rational and justified. In other words dimensional salience may be "motivated." Alternatively, or additionally, it could be that people hold the attitudes they do because of the aspects of issue that have selectively attracted their attention. Support for this latter possibility comes from the studies we have reported on the attitudinal effects of manipulated salience. These, however, we regard as but a small instance of a more general set of processes whereby changes in attitude may follow from changes in cognitive structure—a theme pursued in more detail in the final two chapters.

Salience, then, is a product both of stimulus context and of cognitive process. It may both depend on and shape the attitudes we hold.

References

Ajzen, I., & Fishbein, M. (1977). Attitude-behavior relations: A theoretical analysis and review of empirical research. *Psychological Bulletin, 84,* 888-918.

Ajzen, I., & Fishbein, M. (1980). *Understanding attitudes and predicting social behavior*. Englewood Cliffs, NJ: Prentice Hall.

Anderson, N. H. (1974). Information integration: A brief survey. In D. H. Krantz, R. C. Atkinson, R. D. Luce, & P. Suppes (Eds.), *Contemporary developments in mathematical psychology* (Vol. 2). San Francisco: Freeman.

Asch, S. E. (1946). Forming impressions of personality. *Journal of Abnormal and Social Psychology, 41,* 258-290.

Cialdini, R. B., Petty, R. E., & Cacioppo, J. T. (1981). Attitude and attitude change. *Annual Review of Psychology, 32,* 357-404.

Cohen, R. (1971). An investigation of the diagnostic processing of contradictory information. *European Journal of Social Psychology, 1,* 475-492.

Eagly, A. H., & Himmelfarb, S. (1978). Attitudes and opinions. *Annual Review of Psychology, 29,* 517-554.

Edwards, A. L. (1959). Social desirability and the description of others. *Journal of Abnormal and Social Psychology, 59,* 434-436.

Edwards, W. (1954). The theory of decision-making. *Psychological Bulletin, 51,* 380-417.

Eiser, J. R., & Bhavnani, K. K. (1974). The effect of situational meaning on the behavior of subjects in the Prisoner's Dilemma Game. *European Journal of Social Psychology, 4,* 93-97.

Eiser, J. R., Eiser, C., Patterson, D. J., & Harding, C. M. (1983). *Effects of selective nutritional information on evaluative judgements of common foods: Attitude change through manipulated salience*. Manuscript submitted for publication.

Eiser, J. R., & Mower White, C. J. (1974a). Evaluative consistency and social judgment. *Journal of Personality and Social Psychology, 30,* 349-359.

Eiser, J. R., & Mower White, C. J. (1974b). The persuasiveness of labels: Attitude change produced through definition of the attitude continuum. *European Journal of Social Psychology, 4,* 89-92.

Eiser, J. R., & Pancer, S. M. (1979). Attitudinal effects of the use of evaluatively-biased language. *European Journal of Social Psychology, 9,* 39-47.

Eiser, J. R., & van der Pligt, J. (1979). Beliefs and values in the nuclear debate. *Journal of Applied Social Psychology, 9,* 524-536.

Eiser, J. R., van der Pligt, J., & Friend, P. (1983). Adolescents' arguments for and against smoking. *Journal of the Institute of Health Education, 21,* 73-78.

Eiser, J. R., van der Pligt, J., & Gossop, M. R. (1979). Categorization, attitude and memory for the source of attitude statements. *European Journal of Social Psychology, 9,* 243-251.

Eiser, J. R., & Ross, M. (1977). Partisan language, immediacy and attitude change. *European Journal of Social Psychology, 7,* 477-489.

Feather, N. T. (1959). Subjective probability and decision under uncertainty. *Psychological Review, 66,* 150-164.

Fischhoff, B., Goitein, B., & Shapira, Z. (1982). The experienced utility of expected utility approaches. In N. T. Feather (Ed.), *Expectations and actions: Expectancy-value models in psychology*. Hillsdale, NJ: Lawrence Erlbaum.

Fishbein, M., & Ajzen, I. (1975). *Belief, attitude, intention and behavior*. Reading, MA: Addison-Wesley.

Fishbein, M., & Coombs, F. S. (1974). Basis for decision: An attitudinal analysis of voting behavior. *Journal of Applied Psychology, 4,* 95-124.

Fiske, S. T. (1980). Attention and weight in person perception: The impact of negative and extreme behavior. *Journal of Personality and Social Psychology, 38,* 889-906.

Fiske, S. T. (1981). Social cognition and affect. In J. H. Harvey (Ed.), *Cognition, social behavior, and the environment*. Hillsdale, NJ: Lawrence Erlbaum.

Goldberg, L. R. (1978). Differential attribution of trait-descriptive terms to oneself as compared to well-liked, neutral and disliked others: A psychometric analysis. *Journal of Personality and Social Psychology, 36,* 1012-1028.

Heider, F. (1958). *The psychology of interpersonal relations*. New York: Wiley.

Higgins, E. T., Herman, C. P., & Zanna, M. P. (1981). *Social cognition: The Ontario Symposium* (Vol. 1). Hillsdale, NJ: Lawrence Erlbaum.

Hodges, B. H. (1974). Effects of valence on relative weighting in impression formation. *Journal of Personality and Social Psychology, 30,* 378-381.

Jaccard, J. A., & Davidson, A. R. (1972). Toward an understanding of family planning behaviors: An initial investigation. *Journal of Applied Social Psychology, 2,* 228-235.

Judd, C. M., & Johnson, J. T. (1981). Attitudes, polarisation and diagnosticity. *Journal of Personality and Social Psychology, 41,* 26-36.

Lichtenstein, S., Fischhoff, B., & Phillips, L. D. (1977). Calibration of probabilities: The state of the art. In H. Jungermann & G. de Zeeuw (Eds.), *Decision-making and change in human affairs*.Dordrecht: D. Reidel.

McArthur, L. Z., & Post, D. L. (1977). Figural emphasis and person perception. *Journal of Experimental Social Psychology, 13,* 520-535.

McKennell, A. C., & Thomas, R. K. (1967). *Adults' and adolescents' smoking habits and attitudes*. Government Social Survey, SS 353/B. London: HMSO.

Miller, G. A. (1956).The magical number seven, plus or minus two: Some limits on our capacity for processing information. *Psychological Review, 63,* 81-97.

Nisbett, R. E., & Ross, L. D. (1980). *Human inference: Strategies and shortcomings of human judgment*. Englewood Cliffs, NJ: Prentice-Hall.

Osgood, C. E., & Tannenbaum, P. H. (1955). The principle of congruity in the prediction of attitude change. *Psychological Review, 62,* 42-55.

Otway, H. J., Maurer, D., & Thomas, K. (1978). Nuclear power: The question of public acceptance. *Futures, 10,* 109-118.

Pruitt, D. G. (1967). Reward structure and cooperation: The decomposed Prisoner's Dilemma game. *Journal of Personality and Social Psychology, 7,* 21-27.

Rosenberg, J. (1956). Cognitive structure and attitudinal affect. *Journal of Abnormal and Social Psychology, 53,* 367-372.

Simon, H. A. (1957). *Models of man*. New York: Wiley.

Slovic, P. (1974). Hypothesis testing in the learning of positive and negative linear functions. *Organizational Behavior and Human Performance, 11,* 368-376.

Smetana, J. G., & Adler, N. E. (1980). Fishbein's value and expectancy model: An examination of some assumptions. *Personality and Social Psychology Bulletin, 6,* 89-96.

Smith, J. L. (1982). A structuralist interpretation of the Fishbeinian Model of Intention. *Journal Theory of Social Behaviour, 12,* 29-46.

Suchman, E. A. (1950). The intensity component in attitude and opinion research. In S. A. Stouffer, L. Guttman, E. A. Suchman, P. F. Lazersfield, S. A. Starr, & J. A. Clausen (Eds.), *Studies in social psychology in World War II: Vol. 4. Measurement and prediction.* Princeton, NJ: Princeton University Press.

Sundstrom, E., DeVault, R., & Peele, E. (1981). Acceptance of a nuclear power plant: Applications of the expectancy-value model. In A. Baum & J. E. Singer (Eds.), *Advances in environmental psychology* (Vol. 3). Hillsdale, NJ: Lawrence Erlbaum.

Tajfel, H., & Wilkes, A. L. (1964). Salience of attributes and commitment to extreme judgments in the perception of people. *British Journal of Social and Clinical Psychology, 3,* 40-49.

Taylor, S. E. (1981). The interface of cognitive and social psychology. In J. Harvey (Ed.), *Cognition, social behavior, and the environment.* Hillsdale, NJ: Lawrence Erlbaum.

Taylor, S. E., & Fiske, S. T. (1975). Point-of-view and perceptions of causality. *Journal of Personality and Social Psychology, 32,* 439-445.

Taylor, S. E., & Fiske, S. T. (1978). Salience, attention, and attribution: Top of the head phenomena. In L. Berkowitz (Ed.), *Advances in experimental social psychology* (Vol. 11). New York: Academic Press.

Tversky, A., & Kahneman, D. (1974). Judgment under uncertainty: Heuristics and biases. *Science, 185,* 1124-1131.

van der Pligt, J. (1981). Actors' and observers' explanations: Divergent perspectives or divergent evaluations? In C. Antaki (Ed.), *The psychology of ordinary explanations of social behaviour.* London: Academic Press.

van der Pligt, J., & Eiser, J. R. (1980). Negativity and descriptive extremity in impression formation. *European Journal of Social Psychology, 10,* 415-419.

van der Pligt, J., Ester, P., & van der Linden, J. van. (1983). Attitude extremity, consensus and diagnosticity. *European Journal of Social Psychology,* in press.

van der Pligt, J., van der Linden, J., & Ester, P. (1982). Attitudes to nuclear energy: Beliefs, values and false consensus. *Journal of Environmental Psychology, 2,* 221-231.

van der Pligt, J., & van Dijk, J. A. (1979). Polarization of judgment and preference for judgmental labels. *European Journal of Social Psychology, 9,* 233-242.

van der Rijt, G. A. J. (1979). *Jeugd en Antirookinformatie.* Doctoral dissertation, Sociologisch Instituut, Katholieke Universiteit Nijmegen.

Wertheimer, M. (1923). Untersuchungen zur Lehre von der Gestalt—II. *Psychologische Forschung, 4,* 301-350.

Woo, T. O., & Castore, C. H. (1980). Expectancy-value and selective exposure as determinants of attitudes toward a nuclear power plant. *Journal of Applied Social Psychology, 10,* 224-234.

Zajonc, R. B. (1980). Feeling and thinking: Preferences need no inferences. *American Psychologist, 35,* 151-175.

Chapter 9

Attitudes and Attitude Change: Mindlessness-Mindfulness Perspective

Mark Palmerino, Ellen Langer, and Daniel McGillis

The study of attitudes has had a long and honored tradition among social psychologists, even to the extent of being defined as the core of social psychology itself (Allport, 1935; Bogardus, 1931; Folsom, 1931; Thomas & Znanieki, 1918). Since the early days of social psychology, the concept of attitude has gone through many changes. Research on attitudes was vigorous during many decades but is less prevalent at present. The reduced prominence of attitude research has prompted a theoretically oriented reconceptualization of the role of attitudes in social psychology. Accordingly, this chapter conceptualizes attitudes as part of a contextual whole and links attitude theory to the theory of mindfulness-mindlessness (M-M). This linkage illustrates how the concept of a situated attitude can be useful in a theoretically deeper understanding of the attitude-behavior link and the mechanics of attitude change.

What Is an Attitude?

Current definitions of attitude are plentiful (e.g., Allport, 1935; Krech, Crutchfield, & Ballachey, 1962; Smith, Bruner, & White, 1956), and all essentially indicate that attitudes have three major features. First, an attitude develops through *experience* with an object. Second, it *predisposes one to act* in a predictable manner with respect to an object. Third, an attitude consists of *positive or negative* evaluations. Fishbein and Ajzen (1975) note "that the major characteristic that distinguishes attitude from other concepts is its evaluative or affective nature" (p. 11). They suggest, then, that the proper way to measure an attitude would be to locate the holder of the attitude on a bipolar affective or evaluative dimensions with respect to the object.

What is notably lacking in present day conceptualizations of attitude is reference to, broadly speaking, the *context* surrounding the attitude. That is, we need not only speak about an attitude with respect to an object but we need to locate this relationship, between the holder of the attitude and the object, within a specific context. The form of this relationship can be radically different given different contexts.

Former definitions have assumed that this link between a person and an object, by itself and apart from a context, guides behavior. However, it is not this link alone that guides behavior. Rather it is this link embedded in a larger contextual structure (cf. Fishbein & Ajzen, 1975, for a detailed discussion of the need to take situational features into account in assessing attitudes). To appreciate a contextual formulation one should consider gestalt and field theories.

Gestalt and Field Theoretical Influences

Many of the ideas that are being applied to the study of attitudes are rooted in gestalt theory and field theory. A brief characterization of some of the more formal elements of these systems of thought seems to be in order.

Perhaps the best summary statement of gestalt theory is that the whole cannot be reduced to the sum of its parts (Wertheimer, 1944).

The ideas inherent in gestalt theory can be understood by contrasting them with the reductionist mode of scientific inquiry characterized by viewing a phenomenon as an aggregate entity that is dissected into disparate elements that then are the subject of study. An understanding of the original phenomenon is arrived at only by rebuilding the framework of which the elements were once a part. The gestalt theorist asks, "Is this cutting into pieces the only method we have?" (Wertheimer, 1944, p. 79). The answer is not only "no," but one might argue that this method of "cutting into pieces" is often misleading and can potentially cloud the issue under study.

The impact of these ideas is clearly evident in Lewin's field theory. According to Lewin, to understand human conduct fully we must begin with an analysis of the situation within which the behavior (B) occurs. This situation, or life space (LSp), is composed of two broad factors, the environment (E), and the person (P), which can only be understood as an *interdependent* field. Thus, in Lewin's terms, the equation $B = f(P,E) = f(LSp)$ represents symbolically the core of the field-theoretical approach. Also, in a similar spirit with Wertheimer's dismissal of viewing a phenomenon as an aggregate of separate facts, Lewin held that the occurrence of a particular behavior depends not upon a certain fact or number of facts but upon the structure of the psychological field as a whole (Lewin, 1939).

Field theory encompasses many formal components including tension, vectors and valence. The concept of valence in field theory has a striking kinship to that of attitude as is evident in the following statement:

> Valences are directional field forces motivating or regulating conduct and mental activity. Stimuli per se are devoid of a permanent positive or negative valence, for they may be either, depending on the time and situation. (Sahakian, 1974, p. 304)

Note the similarity between these concepts in that valences, like attitudes, are theorized to guide behavior and that valances can take either positive or negative values. One dissimilarity between these concepts is that the notion of attitude, as contemporary definitions seem to suggest, implies that a person would act predictably toward some object. The description of valence explicitly indicates that objects may have both positive and negative valences associated with them. A second dissimilarity is that attitudes are said to reside in the *person* while valences are said to reside in objects.

As will be seen, it is precisely these points of departure that indicate the major deficiencies in the concept of attitude and suggest ways of reconceptualizing attitudes to enable the concept to take into account the context of actions.

A Reconceptualization of Attitude

Present day definitions of attitude effectively ignore the role of context. Drawing upon the basic concepts from gestalt theory and field theory, this section provides a new way of viewing attitudes that includes the critical role of context. This approach has been suggested by Lewin and others but is not currently the dominant view of attitudes in social psychology. Mindfulness-mindlessness theory may provide new and valuable insights into how context affects attitudes. Following the general discussion of how attitudes may be redefined, the contribution of M-M theory to an understanding of attitudes is explored.

According to the revised conceptualization of attitudes, an attitude should be defined as a relationship between two entities where one entity is a person and the other is a person or object. Note that this definition pulls the attitude out of the person and defines the attitude with respect to a relationship. In addition, unlike valence as defined by Lewin, an attitude is not exclusively attached to the nonperson object. Rather, an attitude is the relation *between* two entities. Furthermore, these two entities not only are attached to one another but the person and the object become part of an extended structure that is the context. However, in keeping with both the former definition of attitudes and valence this relationship can be said to vary along a positive-negative dimension.

The idea that objects do not have a permanent positive or negative valence attached is critical. Objects are unquestionably ambiguous by and of themselves. They cannot have a permanent valence and similarly it makes little sense to speak of someone's attitude toward an object as if the attitude is immutable. Instead, objects take on particular "shapes," or affective loadings, as a consequence of being an integral part of a structure, a context. Certain illusions serve as fine examples of this point. The line drawing introduced by Boring (1930), for example, is seen as either a young woman or an old woman depending on variations in the context.

Only objects that have been contextually defined can have a specific valence attached to them. Being contextually defined means that the object is related to every other part of the field in a more-or-less rigid manner. An attitude is the relationship between this contextually disambiguated object and some other entity defined by the context (more specifically, a person). Thus, in this sense an attitude cannot exist outside of a particular context because an attitude requires two contextually defined objects.

It is the object "in context" that can have a specific valence attached to it. When the disambiguated object is related to some other entity in the context (a person) they comprise what is to be called an attitude. In this sense an attitude cannot exist outside of a particular context because an attitude requires two contextually defined objects.

This picture of attitudes points to particular shortcomings in current research directed at the understanding of attitudes. Because an attitude requires two contextually defined objects and the contextually defined link between them, it is easy to understand that if a new context alters one or more of these components then a different, sometimes radically different, attitude results. An example of how this might work follows. Consider that we have an object which can take on as radically different meanings as the Boring young woman/old woman illusion (which, of course, in reality virtually any object can and does). It can be seen that if one context defines the object as a young woman while another defines the object as an old woman quite different attitudes are likely to result. In the same way, the person who is viewing this object is as ambiguous away from a particular context as any other object. Thus, two different contexts may leave the object of the Boring illusion seemingly unchanged (say as a young woman) but may define the person in one context as a father and in another context as a doctor. Attitudes and behaviors in these two contexts, with respect to the exact "same"object, would be quite different.

Finally, an attitude not only consists of two contextually defined objects but also the contextually defined relationship between them. This gives rise to a third way in which attitudes can vary across contexts. It is, in principle, possible for both of the objects to be the "same" in two different contexts (say as doctor and young woman) but they may "hang together" quite differently as a function of the contexts. As an example, consider the situation where a daughter has misbehaved and is reprimanded by her father versus the situation where she has done something praiseworthy and is complimented by him. These different contexts should and do give rise to different attitudes.

Schuman's (1972) research on attitudes toward racial issues has powerfully illustrated the impact of different contextual settings on the strength of attitudes toward affirmative action. In his research, Schuman found that 85% of subjects stated strong support for the concept of affirmative action when it was presented in the abstract. When specific behavioral contexts that dealt with affirmative action decisions in the presence of other values were described to subjects, subjects' judgments regarding the appropriateness of affirmative action changed drastically. For example, if subjects were asked whether racist co-workers should be able to vote on the promotion of a minority-group worker only 45% of subjects stated an affirmative action position while others agreed such a vote was proper. In this context the value of democratic decision-making was pitted against the value of affirmative action and resulted in a very different perception of the structure. Similar findings occurred when vignettes dealing with other values such as worker harmony were presented to subjects.

This analysis underscores why there is relatively little attitude-behavior consistency evident in laboratory research concerning attitudes (Langer & Newman, 1979; Schuman & Johnson, 1976; Wicker, 1969). Typically, an experiment investigating this link includes an attempt to infer a person's attitude toward some object (e.g., religion, Germans, birth control, etc.) often through a paper and pencil measure. Then some measure of the person's behavior with respect to this object is gathered (e.g., attendance at church, amount of money donated) which is then related in some statistical fashion with the measure of attitude.

It should be clear that the three elements (i.e., the person, the object, and the relationship between them) must retain the same identity at both the attitude inference stage and the behavioral measurement stage in order for a research method of this sort to demonstrate an attitude-behavior link.

The Theory of Mindfulness-Mindlessness

Mindfulness-mindlessness theory is one of situated action and as such can be instructive in increasing our understanding of attitudes. This section presents a brief review of the theory and summarizes some of the research it has generated.

Mindfulness-mindlessness theory is based upon the fundamental proposition that similar actions can be accompanied by vastly differing degrees of cognitive activity. Indeed, much of human activity that appears thoughtful, conscious, and intentional is in fact conducted in what has been called a mindless fashion. Whether an activity is executed in a mindless or mindful state has critical consequences for adaptive human functioning (Langer, 1980). Mindlessness may be defined as a state of reduced cognitive activity in which the individual processes cues from the environment in a relatively automatic manner without paying attention to potentially novel aspects of those cues. Mindfulness, on the other hand, is a state in which the individual consciously processes environmental cues. Here the person is engaged in actively *constructing* his or her environment, forming new categories and drawing novel distinctions. When one first comes in contact with a cup, for instance, one is mindful. This is in marked contrast to the mindless state in which one deals with the cup predictably as a cup without making new differentiations. When mindless, the individual is faced with an already-constructed environment.

Mindless information processing may arise either after many repetitions of a particular experience, or in certain instances, after a single exposure. In the former case, as an individual's experience with certain situations accumulates, a cognitive structure of the situation is formed which represents its underlying "semantics" (one may come to "know" a cup over time). The appearance of similar cues on subsequent occasions will then trigger a mindless sequence of behaviors. Once an activity becomes mindless the underlying semantics may no longer be available for conscious cognitive manipulation or even for examination.

In the latter single-exposure case, reduced cognitive activity does not result from reliance on cognitive structures built up over time, but from reliance on a cognitive structure that one has appropriated from another source (e.g., someone tells you what a cup is and that "this" is a cup). When this occurs, the individual does not scrutinize the information available at the time sufficiently, and, therefore, does not have that additional information available for later scrutiny. If on a subsequent occasion adaptive behavior requires examination of the information, the individual may be incapable of this.

Mindlessness is pervasive. In fact, for the typical individual, mindfulness is expected to occur only (a) when significantly more effort is demanded by the situation than was originally demanded; (b) when the external factors in the situation disrupt initiation of the mindless sequence; (c) when external factors prevent the completion of the behavior; or (d) when negative or positive consequences are experienced that are sufficiently discrepant with the consequences of prior enactments of the same behavior (Langer, 1978).

Although research by others has addressed reduced levels of cognitive activity (e.g., automaticity, preattentive processing, and overlearning), M-M theory is distinct in several ways. First, mindlessness suggests a more molar unit of analysis than has been examined in the past. Second, mindlessness may come about with as well as without repeated exposure. Third, mindlessness and mindfulness appear to be qualitatively different, rather than just quantitatively different. (For example, that which has been processed mindlessly may no longer be available for active conscious cognitive work.) Fourth, those studying reduced cognitive activity have focused on behavior, while here the focus is on the state of the actor. And fifth, other researchers studying automaticity, for example, have focused on the adaptive function automatic processing serves in freeing conscious attention. While this is certainly true, all of the research we have conducted thus far suggests that is also may be quite maladaptive.

We have pursued the study of M-M in several domains: its consequences for competent performance, for the perception of deviance, for the course of physical disease, and its implications for the very study of social-psychological processes. Each topic area is considered here, briefly, in turn.

Research (Langer, Blank, & Chanowitz, 1978; Langer & Weinman, 1981) has revealed that either face-to-face or written interactions between people may be mindless as long as the structure of the interaction triggers some overlearned sequence of behavior whether the communications are semantically sound or senseless. With respect to potentially relevant information, people failed to hear what was said and to read what was written.

Since with each repetition the individual components of an activity progressively drop out, the result is that not only is the individual responding over time to some abstracted structure but also that the steps of the task become relatively inaccessible. Thus, in other research (Langer & Imber, 1979), we found that counter to an analysis that ignores the mindless-mindful distinction, a great deal of practice at a task may render the individual more vulnerable to external factors that bring competence into question. Groups that were moderately practiced at a task were able to describe the steps of the task as evidence of competence and therefore did not show performance decrements when their confidence was shaken, while no-practice and overpracticed groups could not supply the components of the task and therefore showed clear debilitation.

Regarding the perception of deviance, we reasoned, first, that deviance (novelty) breeds mindfulness. If people are typically mindless vis-à-vis normal individuals, then the people who are deviant in any respect may be perceived as deviant in many respects (and therefore labeled, avoided, etc.) not so much because of their deviance but because of the thorough scrutiny that is prompted by the mindful state. Such a close examination of any individual would lead one to notice characteristics that typically go unnoticed and to the inappropriate judgment of these characteristics as extreme or unusual. As predicted, we found that the perception of the deviant was accurate but the typical characteristics and gestures that were noticed were evaluated as extreme and unusual. This occurred whether the subject of the deviance was positive (e.g., an eccentric millionaire) or negative (e.g., an ex-mental patient) but did not occur when the same stimulus person was unlabeled (Langer & Imber, 1980).

In work on mindlessness upon initial exposure, we found that when individuals were initially given information (symptoms of a disorder) that was apparently irrelevant to them (in contrast to groups who were encouraged to consider the information mindfully) they then became vulnerable at a later time when the information became relevant (they discovered they had the disorder). Groups that initially were encouraged to process the information mindfully did not show the debilitation (Chanowitz & Langer, 1981). The same effect was found for responses to one's old age and to alcoholism. Regarding both of these, we found that one's earliest exposure to information about these states determined their subsequent responses once they became old or alcoholic (Langer, Perlmuter, Chanowitz, & Rubin, 1982). Subjects apparently mindlessly processed the initial information as if they took a photograph early on and then when they "looked at it" in the future they used the unchanged photo to know how to perform.

In past research we also have found that mindfulness may be positively related to longevity. In several studies we have found that by increasing mindfulness our elderly subjects have lived longer. In the first study we increased mindfulness by increasing decision-making (Langer & Rodin, 1976; Rodin & Langer, 1977). Mindfulness was manipulated in the second study by increasing the cognitive demands made on our subjects (Langer, Beck, Janoff-Bulman, & Timko, 1982; Langer, Rodin, Beck, Weinman, & Spitzer, 1979). The third study varied mindfulness most explicitly and the results were the same. Those given the mindfulness treatment lived longer than comparison groups (Alexander, Langer, Newman, & Chandler, 1982).

Psychological researchers have typically conceived of their experimental subjects as thinking people. Given that people may at any point be either mindless or mindful, the generalizability of most experimental results that have failed to consider the distinction becomes questionable. Experimental situations, because of their novelty for subjects, typically occasion mindful responding. However, experimenters may then be in the uncomfortable position of generalizing their findings from mindful subjects to a world of mindless individuals without assurance of any correspondence between the two (see Langer, 1978; Langer & Newman, 1979). And, taken together, the research accumulated thus far suggests that the distinction may be important.

Implications of Mindfulness-Mindlessness Theory for the Study of Attitudes

It has been suggested that an attitude should be considered to be the relationship between a person and an object that derives its form from the surrounding context. An attitude, as part of the structure of the context, shares in the context's ability to direct the behavior of the person. However, M-M theory clearly demarcates boundary conditions for the operation of attitudes by noting the quantitative and qualitative dividing line between mindfulness and mindlessness. Mindlessness is a state of mind in which one deals with an already constructed environment. Thus, M-M theory posits one important qualification to situated action paradigms in that in order for the structure of the environment to guide behavior one must be engaging with the environment in a mindless fashion.

The view of the person that emerges from theories of situated action characterizes people as

> performers of human actions . . . active agents who are capable of making plans and pursuing objectives, of acting as well as reacting, of doing things for reasons as well as having been forced to do them by causes. (Ginsburg, 1980, p. 298)

Mindless interaction with the environment places individuals in the position of "reacting" and being "forced" to take certain actions. They are reacting to an already preformed structure that the situation seems to demand. In contrast, individuals behaving mindfully are in the process of actively constructing an environment. In erecting this structure there is less reaction and more reasoning and pursuing of objectives.

Attitudes, and contexts in general, have greater influence upon behavior when a person is mindless. This tendency contributes to attitude-behavior inconsistency. In order for a researcher to measure the effects of an attitude on behavior reliably the relationship between the person and the object must be comparable when a researcher measures the attitude and later measures the behavior. For example, if a person mindlessly asserts a sexist or racist social stereotype the underlying attitude is quite directly translated into behavior (see Allport's, 1954 classic work). On the other hand, mindful attitude statements can be quite variable and influenced by the setting. Mindless functioning results in congruity in both attitude and behavior measures because the person is responding in a routinized fashion and not varying his or her behavior in light of changing environmental conditions. Mindful functioning, however, is more likely to result in attitude-behavior inconsistency because unique features of the context are actively considered and cause attitude variability.

Ironically enough, the very situation in which researchers have often tried to establish an attitude-behavior link may be a situation that inherently elicits mindfulness. Laboratories may induce self-consciousness in our subjects and as such may be thought-provoking and habit-inhibiting.

Attitude Change

Attitude change is a shifting in the form or shape of the relationship between two objects. Thus, whenever there is a context change, whenever the structure of the psychological field shifts, attitudes are also likely to change. Changes may occur in the form of the object, the person, or the form of the relationship between the two. Although at first glance the first two may not be regarded as attitude change, in point of fact, when an "attitude" changes it may be the result of a change in any one of these three elements. If the context changes and what was once seen as a young women becomes an old woman, or what was once defined as a father is now defined as a doctor then we expect concomitant changes in the relationship between the two objects, that is changes in attitudes. However, this is not what is usually meant when researchers speak of a person's attitude toward an object (for example, Castro) changing from a negative to a positive one. That is, the definition of the person has not changed much, nor, presumably, has the shape of Castro. Rather, it is the relationship between the person and Castro that is different.

However, it does not make much sense to speak *only* of the relationship changing. When the relationship changes, a new structure is born and as a consequence both Castro and the individual are reshaped from the perspective of the researcher. (This illustrates the general principle of structural mechanics, namely, that a change in any one part of the structure necessarily effects changes or restructuring in the whole.) This is one type of attitude change that occurs when there are context shifts. Another type of attitude change is that of mindfulness.

A person in the process of building up a structure is also in the process of building up attitudes. There are times when this new structure is being built up from the ashes of an old structure (as in the case of the occasions which engender mindfulness) and there are times when a situation is so novel that there are no already existing structures available. In the former case, attitudes are changing, that is, "old" objects are being embedded in a new structure, which gives rise to unique attitudes. In the latter case attitudes are being created.

Implications for Producing Attitude Change

Generally speaking then, provoking mindfulness will often lead to attitude change with respect to relevant objects in the psychological field. Note, however, that although provoking mindfulness would lead to changes in the structure of the psychological field there is no reason to expect that, in general, these relationships would change from positive to negative. Attitude-measurement techniques currently in use often are useful in registering only these types of gross change. Attitude-measurement techniques that will register any type of change in attitudes are needed. Thus, mindfulness is expected to lead to attitude change though not necessarily changing positive attitudes to negative ones or vice versa.

Attitudes can be changed by building up a new structure to characterize the current psychological field (as in mindfulness) or by making changes in the existing structure of the psychological field (which in essence causes a reshaping of the entire field). A third method of attitude change, or possibly attitude induction, is suggested by the work done on premature cognitive commitments (Chanowitz & Langer, 1981). This research indicates that a structure built up in one psychological field may be appropriated and used for a psychological field that does not have a structure in order to process information. This is another way in which a person can be mindless. Instead of constructively acting to erect a structure on a new psychological field, the mindless individual borrows an already existing structure and imposes it on the present field. This borrowed structure then *imposes* certain relationships between objects in the field. Chanowitz and Langer (1981) presented subjects with either "relevant" or "irrelevant" information concerning, for example, a perceptual deficit. It was expected that the irrelevant information would be accepted at face value (if borrowed from the source). At a later point in time all subjects were informed that they had the deficit and experimental data revealed that those subjects who were initially led to believe that the information concerning this deficit was irrelevant showed perceptual deficiencies on follow-up tasks. That is, they behaved in the way that was dictated by the information. This is an example of how the structure into which this information was presented imposed a relationship upon the information with other objects in the field. When processed mindlessly because of its irrelevance, the information could only be used in a very rigid manner that produced perceptual deficits. That is, the structure was imposed onto the psychological field of these subjects.

Thus we see that applying M-M theory to this area helps to sharpen our understanding of the relevant processes involved in the attitude-behavior consistency issue and attitude change. There is, however, another way in which M-M theory can be applied to the field. This is as a categorization scheme to impose some structure on the many existing theories of attitudes—for example, balance theory (Heider, 1958), cognitive dissonance (Festinger, 1957), innoculation theory (McGuire, 1964), reactance theory (Brehm, 1966), and self-perception theory (Bem, 1967). The central difficulties faced by the numerous attitude theories is noted by Eagly and Himmelfarb (1974):

> After several decades of research, there are few simple and direct empirical generalizations that can be made concerning how to change attitudes. In fact, one of the most salient features of recent research is the great number of studies demonstrating that the empirical generalizations of earlier research are not general, but contingent on conditions not originally apparent. (p. 594)

Regardless of whether this state of affairs has arisen because of one-shot type studies (Katz, 1972), the posing of trivial hypotheses (Fishbein & Ajzen, 1975), or inadequate experimental methods (McGuire, 1973), M-M theory provides a means to help distinguish some fundamental differences among theories that are often overlooked. Table 9-1 roughly categorizes a number of major attitude theories and heavily researched attitude-change strategies in terms of whether they are based primarily upon mindful or mindless process. The task of categorizing the theories and strategies can be complex, as is illustrated in the following, but the effort to distinguish the theories in terms of degrees of mindfulness-mindlessness may yield interesting insights.

For example, theories categorized as primarily mindful include dissonance theory (Festinger, 1957), balance theory (Heider, 1958), various expectancy-value theories (e.g., Rosenberg, 1956), and attribution theories (e.g., Jones & Davis, 1965; Kelley, 1967). In each case the perceiver is postulated to process incoming information actively and consciously to arrive at a belief or attitude judgment. For example, dissonance theory research stresses the role of consciously perceived choice and foreseeability as a precondition for the occurrence of dissonance attitude-change phenomena (see Kiesler, Collins, & Miller, 1969).

The task of categorizing the theories is complex due to the subtle characteristics of many of the theories, and because some theories combine mindful and mindless processes. Initial information-processing leading to cognitive dissonance must be mindful although it may be content-free mindfulness. The distinction between the past and present feeling state is mindfully experienced even though it may not be proposi-

Table 9-1. Attitude Theories and Strategies Categorized by Mindfulness-Mindlessness

Primarily mindful	Primarily mindless
Theories	
Dissonance theory (e.g. choice, forseeability)	Classical conditioning theories
Balance theory	Operant conditioning theories
Expectancy-value theories	
Attribution theories	
Social judgment theory	
Mindful	**Mindless**
Strategies	
Implicit conclusions	Explicit conclusions
Two-sided arguments	One-sided arguments
Active audience role	Passive audience role
Innoculation-forewarning	Repetition
	Distraction effects (inhibits counterarguing)
	Communicator effects

tionally articulated. Bem's position basically relies on mindless behavior. The subject in the Bem situation has no mindful experience to which to appeal when assessing his or her attitude. Therefore he or she relies solely on the information in the current situation (e.g., "I must like brown bread because I'm eating it"). Similarly, balance theory presumes a conscious mindful assessment of propositions by a perceiver of the valences attached to the relationships among the perceiver, another person, and an entity, but a content-free mindful response to the overall "goodness" of the resulting pattern of valences. Responses to tensions to bring intuitively perceived imbalanced gestalt pattern into balance are presumably mindful (see Kiesler et al., 1969, for a review of the theory).

Expectancy-value theories of attitude change and attribution theories also tend to assume that mindful processes are the primary contributors to belief and attitude change (see Shaver, 1975, on this point). Such strong reliance upon a rational model of man has led to considerable criticism of such theories (e.g., Hastorf, Schneider, & Polefka, 1970). Our position is that while people may be rational or irrational, they also may be nonrational (i.e., mindless) and the distinctions are important when trying to predict behavior.

Mindfulness-Mindlessness Theory and the Attribution of Attitudes to Others

Mindfulness-mindlessness theory has intriguing implications for the attribution of attitudes. A substantial literature on attitude attributional processes has evolved (e.g., see Schneider, Hastorf, & Ellsworth, 1979), and Jones and Davis' correspondent inference theory (1965) indicates the circumstances under which attitudes are likely to be clearly and confidently attributed to another. Jones and Davis refer to such clear attributional judgments as "correspondent inferences," and major factors limiting the clarity and confidence of attitude attributions include coercion of the attitude statement by outside forces and the existence of external incentives to make the attitude statement.

As was noted, attribution theories are primarily "mindful" and describe active, conscious processes whereby perceivers form belief and attitude judgments. In forming such attributional judgments, however, the perceiver can take into account the degree of mindfulness or mindlessness associated with the behavior of the person being perceived. Such information can be independently valuable over and above the factors suggested by Jones and Davis. In particular, we hypothesize that if an attitude assertion is considered to be the result of "mindless" behavior (e.g., knee-jerk liberalism, blind bigotry, nonconscious ideologies; see Bem, 1970), a perceiver will presume a greater correspondence between the observed behavior and relevant attitudes than if the attitude assertion was the result of "mindful" behavior.

The reason for this hypothesis is straightforward. Mindless attitude assertions are, by definition, the product of routinized, relatively automatic cognitive processes, and tend to reflect the underlying attitude directly. Mindful attitude assertions, on the other hand, are the product of active information processing on the part of the person being perceived. Such attitude statements are inherently less stable than ones generated by mindless processes, and the very act of mindfully assessing an attitude position in light of varying factors can result in different attitudes being asserted at different times depending upon the weight given to the various factors contributing to the attitude. For example, we predict that an attitude statement favorable to a social policy (e.g., an endorsement of the federal food stamp program) is likely to be viewed as more clearly and confidently reflective of the target person's underlying "true" attitude if it is considered to be the result of "knee-jerk liberalism" and thus mindless behavior, than if it is considered to be the result of careful, "mindful" assessment of the advantages and disadvantages of federal food stamp policy. Mindlessly generated attitudes are considered to be "hard wired" in the target person and more predictive of future attitude assertions than mindfully produced attitudes according to this hypothesis.

To our knowledge, no experiments have been conducted to assess the impact of variations in the mindfulness-mindlessness of attitude-related behaviors upon the attributions of attitudes by persons perceiving the behavior. A study to test our hypothesis would require the presentation of attitude-related behaviors varying in their apparent mindfulness-mindlessness and the collection of dependent measures that assess the strength of attitude attributions (i.e., the level of correspondence of inference) and the degree to which subjects perceive variations in mindfulness. Mindless behaviors should result in greater correspondence of inference.

The hypothesis presented here seems, on the surface, to be incompatible with Jones and Davis' presupposition that intentionality of behavior is required for correspondent inferences to be possible. The Jones and Davis analysis assumes that the person being observed in fact does have knowledge of the effects of his or her actions and intends specific outcomes. Mindful behavior, by definition, involves active information processing and would meet the intentionality requirement but mindless behavior is far less intentional and can be routinized and quite automatic. The apparent resolution of this paradox in our hypothesis is that relatively mindless and stereotypic attitude assertions are still intentional acts, albeit less carefully formulated than mindful attitude assertions. Perceivers assume that people have at least minimal intentional control over their verbal behavior (with the exception of reflexive vocalizations associated with pain), and thus even the most mindless attitude assertions are considered somewhat intentional on the part of the person being observed.

If our hypothesis is accurate, it provides an interesting qualification upon Jones and Davis' presupposition regarding intentionality. One must be able to view a behavior as minimally intentional before correspondent inferences are possible (the behavior cannot be a muscular reflex, an accident, or totally coerced by external pressure). But once this minimal standard is reached, the less the mindfulness of the attitude behavior (i.e., the less the intentional detailed information processing on the part of the person being observed) the more clear and confident the attitude attribution based upon observing the behavior.

The bottom portion of Table 9-1 notes a variety of attitude-change strategies that have been repeatedly investigated by social psychologists. As in the case of the major attitude theories, the strategies resist simple categorization into primarily mindful or mindless functioning, but nevertheless can be fit into the two categories. Strategies listed as primarily mindful in operation include: (a) efforts to leave conclusions of a persuasive communication implicit, this requiring active information processing by the perceiver, (b) persuasion efforts employing two-sided arguments, (c) techniques calling on the audience to have an active role in dealing with the persuasive stimuli (e.g., audience role-playing, essay-writing, etc.), and (d) strategies employing inoculation and forewarning that may stimulate the active construction of counterarguments to a potentially threatening communication (such strategies are reviewed in Zimbardo & Ebbesen, 1969).

In contrast, strategies that are viewed as primarily mindless include: (a) techniques involving the drawing of explicit conclusions, (b) the presentation of one-sided arguments, (c) cases involving a passive audience role, (d) repeated presentation of attitude-change communications that may lead to habituation on the part of the perceiver, and (e) efforts at distraction that inhibit the ability to counterargue against the communication (see Zimbardo & Ebbesen, 1969). As in the case of the attitude theories, combinations of mindful and mindless responses can occur in each of the above strategies, but the strategies differ in their central tendencies to be either mindful or mindless.

Variations in the prevalence of mindful versus mindless persuasion strategies may be an important social indicator of the level of rational discourse in a given society. The image of a totalitarian society calls to mind a heavy reliance upon mindless propaganda strategies (one-sided arguments, repetition, and the like) and efforts to condition classically the militant attitudes of the young. In contrast, the ideal of an open society calls for conscientious public debate of issues in a highly mindful fashion (two-sided arguments, active participation by citizens in formulating positions, etc.) and careful efforts to publicly explore and evaluate issues. Studies using content-analysis approaches could begin to develop indicators of the prevalence of the varying forms of strategies in popular media, public campaign debates, and related settings across societies over time. Presumably a strong educational system based upon the teaching of mindful information processing serves as a partial antidote to the mindless processing of persuasive communication, but both forms of persuasion are pervasive in all societies and only balances among them vary over time and across societies.

Proponents of theories naturally feel that the processes they have hypothesized are quite good at explaining the phenomenon of interest. Table 9-1 illustrates, however, that it may be more useful to ask when a particular system is likely to be activated. Classifying attitude theories or strategies of attitude change on the basis of M-M makes it clear that we might expect a certain theory to be useful for a situation in which people are mindful but not if they are mindless. Similarly, we might expect certain attitude-change strategies when a person is mindless.

By attending to the different ways the same behavior can be produced we should be able to circumvent the biases that may be all too prevalent when we don our researcher-observer role (cf. Ross, 1977).

Summary

This chapter has presented a reconceptualization of the social-psychologically important concept of attitude. An attitude is a contextually defined relationship between two contextually defined entities (one of which is a person). This reconceptualization highlights the role of a contextual structure in guiding human conduct. Concepts from M-M theory, gestalt theory, and Lewin's field theory helped shape this view of attitudes. Application of the attitude concept as a structural component to the problem of attitude-behavior consistency and attitude-change phenomena appears to be theoretically fruitful.

In the case of the attitude-behavior consistency problem this application noted fundamental shortcomings in past research caused by lack of attention to the impact of context upon the definition of objects. In the case of attitude-change phenomena, the shifting in form or shape of the relationship between two objects was explored. And finally, in the case of the attribution of attitudes it was proposed that attitudes that are considered the result of mindless processes would lead to greater correspondent inferences than mindful attitudes.

This chapter was born out of a concern over the apparent static nature of recent views of attitude and stresses the importance of viewing attitudes in context, a viewpoint promoted by Kurt Lewin in social psychology's infancy and worth enlivening in its adulthood. This becomes more apparent when attitudes are viewed through the mindfulness-mindlessness perspective.

References

Alexander, C., Langer, E., Newman, R., & Chandler, H. (1982). *Mindfulness and meditation: An experimental intervention with the institutionalized elderly.* Unpublished manuscript, Harvard University.

Allport, G. W. (1935). Attitudes. In C. A. Murchison (Ed.), *A handbook of social psychology*. Worcester, MA: Clark University Press.

Allport, G. W. (1954). *The nature of prejudice*. Reading, MA: Addison-Wesley.

Bem, D. J. (1967). Self-perception: An alternative interpretation of cognitive dissonance phenomena. *Psychological Review, 74,* 183-200.

Bem, D. (1970). *Beliefs, attitudes and human affairs*. Belmont, CA: Brooks/Cole.

Bogardus, E. S. (1931). *Fundamentals of social psychology* (2nd ed.). New York: Century.

Boring, E. G. (1930). A new ambiguous figure. *American Journal of Psychology, 42,* 444-445.

Brehm, J. W. (1966). *A theory of psychological reactance*. New York: Academic Press.

Chanowitz, B., & Langer, E. (1981). Premature cognitive commitments. *Journal of Personality and Social Psychology, 41,* 1051-1063.

Eagly, A., & Himmelfarb, S. (1974). Current trends in attitude theory and research. In S. Himmelfarb & A. Eagly (Eds.), *Readings in attitude change*. New York: Wiley.

Festinger, L. (1957). *A theory of cognitive dissonance*. Stanford, CA: Stanford University Press.

Fishbein, M., & Ajzen, I. (1975). *Belief, attitude, intention, and behavior: An introduction to theory and research*. Reading, MA: Addison-Wesley.

Folsom, J. K. (1931). *Social psychology*. New York: Harper.

Ginsburg, G. (1980). Situated action, an emerging paradigm. In L. Wheeler (Ed.), *Review of personality and social psychology* (Vol. 1). Beverly Hills, CA: Sage.

Hastorf, A. H., Schneider, D. J., & Polefka, J. (1970). *Person perception*. Reading, MA: Addison-Wesley.

Heider, F. (1958). *The psychology of interpersonal relations*. New York: Wiley.

Jones, E. E., & Davis, K. E. (1965). From acts to dispositions: The attribution process in person perception. In L. Berkowitz (Ed.), *Advances in experimental social psychology* (Vol. 2). Academic Press.

Katz, D. (1972). Some final considerations about experimentation in social psychology. In C. McClintock (Ed.), *Experimental social psychology*. New York: Holt, Rinehart & Winston.

Kelley, H. H. (1967). Attribution theory in social psychology. In D. Levine (Ed.), *Nebraska Symposium on Motivation*. Lincoln: University of Nebraska Press.

Kiesler, C. A., Collins, B. E., & Miller, N. (1969). *Attitude change*. New York: Wiley.

Krech, D., Crutchfield, R., & Ballachey, E. (1962). *Individual in society*. New York: McGraw-Hill.

Langer, E. (1978). Rethinking the role of thought in social interaction. In J. Harvey, W. Ickes, & R. Kidd (Eds.), *New directions in attribution research* (Vol. II). Hillsdale, NJ: Lawrence Erlbaum.

Langer, E. (1980). Playing the middle against both ends: The usefulness of adult cognitive activity as a model for cognitive activity in childhood and old age. In S. Yussen (Ed.), *The development of reflection*. New York: Academic Press.

Langer, E. (1981). Old age: An artifact? In J. McGaugh & S. Kiesler (Eds.), *Aging: Biology and behavior*. New York: Academic Press.

Langer, E., Beck, P., Janoff-Bulman, R., & Timko, C. (1981). *The relationship between cognitive deprivation and longevity in senile and nonsenile elderly populations*. Unpublished manuscript, Harvard University.

Langer, E., Blank, A., & Chanowitz, B. (1978). The mindlessness of ostensibly thoughtful action: The role of placebic information in interpersonal interaction. *Journal of Personality and Social Psychology, 36,* 635-642.

Langer, E., & Imber, L. (1979). When practice makes imperfect: Debilitating effects of overlearning. *Journal of Personality and Social Psychology, 37,* 2014-2025.

Langer, E., & Imber, L. (1980). Role of mindlessness in the perception of deviance. *Journal of Personality and Social Psychology, 39,* 360-367.

Langer, E., & Newman, H. (1979). The role of mindlessness in a typical social psychological experiment. *Personality and Social Psychology Bulletin, 5,* 295-298.

Langer, E., Perlmuter, L., Chanowitz, B. C., & Rubin, R. (1982). *Two new applications of mindlessness theory: Aging and alcoholism*. Unpublished manuscript, Harvard University.

Langer, E., & Rodin, J. (1976). The effects of choice and enhanced personal responsibility for the aged. *Journal of Personality and Social Psychology, 34,* 191-198.

Langer, E., Rodin, J., Beck, P., Weinman, C., & Spitzer, L. (1979). Environmental determinants of memory improvement in late adulthood. *Journal of Personality and Social Psychology, 37,* 2003-2013.

Langer, E., & Weinman, C. (1981). When thinking disrupts intellectual performance: Mindfulness on an overlearned task. *Personality and Social Psychology Bulletin, 9,* 240-243.

Lewin, K. (1939). Field theory and experiment in social psychology. *American Journal of Sociology, 44,* 868-897.

McGuire, W. J. (1964). Inducing resistance to persuasion: Some contemporary approaches. In L. Berkowitz (Ed.), *Advances in experimental social psychology*. New York: Academic Press.

McGuire, W. J. (1973). The yin and yang of progress in social psychology: Seven koan. *Journal of Personality and Social Psychology, 26,* 446-456.

Rodin, J., and Langer, E. (1977). Long-term effects of a control-relevant intervention with the institutionalized aged. *Journal of Personality and Social Psychology, 35,* 897-902.

Rosenberg, M. J. (1956). Cognitive structure and attitudinal affect. *Journal of Abnormal and Social Psychology, 53,* 367-372.

Ross, L. (1977). The intuitive psychologist and his shortcomings: Distortions in the attribution process. In C. Berkowitz (Ed.), *Advances in experimental psychology* (Vol. 12). New York: Academic Press.

Sahakian, W. (1974). *Systematic social psychology*. New York: Chandler.

Schneider, D., Hastorf, A., & Ellsworth, P. (1979). *Person perception* (2nd ed.). Reading, MA: Addison-Wesley.

Schuman, H. (1972). Attitudes vs. actions versus attitudes vs. attitudes. *Public Opinion Quarterly, 36,* 347-354.

Schuman, H., & Johnson, M. P. (1976). Attitudes and behavior. *Annual Review of Sociology, 2,* 161-207.

Shaver, K. G. (1975). *An introduction to attribution processes*. Cambridge, MA: Winthrop.

Smith, M., Bruner, J., & White, R. (1956). *Opinions and personality*. New York: Wiley.

Staats, A. W. (1967). An outline of an integrated learning theory of attitude formation and function. In M. Fishbein (Ed.), *Readings in attitude theory and measurement*. New York: Wiley.

Thomas, W. I., & Znanieki, F. (1918). *The Polish peasant in Europe and America* (Vol. 1). Boston: Badger.

Wertheimer, M. (1944). Gestalt theory. *Social Research, 11,* 78-99.

Wicker, A. (1969). Attitudes versus action: The relationship of verbal and overt behavioral responses to attitude objects. *Journal of Social Issues, 25,* 41-78.

Zimbardo, P., & Ebbesen, E. B. (1969). *Influencing attitudes and changing behavior*. Reading, MA: Addison-Wesley.

Chapter 10

Schematic Bases of Belief Change

Jennifer Crocker, Susan T. Fiske, and Shelley E. Taylor

It is a truism of human existence that people are seldom open-minded. We approach new situations and people, bringing to bear all our past experiences, knowledge, beliefs, and feelings about similar situations and people. For example, we go to a sporting event with a wealth of knowledge about the game, the players' positions, and individual plays. That knowledge, which may have been gained through direct experience or secondhand sources, provides us with a variety of expectations about what will happen, who will be there, and what they will be like. It also guides our attention and interpretations of information while we are at the event and our memory of it after we leave.

Our knowledge about the social world is represented in cognitive structures called schemas. A schema is an abstract or generic knowledge structure, stored in memory, that specifies the defining features and relevant attributes of some stimulus domain, and the interrelations among those attributes (cf. Fiske & Linville, 1980; Hastie, 1981; Rumelhart & Ortony, 1978; Taylor & Crocker, 1981). Social schemas may be representations of types of people, social roles, or events (Cantor & Mischel, 1979; Markus, 1977; Schank & Abelson, 1977; Taylor & Crocker, 1981). Social schemas are very useful to perceivers: They help us to structure, organize, and interpret new information; they facilitate encoding, storage, and retrieval of relevant information; they can affect the time it takes to process information, and the speed with which problems can be solved. Schemas also serve interpretive and inferential functions. For example, they may fill in data that are missing or unavailable in a stimulus configuration. (For discussions of these functions, see Minsky, 1975; Neisser, 1976; Rumelhart & Ortony, 1978; Schank & Abelson, 1977; Taylor & Crocker, 1981.)

Social perceivers vary in the extent to which they have well-developed schemas for particular stimulus domains (Markus, 1977). One person highly familiar with football may have schemas for particular positions and plays, and follow the action easily, whereas an individual with no schema (aschematic) and little experience with the sport may fail to see the plays developing, and simply wish the players would stand still long enough to be counted. The functions of schemas in facilitating social information processing, as well as the liabilities of schematic processing have been discussed elsewhere in more detail (Taylor & Crocker, 1981). This chapter concerns how social schemas change.

There are two main ways that schemas can change (cf. Anderson, Kline, & Beasley, 1979). Schemas develop with increasing experience with instances. Some of those instances fit the schema very well, whereas others fit poorly. The maturing schema evolves to fit the variety of instances to which the perceiver is exposed (cf. Fiske & Dyer, 1982; Martin, Harrod, & Siehl, 1980; Taylor & Winkler, 1980). The second form of change is through exposure to incongruent information. By incongruent, we mean information that is improbable given the schema (cf. Hastie, 1981). That is, when the schema specifies that some stimulus configuration is unlikely to occur in an instantiation of the schema, that stimulus is incongruent with the schema. For example, one's schema for friendly people may specify that it is unlikely they will do something hostile. Incongruence may occur because a perceiver holds an incorrect or overgeneralized schema, and accordingly the instances to which he or she is exposed are repeatedly disconfirming. Alternatively, the environment may change so that a once correct schema no longer is. Most commonly, when the cues in an environment are conflicting or ambiguous a wrong schema may be called up for a particular instance.

In this chapter, we will be concerned with the second type of change—how and when existing knowledge structures are modified to accommodate information that is incongruent with them. First, we will consider briefly how and why schemas typically resist change and with what consequences for the social perceiver. Then, we will describe the features of schemas that can change. Next, we will address the conditions under which perceivers attend to and process incongruent information. We will consider three models of how schemas change in response to incongruent information. Then we will consider characteristics of schemas and characteristics of data that determine how and when incongruent information leads to schema change. Finally, we will discuss the relationship of the topic of schema change to social psychology's longstanding concern with attitude change.

Schemas Resist Change

Any discussion of schematic responses to inconsistent information must begin with the concepts of assimilation and accommodation articulated by Piaget (Flavell, 1963; Inhelder & Piaget, 1958). Assimilation refers to adapting the stimulus to fit the perceiver's schema. Accommodation refers to modifying or altering the schema in response to the demands of the environment. When the perceiver assimilates schema-inconsistent information into the schema, the schema resists change. Schema change occurs when the perceiver accommodates the schema to the inconsistent information. According to Piaget, assimilation and accommodation occur together as the person adapts to the environment.

Most research and theorizing about social schemas have emphasized schemas' ability to resist change by assimilating incongruent information, rather than accommodating to it. A remarkable number of studies have demonstrated the ways that social schemas can bias and distort the encoding, retention, and retrieval of schema-relevant information, as well as inferences and judgments about schema-relevant stimuli (for reviews, see Fiske & Taylor, 1984; Hastie, 1981; Nisbett & Ross, 1980; Taylor & Crocker, 1981).

The ability of social schemas to resist change is usually quite functional for the social perceiver. Stable schemas lend a sense of order, structure, and coherence to social stimuli that would otherwise be complex, unpredictable, and often overwhelming. If cognitive representations of the social world shifted in response to each piece of information that was not exactly consistent, then this order and predictability would be lost.

On the other hand, it seems clear that schemas will be dysfunctional to the perceiver if they are completely resistant to change. Sometimes people acquire schemas that are incorrect, either because they were exposed to nonrepresentative instances, because they were taught an incorrect schema, or because reality has changed and a once correct schema no longer is consistent with reality. To the extent that the schema guides decisions and behavior, operating with an incorrect schema can lead to a variety of negative consequences.

One consequence of having an incorrect schema is inefficiency. That is, the time required to process information and solve problems may be increased when the schema is incorrect for incoming information. A study by Taylor, Crocker, and D'Agostino (1978) demonstrates the consequences of having an incorrect schema for problem-solving time. Subjects were presented with attribute lists describing four people and were given the task of finding the common attribute in the four lists (i.e., the synonym). Some subjects were told that the four people had the same occupation (e.g., salesmen), which presumably activated subjects' schema for the occupation, and suggested an attribute the four people might have in common (e.g., extroverted). Sometimes this clue was, in fact, useful for finding the correct answer (i.e., the common attribute was related to the activated schema) but in other cases it suggested the wrong answer. When the clue suggested the wrong schema, the common attribute was not related to the activated schema. It took subjects significantly longer to find the common attribute when the clue suggested the wrong schema than when the clue suggested the right schema (see also Bruner & Potter, 1964).

A second possible consequence of having an incorrect schema is inaccuracy. People may so distort incoming information to be consistent with the schema that they make serious errors of inference. One domain in which schemas may affect inferences is in psychiatric intake decisions. Langer and Abelson (1974) had therapists listen to a tape of two men interacting, having told one group of subjects that the tape was a job interview, and another group that the tape was a psychiatric intake interview. Subjects "found" more pathology in the target individual when they believed they had heard a psychiatric intake interview than when they believed they had heard a job interview. Once a schema has been incorrectly applied, and decisions based on that schema have been made, it may be very difficult to disconfirm the schema and reverse the consequences of the decision. In the case of the "mentally ill" schema, once an individual has been committed to an institution, there may be very little he or she can do that "proves" that the label is incorrect (Rosenhan, 1973).

A further consequence of having an incorrect schema, which compounds the seriousness of the error, is that once the schema has been misapplied the perceiver may actually alter reality to fit the schema. In the case of mental illness, institutionalization itself may produce "secondary deviance" that confirms the label (Schur, 1980). This "self-fulfilling prophecy" effect has been demonstrated in a variety of contexts, including the effect of teacher expectations on student performance (Rosenthal & Jacobson, 1968), the effect of anticipating that another will be hostile or competitive upon subsequent behavior toward that person (Snyder & Swann, 1978), the effect of believing that attractive people are charming and bright (Snyder, Tanke, & Berscheid, 1977) and the effect of stereotyped expectations on interracial interaction (Word, Zanna, & Cooper, 1974). (See Darley & Fazio, 1980, for a review.)

Given the high costs of having an incorrect schema, it is fortunate that schemas can and do accommodate in response to new information. Although previous research and theorizing have emphasized the "theory-driven" quality of schematic processing (i.e., the distortion of information to fit the theory or schema), it is also the case that social information processing can be "data-driven." That is, schemas are at least somewhat responsive to the characteristics of the stimuli that they process (Neisser, 1976; Rumelhart & Norman, 1978; Rumelhart & Ortony, 1977). Simply stated, people learn things, and one form that learning takes is the modification of existing knowledge structures in response to disconfirming information.

Features of Schemas that Can Change

Any discussion of schema change raises the issue of what elements or characteristics of schemas could be altered in response to incongruent information. Answering this question depends on describing what a schema is, and what it looks like. In this section we will sketch out what the components or features of a schema are, and how these features may change in response to incongruent information.

Schemas have variables

A schema specifies the relevant attributes of some stimulus domain. We will call those features and attributes "variables" after Rumelhart and Norman (1978). A schema for birthday parties, for example, might include the attribute "refreshments." Refreshments are a variable, in the sense that they can vary in quantity, type, and so forth. Any particular instantiation of the schema "birthday party" will provide specific values for the variable. For example, at one birthday party, the refreshments might be chocolate cake, chocolate chip ice cream, and coffee. Schemas differ in their complexity (i.e., the number of uncorrelated variables they have), and perceivers may differ in the complexity of the schemas they have for the same stimulus domain (Linville, 1982a, 1982b; Linville & Jones, 1980).

One way that schemas can change is that variables can be added to or dropped from the schema. This type of change might occur when one is exposed to a new set of instances that consistently have some new feature or fail to include some old expected feature of the schema. Alternatively, exposure to such new data might simply lead to a change in the *strength* of association between a given attribute and the schema (Anderson, Kline, & Beasley, 1979).

Variables have default values

Perhaps the most widely agreed upon feature of schemas is that there are "expected" or "default" values associated with the schema's variables (Minsky, 1975; Rumelhart & Norman, 1978; Rumelhart & Ortony, 1977; Schank & Abelson, 1977; Taylor & Crocker, 1981). When a schema is incompletely instantiated, the schema fills in missing information with default values. For example, the default value for refreshments at a birthday party might be cake and ice cream. When information that is incongruent with the schema is encountered, one aspect of the schema that can change is the default value for a variable. Default values may, however, be rather difficult to change. A single instance that contains a nondefault value (e.g., cheesecake for refreshments) does not directly contradict the default option, because the default only holds true, by definition, when no other value is specified. Similarly, an instance that happens to have no value specified does not contradict the default. Thus, many instances with incongruent values may be needed in order to change the default. Later we will address the issue of how great a quantity of incongruent instances, and in what form, are required to change the default values of a schema.

Variables have constraint values

Another feature of schemas that may change is constraint values; that is, variables have some range of possible values that they can assume. Not every instantiation will match the expected values for the variables, and so there are constraints or limits on what values are acceptable (Rumelhart & Norman, 1978). Those constraints may be "fuzzy" limits rather than strictly defined ones (Rosch & Mervis, 1975; Rosch, Mervis, Gray, Johnson, & Boyes-Brehm, 1976). Values on variables are probabilistically associated with the schema. The constraint values determine decisions about what is and what is not an instantiation of the schema (Freid & Holyoak, in press), and they may be interdependent. For example, one's schema for "birthday party" may have a variable for refreshments, which has as default values that there be cake and ice cream. A gathering may be an instance of a birthday party if it has either cake or cake and ice cream, but if it has ice cream only, it may have to be recategorized because the value of the refreshment variable falls outside the acceptable constraints. Nevertheless, repeated exposure to ice cream only birthday parties may change that particular constraint. Thus, another way that schemas can change in response to incongruent information is that the constraint values associated with variables can change, as by expanding through repeated contact with less expected values.

Variables have interrelations

In addition to specifying the default and constraint values for variables, the schema specifies how variables are related to one another. Variables may be related in time (cf. Schank & Abelson, 1977), in space (cf. Minsky, 1975), they may be correlated (Medin, Altom, Edelson, & Freko, 1982), or they may be causally related (Read, 1983; Schank & Abelson, 1977). For example, one's schema for a birthday party may specify that the games are played before the food is eaten, that the ice cream is served on top of the cake, that the smaller the box the nicer the present, and that eating too much cake and ice cream can make one sick. These relationships among variables may change in response to incongruent information.

Schemas have vertical and horizontal structure

Schemas include information that has two types of structure. By vertical structure we mean the number of levels of abstraction contained in the schema. At the most abstract level is a generic concept (e.g., birthday party) that has typical features (e.g., a gathering to celebrate someone's birthday) and relevant attributes (e.g., refreshments, birthday person). At the most abstract level (i.e., the generic concept), the constraint values associated with the variables may accept a wide range of values (e.g., the birthday person could be anyone). A schema with vertical structure will have more specific levels within it and the number of levels of abstraction may vary from schema to schema (Cantor & Mischel, 1979; Rosch, 1978; Schank & Abelson, 1977). For example, one's birthday party schema may include more specific information about types of birthday parties, such as a child's or an adult's birthday party. The default values for refreshments at a child's birthday party (e.g., cake and ice cream) may be quite different from default values for refreshments at an adult's birthday party (e.g., alcohol and hors d'oeuvres). Someone with a lot of experience with birthday parties (e.g., a caterer) might have many levels of abstraction in his or her schema for birthday parties, including very specific types (e.g., under adult birthday party, a movie star's birthday party, and a businessman's birthday party, etc.). One way that schemas can change is to develop more vertical structure, or more levels of abstraction.

Change in vertical structure is likely to occur in conjunction with changes in the horizontal structure of the schema. By horizontal structure we mean the number of different subcategories at any given level of abstraction. One way schemas may respond to incongruent information is to create a more differentiated structure by adding subcategories at a more specific level of abstraction. For example, one's schema for birthday parties might specify that close friends and relatives attend. One might subsequently learn that hundreds of strangers and acquaintances attended a movie star's birthday party. In response to this new information, one's birthday party schema might develop subcategories for more specific types of birthday parties: birthday parties for common folk and birthday parties for celebrities. Alternatively, schemas could change by subtracting subcategories, if some of the existing subcategories were never used.

Schemas may include particular instantiations of the schema

The most specific level of a schema may consist of specific instances or exemplars of the schema. Generally, the instances that are stored with the schema will be "good examples" of the schema, with instantiations of variables that are probably quite close to the default values for the schema (e.g., Rosch, 1978). For example, when one's schema for birthday parties is evoked, the example of your 30th birthday party may become available in memory. When the perceiver encounters information inconsistent with the schema, the particular instances stored with the schema may change. The implications of change at a specific level of a schema for representations at higher levels of abstraction is an issue to which we will return in a later section.

Thus, there are many elements of a schema that could potentially change in response to incongruent information. Variables can be added to or dropped from a schema, the default values associated with variables can change, the vertical and horizontal structure of the schema can change, and the particular instances associated with the schema can change. Since schemas are responsive to disconfirming feedback from the environment, at least under some circumstances, it is crucial to determine when people will process incongruence and when they will ignore it. It appears that people frequently attend to incongruent information, but only sometimes process it fully.

When Will Incongruent Information Receive Attention?

A large volume of research suggests that people's attention is drawn to stimuli that are incongruent with their expectations. As early as Titchener (1908), people were hypothesized to attend to rare or strange stimuli, that is, those that are incongruent with their expectations. Later theories also suggested that novel (i.e., unexpected) stimuli attract attention (e.g., Berlyne, 1970). In social settings, incongruent people and incongruent attributes of people capture attention (McArthur, 1981; Taylor & Fiske, 1978). Although much of this research concerns attention to stimuli that are statistically infrequent or improbable, stimuli that are improbable with respect to a particular schema also attract attention (Crocker & Vitkus, 1983; Fiske & Gup, 1980). Overall, then, there is substantial basis for the hypothesis that schema-incongruent information attracts more attention than schema-congruent information.

Although incongruent stimuli may initially draw attention, they are not always fully processed. When do people make the effort to incorporate incongruent information into a schema? Three conditions should affect whether or not perceivers incorporate incongruent information: current processing load, organization of schematic material, and motivation. All of these hinge on the perceiver's committing additional resources, beyond what would be necessary if the information were congruent, as will be seen.

First, the current processing load must allow the perceiver to invest the extra time needed to handle the incongruent information (Hastie, 1981). Evidence that incongruent information takes longer to process than congruent information comes from a study by Brewer, Dull, and Lui (1981). They gave subjects information that was congruent or incongruent with their old-person stereotype. In forming an impression of an elderly woman, incongruent phrases such as "has a lot of nervous energy," "runs a small business," and "keeps up with fashions in dress" took longer to process than did congruent information such as "likes to knit" or "is a good cook" (see also Crocker & Vitkus, 1983).

If increased processing time must be spent on incongruent information, then it follows that any pressure on an individual to process information quickly will favor processing of congruent over incongruent information. Thus, incongruent information is likely to be processed if a person is not under time pressure and/or if he or she is not simultaneously trying to process a lot of other information. Support for this hypothesis is provided by Srull (1981) who found that, consistent with previous studies, incongruent information is more likely to be recalled than congruent information, suggesting that incongruent information receives more processing than congruent information. (This finding will be discussed at length later in this chapter.) More relevant to the present discussion is Srull's further finding that the advantage of incongruent items in memory disappears when subjects are required to allocate a portion of their processing capacity to an irrelevant task. Apparently, incongruent information receives additional processing only when processing capacity is not taxed by other demands.

Given a low capacity load, the individual must also have the ability to make sense of the incongruent information. Specifically, a person must have a well-developed understanding of schema-congruent information before being able to handle incongruent information. In support of this point, Fiske, Kinder, and Larter (1983) found that experts in politics were more able to process incongruent information than were novices in politics. For example, when confronted with a communist country that did not fit their schema for communism, experts focused on the incongruent information. They recalled more inconsistent information, and they moderated their judgments according to the extent that they organized their memories around the inconsistencies. Novices, in contrast, showed a rather indiscriminate use of the schema, applying it despite its incongruence with the data (see also Taylor & Winkler, 1980).

Why does expertise lead people to process incongruent information more effectively? One possible reason concerns the fact that the schematic knowledge of experts is more practiced than that of novices and forms a more compact unit in memory (Chase & Simon, 1973; Hayes-Roth, 1977). In dealing with new information, the expert has compact knowledge structures containing congruent information that can be used efficiently and with little strain on processing capacity. Thus, there is enough capacity left over to deal as well with the incongruent information (Fiske et al., 1983). Hence, experts (or schematics) may be able both to organize information into larger units, or "chunks," and to attend to important details such as incongruencies better than novices, or aschematics. In contrast, novices have less practiced, less compact, and more fragile schemas that may occupy more of their on-line capacity; thus, there may be enough capacity to process new incoming congruent information, but not the additional amount needed for incongruent information.

A recent study by Markus, Smith, and Moreland (1983) supports the notion that individuals who have well-developed schemas on some social domain are like experts. They found that people who had self-schemas on a dimension tended to organize schema-relevant information about others into larger chunks than aschematics. However, schematics also showed greater flexibility in their organization of information. When asked to, they could also organize into smaller chunks than could aschematics. Thus, the ability of experts to process schema-relevant information efficiently may free up capacity to process incongruent information.

Finally, for incongruent information to be fully processed, the perceiver's motivation or goals have to favor accuracy over maintenance of the schema. Unfortunately, little research has addressed what conditions might prompt an accuracy orientation. One likely condition is outcome-dependency; that is, when one's outcomes are directly dependent upon one's inferences, one may be highly motivated to be accurate. In fact, preliminary evidence suggests that outcome-dependency does encourage attention to incongruent information (Erber & Fiske, 1983).

Task demands may also influence the motivation to process incongruent information. Surprisingly, deliberate attempts to learn information accurately may result in less processing of incongruent information than other goals a perceiver might have. In one study, subjects who were instructed to remember information as accurately as they could were less likely to recall information that was incongruent with an impression than subjects who were instructed to form an impression based on the same information (Srull, 1981). In general, tasks that require integration of incongruent information with a schema may result in high levels of processing of incongruent information (cf. Bernstein & Schul, 1983; Hastie & Kumar, 1979).

When people have the time, capacity, and motivation, they will attend to and process incongruent information. However, attention may be a necessary but not a sufficient condition for incongruent information to produce schema change. In fact, in some cases, greater attention to incongruent information may be related to less change in the schema (Crocker & Vitkus, 1983). Just as crucial as whether people attend to incongruent information is the issue of what they do with it once they have attended to it. In the next section, we will review how incongruent information, once attended to, may lead to changes in a schema.

Models of Schema Change

Now that we have reviewed briefly the features of schemas that can change, as well as when people will attend to incongruencies, which features actually do change when the perceiver attends to information incongruent with the schema? Information may be incongruent with a very specific level of a schema, or with more abstract levels. For example, information may contradict the instances stored with the schema, or information may contradict generalities about the entire category.

Change in the instances stored with the schema

When information contradicts an instance stored with a schema, will the instance be revised or eliminated? For example, a schema for a particular type of person may have associated with it specific examples of that type of person. What will happen if one of those individuals behaves in a way that is incongruent with the schema? Will the representation of the instance be revised but kept within the schema, or will the instance be moved to a new location in memory? Will the schema change at more abstract levels? Will the incongruent information about the instance be stored with the schema?

Generally, when information is incongruent with the schema, the information may be dismissed as "bad data," and the instance stored with the schema will not be revised. In schemas for types of people, for example, when an individual who exemplifies the schema behaves in a way that is incongruent with the schema, the behavior may be attributed to situational or unstable causes (Crocker, Hannah, & Weber, 1983; Deaux & Emswiller, 1974; Feldman-Summers & Kiesler, 1974; Hayden & Mischel, 1976; Kulik, 1983). Thus, the incongruent behavior may have little effect on either the representation of the individual (Crocker et al., 1983) or more abstract levels of the schema.

Sometimes, an incongruent behavior may, in fact, be judged to be typical of the individual. Attribution theorists have spelled out a variety of contextual factors that might lead a perceiver to conclude that a behavior reflects enduring characteristics of an individual. For example, if the behavior is consistent over time and across stimuli and is different from how others behave in that situation, the behavior will be attributed to dispositional causes (Kelley, 1967). In this case, the representation or impression of the individual may be revised, and the instance may be no longer stored with the schema; however, the more abstract levels of the schema might remain intact if the individual is judged to be unrepresentative of the schema.

Change in the abstract levels of a schema

How does change at the specific levels of a schema relate to change at more abstract levels? When will information about incongruent instances lead to changes at more abstract levels of the schema? What features of the schema will change in response to these incongruent instances? Three models of when and how schemas change at more abstract levels have been suggested.

Rothbart (1981) has suggested two models for how schemas may respond to incongruent information. These models originally were developed to explain how stereotypes change in response to new information, but they can also be applied to changes in other types of social schemas. The first model, which Rothbart calls the *bookkeeping* model, suggests that change occurs gradually. The default values are adjusted each time an incongruent instance is encountered. In this view, schema revision is a gradual incremental process of minor adjustments or "tuning" in response to each new piece of information (see also Rumelhart & Norman, 1978).

The second model, called the *conversion* model, involves sudden "all-or-none" change. According to the conversion model, instances that are only slightly or moderately incongruent with the schema are assimilated into the schema, and the schema does not accommodate in response to them. Salient, dramatically incongruent instances produce sudden schema revision. When such an instance is encountered, the revision is drastic, similar to the change that occurs during a religious conversion. Conversion may involve either major shifts in default values for variables or the addition or subtraction of variables. The horizontal and vertical structure of the schema remains unaffected by the conversion process. In other words, the number of levels of abstraction, and the number of subcategories at each level in the schema remain the same. Rothbart suggests that, at least with respect to stereotyping, the conversion model is a more accurate description of schema change than the bookkeeping model.

A third model, called *subtyping*, involves the development of subcategories in response to incongruent information (e.g., some engineers are interesting, but most engineers are dull and conservative) (cf. Taylor, 1981). According to this model, incongruent information changes the horizontal and vertical structure of the schema. The schema accommodates the new information by developing new subcategories at a more specific level of abstraction. The new subcategories all have the defining features of the schema (they are engineers), but other attributes that had previously been associated with the entire category (they are dull) are now associated with only a subset of the category; and a new set of perhaps contradictory attributes (they are interesting) is associated with another subset. This type of schema change can be visualized as a branching out of the schema changing from more general, all-encompassing categories to more and more specific, and smaller subcategories. Taylor (1981) has suggested that when stereotypes are disconfirmed we do not merely discard the stereotype or adjust it on some continuum, but develop a subcategory for the disconfirming individuals.

A study by Weber and Crocker (1983) attempted to determine which model of schema change (conversion, bookkeeping, or subtyping) best describes how schemas change when incongruent information is encountered. They gave subjects information about individuals who were members of stereotyped occupations (in this study, librarians and corporate lawyers). Three behaviors of each individual were described, and in the total set of behaviors, one-third were incongruent with the stereotype. The way the incongruent behaviors were distributed across the individuals was varied. In some conditions the incongruent information was dispersed so that each individual performed one incongruent behavior. In other conditions the incongruent information was concentrated within a few individuals, such that one-third of the individuals completely disconfirmed the stereotype, and two-thirds completely confirmed it.

According to the *bookkeeping model*, each item of disconfirming behavior is attended to and incorporated into the schema, regardless of how it is distributed across individuals. Thus, the bookkeeping model predicts equal amounts of schema change in the dispersed and concentrated conditions. According to the *conversion model*, only the dramatically disconfirming instances will lead to revision of the schema. Thus, schema change should be greater when the incongruent information is concentrated within a few individuals rather than dispersed across many. The *subtyping model* predicts the opposite result. According to this model, when all the disconfirming behaviors are concentrated within a few individuals, those individuals will be seen as a separate subcategory, different from the majority of category members. In other words, they will be seen as the exceptions that prove the rule. The schema will still be considered valid for most category members. Thus, the subtyping model predicts more change when the incongruent information is dispersed across many individuals than when it is concentrated in a few.

The results supported the subtyping model. Stereotypes changed more when the incongruent information was dispersed than when it was concentrated. Furthermore, when asked to sort descriptions of all the individuals into meaningfully distinct groups, subjects in the concentrated conditions tended to sort all of the disconfirming individuals into a single pile, further suggesting that they had developed a subcategory for those individuals. When the disconfirming information was dispersed across group members, disconfirming individuals could not be subtyped, and the stereotype changed in accord with the bookkeeping model.

The results of the Weber and Crocker (1983) study suggest that the subtyping model may be the best description of how schemas change when incongruent information is concentrated, and the bookkeeping model may describe how schemas change when incongruent information is dispersed across many instances (see also Crocker & Weber, 1983). However, it seems likely that the conversion model describes schema change under certain conditions not investigated in this study. Both religious conversions and scientific revolutions appear to follow the conversion model (Kuhn, 1962). One interesting aspect of both religious conversions and scientific revolutions is that the old schema seems to be tossed out only when there is a new one available to replace it. A similar suggestion has been made with regard to stereotypes (Rose, 1981). Complete revision of a schema may occur more easily when there is a new fully developed schema available. Determining the circumstances under which each of the models applies is a task for future studies.

Characteristics of Schemas that Lead to or Resist Change

To this point, we have discussed the processes of schema change as if all schemas are essentially the same, and as if all of them change in similar ways under similar conditions. The issue of schema change is, however, complicated by the fact that schemas differ in important ways that cause them to respond to incongruent information differently. As we will see, the level of schema development, the accessibility of a schema, and the disconfirmability of a schema all affect its response to incongruent information.

Well-developed schemas resist change

One determinant of responsiveness to incongruent information is how well-developed the schema is. Individual differences in knowledge range along a continuum from no experience (the person uninitiated with regard to a particular schema) to a person possessing rudimentary knowledge (i.e., a novice) to one who has well-developed knowledge about the schema (i.e., an expert). Degree of experience will have important effects on schematic processing: Expertise affects the quantity, organization, compactness, and use of schematic knowledge, and therefore affects responses to incongruent information.

Experience-based differences in knowledge demonstrate that well-developed schemas contain more information. For example, we are all experts on ourselves, and that means that self-schemas contain many schema-relevant instances and much other detail (Markus, 1977; Markus, Crane, Bernstein, & Siladi, 1982; Markus & Smith, 1981; Markus, Smith, & Moreland, 1983). To the extent that people are experts about a domain, they have more information about it along more dimensions (Chase & Simon, 1973; Chi & Koeske, in press; Hinsley, Hayes, & Simon, 1977; Larkin, McDermott, Simon, & Simon, 1980; Linville, 1982a, 1982b; Linville & Jones, 1980; Neves & Anderson, 1981). Well-developed schemas contain large quantities of schema-congruent information. For an expert, then, any single piece of incongruent information confronts a vast store of congruent information in memory. As a consequence, incongruence is simply less likely to have an impact on the schema than if there were fewer pieces of prior knowledge available (e.g., Markus, 1977).

Furthermore, because they include more information and are based on more experience, experts' schemas may in fact be better adapted to fit reality. In practice then, it may be more difficult to disconfirm the schema of an expert than that of a novice. Should reality change, however, who would be better able to detect that change, an expert or a novice? Experts have more capacity to attend to information incongruent with their schema (Fiske et al., 1983), but they also have a larger store of congruent information, and may also be committed to the schema because they use it often. Novices may lack the processing capacity to attend to incongruence, but their schemas are not shored up by a vast store of congruent information, and they may be less committed to their schemas. No research that we are aware of has investigated this point, but it would seem important to know whether experts or novices are better able to detect a change in reality.

Well-developed or expert schemas also involve more organization. That is, there are more links and stronger links among the components of expert knowledge. If change does occur in one aspect of the well-developed schema, then, it has more repercussions for other aspects of the schema. Thus, for an expert, change has higher costs than for a novice.

Accessibility of the schema

Many social stimuli can be processed with reference to any of a number of schemas. For example, an acquaintance may be thought of as a woman, a lawyer, a skier, or an extrovert. Which schema is used depends on the accessibility of the schemas. There is evidence that schemas may be more or less easily retrieved or accessible to the perceiver (see Higgins & King, 1981; Higgins, King, & Mavin, 1982; Srull & Wyer, 1980; Wyer & Srull, 1981). Consequently, new information may be processed with respect to one or some of the schemas that are potentially relevant, but not all of them.

The importance of schema accessibility for belief change lies in the fact that information that is incongruent with a schema will not change a schema that has not been activated. For example, meeting a white male Protestant psychologist who jogs and expresses his feelings will not change our stereotype that males do not express their feelings if we encode him as an expressive psychologist or an expressive jogger. Several factors can influence the degree of accessibility of a particular schema.

One determinant of schema accessibility is whether the schema has been used *recently*. A study by Carlston (1980) illustrates this point. Subjects made judgments about either helpfulness or dishonesty. Later, subjects were exposed to an ambiguous behavior that could be interpreted either as helpful or dishonest (giving another student the answer to an exam question). Subjects who had previously made helpfulness judgments saw the behavior more positively and rated the person as more helpful, whereas subjects who had made dishonesty judgments saw the person as more dishonest.

The *frequency* with which a schema is used also influences its accessibility perhaps because a schema that is activated frequently is likely to have been activated recently (Higgins & King, 1981; Higgins, King, & Mavin, 1982; Srull & Wyer, 1980; Wyer & Srull, 1981). Variations in frequency of activation, over time, may lead to stable individual differences in the accessibility of schemas for different perceivers. Higgins and King (1981; Higgins, King, & Mavin, 1982) have demonstrated that individuals differ in the constructs they use to describe others, and that the constructs that are accessible to a perceiver are related to the kinds of information the perceiver has retained about others.

Self-schemas also may be viewed as reflecting individual differences in schema accessibility. Markus and her colleagues (Markus & Smith, 1981; Markus, Smith, & Moreland, 1983) have argued that the schemas we bring to bear in processing information about others are those that are important to our self-concepts. In one study, Markus and Fong (1979) showed that subjects who are schematic with respect to independence for themselves make more extreme judgments about the independence of another person than do subjects who are aschematic. Schematics also tend to "chunk" behavior of others into larger units, to make more trait inferences about the behavior, and to engage in more conjecture about behavior when the other's behavior is relevant to the self-schema (Markus, Smith, & Moreland, 1983). Such individual differences in schema accessibility may affect the way perceivers respond to incongruent information, but there is no evidence on this point to date.

Finally, contextual features of the stimulus may make a particular schema more accessible. A stimulus that is distinctive may elicit a schema that is relevant to that distinctiveness. That is, people are likely to categorize themselves and others along dimensions that make them stand out from their current context. For example, people describe themselves along dimensions on which they are distinctive (McGuire, McGuire, Child, & Fujioka, 1978; McGuire & Padawer-Singer, 1976). For another example, a black in an otherwise white group is more likely to elicit the schema "black person" than a black in a group of mixed racial composition or an all black group (Taylor, Fiske, Close, Anderson, & Ruderman, 1975; see Taylor, 1981).

To summarize, schema accessibility is determined by the perceiver's recency and frequency of activating a particular schema and by the features of context that make a given schema salient. Thus, some schemas are not activated frequently or recently and some are not salient in context; these schemas are unlikely to change even if incongruent information is available, simply because the information is unlikely to be processed in regard to those schemas.

Disconfirmability of the schema

One way that schemas differ is that some schemas are more easily disconfirmed than others. There are two types of disconfirmability that a schema may have: It may be logically disconfirmable, and it may be practically disconfirmable. These two kinds of disconfirmability emphasize different issues in the disconfirmation process.

A *logically disconfirmable* schema specifies what stimuli should not occur given the schema. For example, birds do not have teeth, and honest people do not cheat. A logically undisconfirmable schema is less specific about what should not occur. For example, the layperson's schema for a mentally ill person includes the belief that the person will be unpredictable (Nunnally, 1961). This makes the schema quite vague about what a mentally ill person should *not* do in any particular situation. Similarly, the schema for devious person is vague about what should not occur in an instance of the category.

Of course, logical disconfirmability is not an all-or-none attribute of a schema. Rather, schemas vary along a continuum of how specific they are about what should not occur given the schema. Although no research has yet investigated the disconfirmability of social schemas, work by Reeder and Brewer (1979), which identifies different types of trait concepts, is consistent with the notion that some schemas are more logically disconfirmable than others. Reeder and Brewer were concerned with the correspondence between traits and behaviors that could be expected for different traits. Some traits ("partially restrictive" traits) are associated with a rather wide range of behaviors. A person's standing on the trait is determined by the average behavior he or she shows in a variety of situations. For example, "friendly" does not require that a person be outgoing every moment, only that he or she be so on the average. Partially restrictive traits are relatively difficult to disconfirm, because a wide range of behaviors could be consistent with an average standing on the trait. Disconfirmation would require observation of a large number of incongruent behaviors.

"Hierarchically restrictive" traits are traits for which one extreme is behaviorally restricted, and the other is not. For example, an intelligent person may do both intelligent and unintelligent things, but an unintelligent person will not do very intelligent things. Hierarchically restrictive traits are disconfirmable at the restricted extreme, and relatively undisconfirmable at the unrestricted extreme.

The third type of trait that Reeder and Brewer identify is the "fully restrictive" trait, in which "possession of a specific dispositional position on the attribute continuum implies performance of only a narrow range of behavior that is congruent with that disposition" (1979, p. 69). An example of a fully restrictive trait is "neat," because a single disconfirmation would call into question the accuracy of the trait label. Fully restrictive traits are the most disconfirmable of the three types.

Reeder and Brewer's classification of trait concepts could be extended to schemas in general. The disconfirmability of schemas may determine the way they respond to incongruent information. For example, partially restrictive schemas may change according to the bookkeeping model (because all instances are observed and averaged); hierarchically restrictive schemas may change according to the conversion model (because one incongruent behavior shifts the person to a new location on the continuum); and fully restrictive schemas may change according to the subtyping model (because if two different behaviors are observed, they must reflect different subcategories).

The second type of disconfirmability that a schema may have is *practical disconfirmability*. That is, independent of logical issues, how likely is it that a perceiver will have the opportunity to obtain incongruent information? Rothbart and Park (1982) have investigated the disconfirmability of traits, and their analysis examines the likelihood that the perceiver will have the opportunity to observe disconfirming behavior. For example, if a perceiver thinks someone is cowardly, it may be difficult to disconfirm that impression because opportunities for bravery are few and far between. Conversely, opportunities for disconfirming the trait "friendly" are more frequently available.

These two types of disconfirmability suggest that schemas may not change for two reasons. Schemas that are not logically disconfirmable will not change because there is no type of instance that is clearly incongruent with them. Schemas that are not practically disconfirmable will not change because the perceiver may never have the opportunity to observe a disconfirmation. Schemas that are logically disconfirmable, however, will change in response to incongruent information, and schemas that are practically disconfirmable will have frequent opportunities for disconfirmation.

Characteristics of Data that Produce Schema Change

The way that a schema responds to incongruent information depends not only on characteristics of the schema, it also depends on qualities of the information itself. In this section, we will explore some qualities of incongruent information that influence the way a schema changes. The qualities to be considered are the amount of discrepancy between the schema and the incongruent information, the ambiguity of the information, the organization of the information, and the memorability of the information.

Discrepancy between the schema and the new information

Perhaps the most important feature of new information with respect to schema change is the degree of discrepancy between the new information and the schema. What degree of discrepancy is most likely to produce change? Attitude change theorists of the 1950s addressed a similar issue in their studies on the effects of varying degrees of discrepancy between a communication and a person's initial opinion on attitude change. In their classic work on this topic, Sherif and Hovland (1961) conclude that, in general, the greater the degree of discrepancy between a communication and the receiver's initial opinion, the more opinion change will result. However, with increasing discrepancy, the amount of change relative to that advocated by the communication decreases. Moreover, with topics that are highly involving to the receiver, extremely discrepant communications may result in little or no opinion change, or even change in the direction opposite to that advocated by the communication (Sherif & Hovland, 1961).

Why would extreme discrepancy between a communication and one's initial opinion result in no change or even change in the direction opposite to the communication? Sherif and Hovland (1961) invoke the concepts of "latitude of acceptance" and "latitude of rejection" to explain these findings. In essence, they argue that communications close to the receiver's initial opinion can be assimilated into that opinion. Communications that are discrepant are contrasted with the receiver's opinion, and judged to be more extreme than objectively warranted. As a result, the discrepant communication is evaluated more negatively, and is judged less impartial and fair than the communication that is close to the receiver's opinion. In Piaget's terms, when stimuli are slightly or moderately discrepant with a schema both assimilation and accommodation occur. The new information is assimilated to the perceiver's opinion, and the perceiver adjusts his or her opinion to accommodate to the information. When stimuli are extremely discrepant, however, neither assimilation nor accommodation occurs. Instead, the discrepant communication is rejected.

Recent evidence suggests that schematic processing may underlie these assimilation and contrast effects. That is, information that is either very similar or very dissimilar to one's own opinion may be more easily processed than information that is moderately discrepant. Judd and Kulik (1980) found that subjects made faster judgments about and better recalled information that they either strongly agreed with or strongly disagreed with relative to information that fell between these poles. Thus, when very discrepant information is encountered, people may easily identify that information as falling in their latitude of rejection, and discount that information. Moderately discrepant information, on the other hand, may receive more attention and thought. Because moderately discrepant information demands thought, and because it is nearer to the latitude of acceptance, it may be more likely to be accommodated after the cognitive laboring is over.

One caution is in order in generalizing these findings to other types of social schemas. Attitude schemas may be particularly likely to assimilate relevant information to a bipolar subjective agree-disagree dimension (Judd & Harackiewicz, 1980; Judd & Kulik, 1980). When a communication is discrepant with an attitude schema, the subjective, agree-disagree nature of the schema enables the recipient to deny the validity of the communication, that is, to reject it. For other types of schemas, moderately discrepant information may be processed more readily than very discrepant information. Information that is highly discrepant with other types of schemas may not be so easily rejected. For example, if your impression of a person was that he was kind, friendly, and warm, and you saw him verbally attack a student, it would be difficult to say, "That isn't true" because of the relatively objective nature of the information. In cases where discrepant information cannot easily be rejected, highly discrepant information may require more cognitive activity (e.g., explaining the behavior and integrating it into an impression) than moderately discrepant information. Further research on this issue is needed to clarify the relationship between discrepancy and schema change.

Ambiguity of the inconsistent information

A second feature of inconsistent information that may determine its impact on a schema is the ambiguity of the information. Information may be ambiguous because crucial aspects of a stimulus configuration are missing (cf. Minsky, 1975; Neisser, 1976), because the information fits more than one schema equally well (cf. Owens, Bower, & Black, 1979; Snyder & Uranowitz, 1978), because there are conflicting cues in the information (i.e., the information is contradictory; cf. Lord, Ross, & Lepper, 1979), or because it is literally out of focus (Bruner & Potter, 1964).

In general, discrepant information must be unambiguous to produce schema change. Ambiguous information tends to be assimilated into the existing schema, rather than changing it. This phenomenon has been demonstrated with a variety of materials, and a variety of operationalizations of ambiguity (e.g., Cohen, 1981; Lord, Ross, & Lepper, 1979; Owens, Bower, & Black 1979). When ambiguous discrepant information is assimilated to an existing schema, the information may strengthen rather than change the schema.

This phenomenon was demonstrated in a study by Lord, Ross, and Lepper (1979). Subjects who strongly favored or strongly opposed the death penalty read the results of two studies that reported conflicting results concerning whether the death sentence is a deterrent to potential murderers. Results indicated that whichever study supported their own position was perceived by subjects to be more convincing and better conducted than the study that opposed their view. As a consequence, following exposure to the information, subjects held their initial beliefs even more strongly. Presumably, the study that was consistent with the subject's own opinion fell into the subject's latitude of acceptance, and he or she accommodated to it. The study that was discrepant fell into the latitude of rejection, and was neither assimilated nor accommodated.

The organization of new information

New information that is incongruent with an existing schema may have different degrees of impact on the schema, depending on how the new information is organized. Some organizational factors that matter include the information's dispersion and redundancy. As previously noted, information that is incongruent with a schema may be concentrated in a few extremely incongruent instances, or it may be dispersed across many moderately incongruent instances. A study by Weber and Crocker (1983), cited previously, indicates that the way disconfirming information is dispersed has two consequences: First, subjects estimated that they had seen *more* incongruent information when the information was dispersed, rather than concentrated; second, the pattern of results suggested that extremely incongruent instances were seen as the "exceptions that prove the rule," and were classified or categorized as a qualitatively different type of instance. On the other hand, when many instances were moderately incongruent, it was apparently more difficult to dismiss the instances as "exceptions." Therefore, when discrepant information was dispersed, the schema changed more than when it was concentrated within a few instances (see also Crocker & Weber, 1983).

Under some conditions, perceivers may have difficulty keeping track of how the incongruent information is organized. For example, when there is a lot of information, placing a high load on memory, perceivers may use a strategy of attending simply to how much information is incongruent, and pay less attention to how the information is organized. A study by Weber and Crocker (1983, Study 3) provides support for this hypothesis. They found that when instances relevant to a schema were interspersed with instances relevant to other schemas, thus placing more demands on subjects' memory processes, concentrated and dispersed incongruent information were equally effective at changing the schema. Apparently, the increased demands on subjects' memories caused them to shift their strategey for organizing the information from attending to how the incongruent information was organized, to simply attending to how much information was incongruent, regardless of how it was organized.

A similar issue concerns how perceivers deal with redundant information. Presumably, a single instance of incongruent information should have the same impact on a schema, whether we encounter the instance once or several times. Even considering that the instance may be seen as more valid or reliable if we encounter it several times, it should have less impact on the schema than several different incongruent instances each encountered once. A study by Rothbart and his colleagues investigated the effect of redundant information under conditions of high versus low memory load (Rothbart, Fulero, Jensen, Howard, & Birrell, 1978). In their study, subjects learned about the traits of members of a group. In some conditions, subjects were exposed to information about the same members several times. For example, they might be told that John is friendly three times. In other conditions, the traits characterized different members of the group. For example, subjects might learn that John is friendly, Bill is friendly, and George is friendly. Rothbart et al. found that under conditions of low memory load, as expected, redundant instances had less impact on judgments than equivalent but independent instances. However, under conditions of high memory load (i.e., when subjects learned about many members), redundant instances had the same impact on judgments as independent instances, apparently because the redundancy went unnoticed.

Taken together, these studies suggest that the organization and redundancy of incoming information are important determinants of schema change. However, under conditions of high memory load, perceivers may be unable to distinguish between redundant and independent information, or between dispersed and concentrated information. Thus, when our information-processing capacities are taxed, the degree of change in a schema may not be sensitive to variations in the organization or redundancy of incongruent schema-relevant information.

The memorability of information

Memorability is another characteristic of incongruent information that may be related to schema change. The more memorable the information, the more likely it may be to influence the schema. As memorable incongruent information accumulates, it may be retrieved, reviewed, and incorporated into a changed schema.

In general, incongruent information is highly memorable in free-recall tasks (Hastie, 1981). Hastie and Kumar (1979) provide a convincing demonstration of this phenomenon in impression formation. They found that behaviors of a target individual that were incongruent with subjects' impressions of the person were more likely to be recalled than behaviors that were congruent (see also Srull, 1981). If recall is related to schema change, then we would expect that subjects' impressions of the target person should be influenced by their memory of the incongruent behavior. However, in other settings, impressions and recall for the information on which they were based have been shown to be surprisingly independent (Anderson & Hubert, 1963; Dreben, Fiske, & Hastie, 1979; Hastie & Kumar, 1979; Riskey, 1979).

One mechanism in particular might account for the independence of memorability and impact in the case of incongruent information. In the section of this chapter on discrepancy between new information and existing person impressions, we noted that discrepant or incongruent information is often discredited. In particular, behavior that is incongruent with an impression tends to be attributed to situational rather than dispositional causes. When incongruent behavior is attributed to situational causes, its memorability may be independent of its impact on the impression. When incongruent information is attributed to dispositional causes, its memorability should be directly related to impression change.

A study by Crocker, Hannah, and Weber (1983) addressed this issue. They gave subjects a list of behaviors of a person, John, that were congruent with subjects' impression of him. In addition, one behavior was either congruent or incongruent with subjects' impressions, and it was attributed to either a dispositional or a situational cause. Subjects' impressions of John and recall for John's behaviors were assessed. As expected, the incongruent item had more impact on subjects' impressions of John when it was attributed to a dispositional cause than when it was attributed to a situational cause.

The advantage in memory of the incongruent item over the congruent item found by Hastie and Kumar (1979) was replicated only when the items were attributed to dispositional causes. When the items were attributed to situational causes, there was no difference in recall for the congruent and incongruent behaviors. Thus, in both free recall and impressions, the incongruent item had the most impact when it was attributed to a dispositional rather than a situational cause.

These parallel results suggested that the impressions might be mediated by subjects' recall of the items. That is, impressions might be based on the information that subjects recall about the target person. To determine whether this was in fact the case, correlations between recall and impressions were calculated. The results of the correlational analysis indicated a moderately positive relationship between recall and impressions when the item was attributed to a dispositional cause ($r = .27$), but no relationship between recall and impressions when it was attributed to a situational cause ($r = .08$). Thus, recall and impressions were related for items that were relevant to subjects' schema for the person (i.e., items attributed to a dispositional cause) but not when the items were irrelevant to the schema for John (i.e., items attributed to situational causes).

Based on these results, we can speculate that recall of information is related to schema change *if the information is judged to be relevant to the schema*. Under conditions where information is irrelevant to the schema, recall will be unrelated to schema change and instead will be dependent on other determinants of memorability, such as primacy, salience, and so forth. Fiske, Kenny, and Taylor (1982) reach a similar conclusion in their investigations of recall as a mediator of salience effects.

An intriguing finding by Srull (1981) suggests a second reason why recall of incongruent information may be unrelated to schema change. Srull found that the presence of incongruent information actually increases the likelihood that congruent information will be recalled. Apparently, the effort to integrate incongruent information into an existing schema creates more links to congruent information in memory. Thus, thinking about incongruent information may actually strengthen one's memory for congruent information, and bolster the initial belief.[1]

The characteristics of data that are related to schema change is an area that requires further investigation. The discrepancy of information with the schema is related to the amount of schema change, although perhaps in a curvilinear rather than linear fashion. Ambiguous incongruent information produces less change than unambiguously incongruent information. The way information is organized also affects its impact on the schema. Dispersed incongruent information appears to produce more change than concentrated incongruent information. The memorability of incongruent information is not directly related to the amount of schema change for two reasons: first, because incongruent information is often dismissed as irrelevant, and second, because attempts at integrating incongruent information can actually make congruent information more memorable.

A Comment on the Relationship Between Schema Change and Attitude Change

What is the relationship between a schematic approach to belief change and research on attitudes and attitude change? There are both striking differences and reassuring points of similarity between the two approaches. The schematic approach differs from most attitude change theories in that it deemphasizes the affect associated with many beliefs, and it is essentially silent on the issue of motivation. Most theories of attitudes emphasize the evaluative components of attitudes, and many approaches to attitude change attempt to change the evaluative component of attitudes (cf. Kiesler, Collins, & Miller, 1969). The schematic approach to belief change, on the other hand, is concerned with changes in the content and structure of social knowledge in response to information that is incongruent with the schema.

A less obvious difference between the two approaches concerns the extent to which attitudes are similar to other social knowledge structures. For example, as noted earlier, attitude-relevant information may be organized around an agree-disagree dimension (Judd & Kulik, 1980) whereas social knowledge structures may not have this bipolar structure. Further research is needed to compare the representation of attitudinal information in memory with the representation of other social knowledge structures.

Despite these differences, there are similarities between some theories of attitude change, particularly cognitive consistency theories, and the current approach. For example, in a discussion of the types of change that might follow from perceiving unbalanced relations, Heider (1958) suggested that change may occur in sentiment relations (what the person likes and dislikes) or in unit relations (the association between entities or events). The processes involved in changes in unit relations that Heider proposed are similar to some of the types of schema change that we have discussed. Heider suggested, for example, that the perceiver could decide that another

[1] We are grateful to Thom Srull for this suggestion.

was not responsible for an action or event that is incongruent with the perceiver's impression of the other. Thus, the knowledge structure guides inferences about the causes of the incongruent behavior. According to Heider, the perceiver could also develop a more differentiated "picture" of the other. This hypothesized process is directly analogous to the process of subtyping, or developing a more differentiated cognitive structure (see also Rosenberg & Abelson, 1960).

This overlap between cognitive consistency theories and the schematic approach to belief change is reassuring. It suggests that the processes that have been identified by the traditional view and the newer one are robust, enduring phenomena. The contribution of the schematic processing approach is to apply a finer-grained information-processing analysis of changes in the structure and content of schemas.

The similarities between cognitive consistency research and schematic approaches to belief change also suggest some warnings for the schematic approach. Although consistency theories had an enormous impact on the field of attitude change, they eventually fell into disuse. Consistency theories suffered from an inability to specify precisely what constituted cognitive inconsistency, from an inability to predict what method of reducing inconsistency would operate in any given situation, and from the finding that people can in fact tolerate a great deal of inconsistency (cf. Kiesler, Collins, & Miller, 1969). Similar problems may plague researchers taking the schematic processing approach. Definitions of the term "schema" vary, and tend to be vague or imprecise. Consequently, it is difficult to specify what stimuli are incongruent with a schema. Second, as we have noted, there are many ways a perceiver can respond (or not respond) to incongruent information, and research has just barely begun to identify what responses will occur under what conditions. Finally, the schematic processing approach assumes that people spend a great deal of time thinking about the implications of the stimuli around them. However, it may be that people are not always interested in understanding the stimuli they encounter, or in resolving inconsistencies. Rather, people may proceed "mindlessly" through much of their daily lives, ignoring many of the inconsistencies that confront them (Langer, 1978). Thus, initial attempts to specify when people will think about inconsistencies (Fiske, 1982; Hastie, 1980) need to be developed further.

These difficulties for the schematic approach are serious but need not be fatal. Researchers are now faced with the choice of heeding the warnings from consistency theory and doing the rigorous work that may overcome them, or being content to apply the schematic approach to their particular concerns for what it presently offers.

Summary and Conclusions

In this chapter, we have described the circumstances under which, and the processes whereby, social schemas change. Schemas are enduring generic knowledge structures, and as such they resist change. Usually discrepant data are assimilated to the schema, rather than the schema itself accommodating to the discrepant data. Nonetheless, there are circumstances when a schema is clearly incorrect or useless, because it does not fit or no longer fits incoming data well. When this is so, processing of information is slow and error-prone, and under some circumstances, data may even be reinterpreted to fit the incorrect schema.

How then are such inaccuracies detected and schemas correspondingly revised? First, a perceiver must notice incongruent information. Incongruent information is often attention-getting, but it may not be processed very deeply. Incongruent information is most likely to be processed if: it can be processed at a leisurely pace (i.e., the information load on the perceiver is low or there is much processing time); the schema itself is well-developed, so that incongruencies are clear and detectable; and the perceiver is motivated to be accurate (e.g., the perceiver's outcomes depend upon accuracy).

Various aspects of a schema can change: the variables themselves; the "default option" of a particular variable (i.e., the expected or usual value associated with a particular variable); the constraint values associated with a particular variable (i.e., the range of values tolerated for a variable); the horizontal and vertical structure of the schema (how many levels and/or subcategories there are); and the instances that are stored with the schema (the typical examples of it). Typically, changes in instances of schemas occur fairly readily, whereas default values are quite unlikely to change. The other features of schemas that can potentially change fall in between these two extremes.

What features of schemas change when? Incongruent data may change instances associated with schemas if they are seen as relevant to the schema; when the data can be dismissed as irrelevant, instances are less likely to change. With respect to changes in the more abstract aspects of a schema, three models have been proposed. The bookkeeping model maintains that each incongruency changes the schema a little. The conversion model suggest that only dramatically incongruent inconsistencies change schemas in an all-or-none fashion. The subtyping model suggests that inconsistencies are incorporated into subcategories, and thereby are used as a basis for increasing the complexity of the schema. Although current research supports the subtyping and bookeeping models, it seems likely that different types of schemas follow different kinds of patterns with respect to disconfirmation.

Some schemas are more resistant to change than others. Well-developed schemas resist change because they are more organized and compact and because they have more congruent instances stored. Schemas that are not accessed cannot change because inconsistencies will not be detected. Frequently activated, recently activated, and salient schemas have more potential to change because they are more likely to be accessed. Some schemas are more disconfirmable than others. Schemas vary as to how logically disconfirmable they are (i.e., the defining aspects of a schema clearly specify what features ought and ought not to occur) and how practically disconfirmable they are (i.e., the likelihood of actually encountering disconfirming evidence is high or low).

Finally, characteristics of the incongruent data themselves determine how likely a schema is to change. Generally, the more the data are discrepant from the schema, the more schema change will occur; however, at extreme levels of discrepancy, the data may themselves be rejected. Ambiguity of the data also influences schema change; ambiguous information is more likely to be assimilated to the schema rather than perceived as a basis for change. Organization of the inconsistent data influences the extent to which it will change a schema: Dispersed, rather than concentrated data are more likely to produce change, although these effects are weak when memory load is great. New rather than redundant information is more likely to produce change, although redundant data may be misperceived as new when memory load is great. Other features of data that may influence schema change include their extremity and memorability. Extremely incongruent data may be perceived as exceptions that prove the rule. Memorable incongruent data may prompt schema change, but only if those data are perceived as relevant to the schema.

The schema literature provides a theoretically rich basis for predicting when schemas will and will not change, how they change, what features are likely to change, and what kind of data will prompt change. It is therefore somewhat surprising that little empirical work has actually examined these hypotheses. No doubt one problem that faces the researcher potentially interested in addressing schema change is the problem of how to measure a schema. In the absence of clear measurement consensus, one must opt for the ultimately unsatisfying demonstration experiments, rather than the more sophisticated approach of competitive model testing. However, research on schema change may, in fact, point to directions for better measurement procedures.

Moreover, the problem of schema change is central not only to social cognition but to other psychological issues as well, such as stereotyping and attitudes. Thus, in order to ameliorate social problems that have their basis in erroneous beliefs, we must understand the cognitive processes underlying belief change. It is our hope that this chapter has suggested some starting points and directions for this task.

Acknowledgment. We are grateful to Reid Hastie and Carol Sigelman for their helpful comments on an earlier draft of this chapter.

References

Anderson, J. R., Kline, P. J., & Beasley, C. M., Jr. (1979). A general learning theory and its application to schema abstraction. In G. H. Bower (Ed.), *The psychology of learning and motivation*. New York: Academic Press.

Anderson, N. H., & Hubert, S. (1963). Effects of concomitant verbal recall on order effects in personality impression formation. *Journal of Verbal Learning and Verbal Behavior, 2,* 379-391.

Berlyne, D. E. (1970). Novelty, complexity, and hedonic value. *Perception & Psychophysics, 8,* 279-286.

Bernstein, E., & Schul, Y. (1983). The informational basis of social judgments: Memory for integrated and nonintegrated trait descriptions. *Journal of Experimental Social Psychology, 19,* 49-57.

Brewer, M. B., Dull, J., & Lui, L. (1981). Perception of the elderly: Stereotypes as prototypes. *Journal of Personality and Social Psychology, 41,* 656-670.

Bruner, J. S., & Potter, M. C. (1964). Interference in visual recognition. *Science, 144,* 424-425.

Carlston, D. E. (1980). The recall and use of traits and events in social inference processes. *Journal of Experimental Social Psychology, 16,* 303-329.

Cantor, N., & Mischel, W. (1979). Prototypes in person perception. In L. Berkowitz (Ed.), *Advances in experimental social psychology* (Vol. 12). New York: Academic Press.

Chase, W. G., & Simon, H. A. (1973). The mind's eye in chess. In W. G. Chase (Ed.), *Visual information processing*. New York: Academic Press.

Chi, M., & Koeske, R. (in press). Network representation of a child's dinosaur knowledge. *Developmental Psychology*.

Cohen, C. E. (1981). Person categories and social perception: Testing some boundaries of the processing effects of prior knowledge. *Journal of Personality and Social Psychology, 40,* 441-452.

Crocker, J., Hannah, D. B., & Weber, R. (1983). Person memory and causal attributions. *Journal of Personality and Social Psychology, 44,* 55-66.

Crocker, J., & Vitkus, J. (1983). *Attributions, attention, and person memory*. Unpublished manuscript, Northwestern University.

Crocker, J., & Weber, R. (1983). Cognitive structure and stereotype change. In R. P. Bagozzi & A. M. Tybout (Eds.), *Advances in consumer research* (Vol. 10).

Darley, J. M., & Fazio, R. H. (1980). Expectancy confirmation processes arising in the social interaction sequence. *American Psychologist, 35,* 867-881.

Deaux, K., & Emswiller, T. (1974). Explanations for successful performance on sex-linked tasks: What is skill for the male is luck for the female. *Journal of Personality and Social Psychology, 29,* 80-85.

Dreben, E. K., Fiske, S. T., & Hastie, R. (1979). The independence of evaluative and item information: Impression and recall order effects in behavior-based impression formation. *Journal of Personality and Social Psychology, 37,* 1758-1768.

Erber, R., & Fiske, S. T. (1983). *Processing inconsistent information: The impact of outcome dependency on attention, recall, and affect*. Unpublished manuscript, Carnegie-Mellon University.

Feldman-Summers, S., & Kiesler, S. B. (1974). Those who are number two try harder: The effect of sex on explanations of causality. *Journal of Personality and Social Psychology, 30,* 846-855.

Fiske, S. T. (1982). *Stereotypes or piecemeal: Two modes of reacting to others*. Invited address presented to Midwestern Psychological Association, Minneapolis.

Fiske, S. T., & Dyer, L. (1982). Cognitive analyses of involvement in persuasion. Paper presented at a symposium on "Persuasion and cognitive processing," American Psychological Association, Washington, D.C.

Fiske, S. T., & Gup, D. (1980). *Effects of stereotype-behavior timing and consistency on attention, evaluation, and memory*. Unpublished manuscript, Carnegie-Mellon University.

Fiske, S. T., Kenny, D. A., & Taylor, S. E. (1982). Structural models for the mediation of salience effects on attribution. *Journal of Experimental Social Psychology, 18,* 105-127.

Fiske, S. T., Kinder, D. R., & Larter, M. (1983). The novice and the expert: Knowledge-based strategies in political cognition. *Journal of Experimental Social Psychology, 19*, 381-400.

Fiske, S. T., & Linville, P. W. (1980). What does the schema concept buy us? *Personality and Social Psychology Bulletin, 6,* 543-557.

Fiske, S. T., & Taylor, S. E. (1984). *Social cognition.* Reading, MA: Addison-Wesley.

Flavell, J. H. (1963). *The developmental psychology of Jean Piaget.* New York: Van Nostrand-Reinhold.

Fong, G. T., & Markus, H. (1982). Self-schemas and judgments about others. *Social Cognition, 1,* 191-205.

Freid, L. S., & Holyoak, K. J. (in press). Induction of category distributions: A framework for classification learning. *Journal of Experimental Psychology: Learning, Memory and Cognition.*

Hastie, R. (1981). Memory for behavioral information that confirms or contradicts a personality impression. In R. Hastie, T. M. Ostrom, E. B. Ebbesen, R. W. Wyer, Jr., D. L. Hamilton, & D. E. Carlston (Eds.), *Person memory: The cognitive basis of social perception.* Hillsdale, NJ: Lawrence Erlbaum.

Hastie, R. (1981). Schematic principles in human memory. In E. T. Higgins, C. P. Herman, & M. Zanna (Eds.), *Social cognition.* Hillsdale, NJ: Lawrence Erlbaum.

Hastie, R., & Kumar, P. A. (1979). Person memory: Personality traits as organizing principles in memory for behaviors. *Journal of Personality and Social Psychology, 37,* 27-38.

Hayden, T., & Mischel, W. (1976). Maintaining trait consistency in the resolution of behavioral inconsistency: The wolf in sheep's clothing? *Journal of Personality, 44,* 109-132.

Hayes-Roth, B. (1977). Evolution of cognitive structure and processes. *Psychological Review, 84,* 260-278.

Heider, F. (1958). *The psychology of interpersonal relations.* New York: Wiley.

Higgins, E. T., & King, G. (1981). Accessibility of social constructs: Information-processing consequences of individual and contextual variability. In N. Cantor & J. F. Kihlstrom (Eds.), *Personality, cognition, and social interaction.* Hillsdale, NJ: Lawrence Erlbaum.

Higgins, E. T., King, G. A., & Mavin, G. H. (1982). Individual construct accessibility and subjective impressions and recall. *Journal of Personality and Social Psychology, 43,* 35-47.

Hinsley, D., Hayes, J. R., & Simon, H. A. (1977). From words to equations: Meaning and representation in algebra word problems. In M. A. Just & P. A. Carpenter (Eds.), *Cognitive processes in comprehension.* Hillsdale, NJ: Lawrence Erlbaum.

Inhelder, B., & Piaget, J. (1958). *The growth of logical thinking.* New York: Basic Books.

Judd, C. M., & Harackiewicz, J. M. (1980). Contrast effects in attitude judgment: An examination of the accentuation hypothesis. *Journal of Personality and Social Psychology, 38,* 390-398.

Judd, C. M., & Kulik, J. A. (1980). Schematic effects of social attitudes and recall. *Journal of Personality and Social Psychology, 38,* 569-578.

Kelley, H. H. (1967). Attribution theory in social psychology. In D. Levine (Ed.), *Nebraska Symposium on Motivation* (Vol. 15). Lincoln: University of Nebraska Press.

Kiesler, C. A., Collins, B. E., & Miller, N. (1969). *Attitude change*. New York: Wiley.

Kuhn, T. S. (1962). *The structure of scientific revolutions*. Chicago: University of Chicago Press.

Kulik, J. A. (1983). Confirmatory attribution and the perpetuation of social beliefs. *Journal of Personality and Social Psychology, 44,* 1171-1181.

Langer, E. J. (1978). Rethinking the role of thought in social interaction. In J. H. Harvey, W. Ickes, & R. F. Kidd (Eds.), *New directions in attribution research* (Vol. 2). Hillsdale, NJ: Lawrence Erlbaum.

Langer, E. J., & Abelson, R. P. (1974). A patient by any other name . . . : Clinician group differences in labeling bias. *Journal of Consulting and Clinical Psychology, 42,* 4-9.

Larkin, J. H., McDermott, J., Simon, D. P., & Simon, H. A. (1980). Models of competence in solving physics problems. *Science, 200,* 1335-1342.

Linville, P. W. (1982a). The complexity-extremity effect, and age-based stereotyping. *Journal of Personality and Social Psychology, 42,* 193-211.

Linville, P. W. (1982b). Affective consequences of complexity regarding the self and others. In M. S. Clark & S. T. Fiske (Eds.), *Affect and cognition: The 17th annual Carnegie Symposium*. Hillsdale, NJ: Lawrence Erlbaum.

Linville, P. W., & Jones, E. E. (1980). Polarized appraisals of outgroup members. *Journal of Personality and Social Psychology, 38,* 689-703.

Lord, C., Ross, L., & Lepper, M. R. (1979). Biased assimilation and attitude polarization: The effects of prior theories on subsequently considered evidence. *Journal of Personality and Social Psychology, 37,* 2098-2109.

Markus, H. (1977). Self-schemata and processing information about the self. *Journal of Personality and Social Psychology, 35,* 63-78.

Markus, H., Crane, M., Bernstein, S., & Siladi, M. (1982). Self-schemas and gender. *Journal of Personality and Social Psychology, 42,* 38-50.

Markus, H., & Fong, G. (1979). *The role of the self on other perception*. Unpublished manuscript, University of Michigan.

Markus, H., & Smith, J. (1981). The influence of self-schemata on the perception of others. In N. Cantor & J. F. Kihlstrom (Eds.), *Personality, cognition, and social interaction*. Hillsdale, NJ: Lawrence Erlbaum.

Markus, H., Smith, J., & Moreland, R. L. (1983). *The role of the self in social perception: A cognitive analysis*. Unpublished manuscript, University of Michigan.

Martin, J., Harrod, W., & Siehl, C. (1980). *The development of knowledge structures*. Paper presented at a symposium on "The development of knowledge structures," American Psychological Association Convention, Montreal.

McArthur, L. Z. (1981). What grabs you? The role of attention in impression formation and causal attribution. In E. T. Higgins, C. P. Herman, & M. P. Zanna (Eds.), *Social cognition: The Ontario Symposium*. Hillsdale, NJ: Lawrence Erlbaum.

McGuire, W. J., McGuire, C. V., Child, P., & Fujioka, T. (1978). Salience of ethnicity in the spontaneous self-concept as a function of one's ethnic distinctiveness in the social environment. *Journal of Personality and Social Psychology, 36,* 511-520.

McGuire, W. J., & Padawer-Singer, A. (1976). Trait salience in the spontaneous self-concept. *Journal of Personality and Social Psychology, 33,* 743-754.

Medin, D. L., Altom, M. W., Edelson, S. M., & Freko, D. (1982). Correlated symptoms and simulated medical classification. *Journal of Experimental Psychology: Learning Memory and Cognition, 8,* 37-50.

Minsky, M. (1975). A framework for representing knowledge. In P. H. Winston (Ed.), *The psychology of computer vision.* New York: McGraw-Hill.

Neisser, V. (1976). *Cognition and reality: Principles and implications of social psychology.* San Francisco: Freeman.

Neves, D. M., & Anderson, J. R. (1981). Becoming an expert at a cognitive skill. In J. R. Anderson, (Ed.), *Skill acquisition.* Hillsdale, NJ: Lawrence Erlbaum.

Nisbett, R. E., & Ross, L. (1980). *Human inference: Strategies and shortcomings of social judgment.* Englewood Cliffs, NJ: Prentice-Hall.

Nunnally, J. C. (1961). *Popular concepts of mental health.* New York: Holt, Rinehart & Winston.

Owens, J., Bower, G. H., & Black, J. B. (1979). The "soap opera" effect in story recall. *Memory and Cognition, 7,* 185-191.

Read, S. J. (1983). A knowledge-based model of causal reasoning. Unpublished manuscript, Northwestern University.

Reeder, G. D., & Brewer, M. B. (1979). A schematic model of dispositional attribution in interpersonal perception. *Psychological Review, 86,* 61-79.

Riskey, D. R. (1979). Verbal memory processes in impression formation. *Journal of Experimental Psychology: Human Learning and Memory, 5,* 271-281.

Rosch, E. (1978). Principles of categorization. In E. Rosch & B. B. Lloyd (Eds.), *Cognition and categorization.* Hillsdale, NJ: Lawrence Erlbaum.

Rosch, E., & Mervis, C. B. (1975). Family resemblances: Studies in the internal structure of categories. *Cognitive Psychology, 7,* 573-605.

Rosch, E., Mervis, C. B., Gray, W. D., Johnson, D. M., & Boyes-Braem, P. (1976). Basic objects in natural categories. *Cognitive Psychology, 8,* 382-439.

Rose, T. (1981). Cognitive and dyadic processes in stereotyping and intergroup behavior. In D. L. Hamilton (Ed.), *Cognitive approaches to stereotyping and intergroup behavior.* Hillsdale, NJ: Lawrence Erlbaum.

Rosenhan, D. L. (1973). On being sane in insane places. *Science, 180,* 365-369.

Rosenberg, M. J., & Abelson, R. P. (1960). An analysis of cognitive balancing. In M. J. Rosenberg, C. I. Hovland, W. J. McGuire, R. P. Abelson, & J. W. Brehm (Eds.), *Attitude organization and change.* New Haven: Yale University Press.

Rosenthal, R., & Jacobson, L. (1968). *Pygmalion in the classroom: Teacher expectation and pupils' intellectual development.* New York: Holt, Rinehart & Winston.

Rothbart, M. (1981). In D. Hamilton (Ed.), *Cognitive processes in stereotyping and intergroup relations.* Hillsdale, NJ: Lawrence Erlbaum.

Rothbart, M., Fulero, S., Jensen, C., Howard, J., & Birrell, P. (1978). From individual to group impression: Availability heuristics in stereotype formation. *Journal of Experimental Social Psychology, 14,* 237-255.

Rothbart, M., & Park, B. M. (1982). *The disconfirmability of social concepts.* Manuscript in preparation, University of Oregon.

Rumelhart, D. E., & Norman, D. A. (1978). Accretion, tuning, and restructuring: Three models of learning. In J. W. Cotton & R. L. Klatzky (Eds.), *Schematic factors in cognition*. Hillsdale, NJ: Lawrence Erlbaum.

Rumelhart, D. E., & Ortony, A. (1977). The representation of knowledge in memory. In R. C. Anderson, F. J. Spiro, & W. E. Montague (Eds.), *Schooling and the acquisition of knowledge*. Hillsdale, NJ: Lawrence Erlbaum.

Schank, R., & Abelson, R. (1977). *Scripts, plans, goals and understanding: An inquiry into human knowledge structures*. Hillsdale, NJ: Lawrence Erlbaum.

Schur, E. M. (1980). *The politics of deviance*. Englewood Cliffs, NJ: Prentice-Hall.

Sherif, M., & Hovland, C. I. (1961). *Social judgment: Assimilation and contrast effects in communication and attitude change*. New Haven: Yale University Press.

Snyder, M., & Swann, W. B., Jr. (1978). When actions reflect attitudes: The politics of impression management. *Journal of Personality and Social Psychology, 34,* 1034-1042.

Snyder, M., Tanke, E. D., & Berscheid, E. (1977). Social perception and interpersonal behavior: On the self-fulfilling nature of social stereotypes. *Journal of Personality and Social Psychology, 35,* 656-666.

Snyder, M., & Uranowitz, S. W. (1978). Reconstructing the past: Some cognitive consequences of person perception. *Journal of Personality and Social Psychology, 36,* 941-950.

Srull, T. K. (1981). Person memory: Some tests of associative storage and retrieval models. *Journal of Experimental Psychology: Human Learning and Memory, 7,* 440-462.

Srull, T. K., & Wyer, R. S., Jr. (1980). Category accessibility and social perception: Some implications for the study of person memory and interpersonal judgments. *Journal of Personality and Social Psychology, 38,* 841-856.

Taylor, S. E. (1981). A categorization approach to stereotyping. In D. L. Hamilton (Ed.), *Cognitive processes in stereotyping and intergroup behavior*. Hillsdale, NJ: Lawrence Erlbaum.

Taylor, S. E., & Crocker, J. (1981). Schematic bases of social information processing. In E. T. Higgins, C. P. Herman, & M. Zanna (Eds.), *Social cognition*. Hillsdale, NJ: Lawrence Erlbaum.

Taylor, S. E., Crocker, J., & D'Agostino, J. (1978). Schematic bases of social problem solving. *Personality and Social Psychology Bulletin, 4,* 447-451.

Taylor, S. E., & Fiske, S. T. (1978). Salience, attention, and attribution: Top of the head phenomena. In L. Berkowitz (Ed.), *Advances in experimental social psychology* (Vol. 11). New York: Academic Press.

Taylor, S. E., Fiske, S. T., Close, M., Anderson, C., & Ruderman, A. (1975). *Solo status as a psychological variable: The power of being distinctive*. Unpublished manuscript, Harvard University.

Taylor, S. E., & Winkler, J. D. (1980). *The development of schemas*. Paper presented at the American Psychology Association annual meeting, Montreal, Canada.

Titchner, E. B. (1966). Attention as sensory clearness. In P. Bakan (Ed.), *Attention: An enduring problem in psychology*. Princeton, NJ: Van Nostrand. (Reprinted from *Lectures on the elementary psychology of feeling and attention*. New York: Macmillan, 1908)

Weber, R., & Crocker, J. (1983). Cognitive processes in the revision of stereotypic beliefs. *Journal of Personality and Social Psychology, 45*, 961-967.

Word, C. O., Zanna, M. P., & Cooper, J. (1974). The nonverbal mediation of self-fulfilling prophecies in interracial interaction. *Journal of Experimental Social Psychology, 10*, 109-120.

Wyer, R. S., Jr., & Srull, T. K. (1981). Category accessibility: Some theoretical and empirical issues concerning the processing of social information. In E. T. Higgins, C. P. Herman, & M. P. Zanna (Eds.), *Social cognition: The Ontario Symposium* (Vol. 1). Hillsdale, NJ: Lawrence Erlbaum.

Author Index

Subject Index